Doubt is a universal problem, especially when it comes to doubts about God. For many people, doubt is the source of anxiety and guilt. But how should we deal with the doubts we have? Should we keep them a secret? Should we try to forget them? Or simply learn to live with them?

In this book, which has become a classic of Christian writing, Os Guinness argues for a powerful alternative: to recognize our doubts and tackle the issues they raise. He explores seven different 'families' of doubt, showing how each can be faced and worked through. In this way, doubt is not merely resolved; it becomes a path towards mature faith.

'At its most basic, doubt is a matter of truth, trust and trustworthiness. Can we trust God? Are we sure? How can we be sure? Do we trust him enough to rely on him utterly? Are we trusting him enough to enjoy him? Is the whole of living different for that trust?'

Os Guinness was born in China and is a graduate of the Universities of London and Oxford. He is now a freelance writer and lecturer living in Washington DC. He is the author of several books, particularly *The Dust of Death* and *The Gravedigger File*, which have won him a wide readership on both sides of the Atlantic.

To my mother and father with love and deep gratitude

DOUBT

OS GUINNESS

A LION PAPERBACK

Tring • Batavia • Sydney

Copyright © 1976 Inter-Varsity Christian Fellowship of the USA

Published by
Lion Publishing plc
Icknield Way, Tring, Herts, England
ISBN 0 7459 1036 X
Lion Publishing Corporation
1705 Hubbard Avenue, Batavia, Illinois 60510, USA
ISBN 0 7459 1036 X
Albatross Books Pty Ltd
PO Box 320, Sutherland, NSW 2232, Australia
ISBN 0 86760 908 7

First published under the title *In Two Minds*
First UK edition 1976
Second edition 1983
Third edition 1987

Acknowledgement is made for permission to reprint copyrighted
material to Tavistock Publications Ltd and Pantheon Books for 'If I
Don't Know . . . I Don't Know' copyright © 1970 by R. D. Laing
Trust, from *Knots* by R. D. Laing; and to Miss D. E. Collins and
Dodd Mead and Co. Inc. for four lines from 'The Free Thinker'
from *The Collected Poems of G. K. Chesterton*.

Cover engraving by M. C. Escher
© M. C. Escher Heirs c/o Cordon Art, Baarn, Holland

Printed and bound in Great Britain by
Cox & Wyman Ltd, Reading

Contents

'The man who is asked by another
what he thinks of his work,
is put to the torture and is not obliged
to speak the truth.'
Samuel Johnson

'As iron sharpens iron,
So one man sharpens the wits of another.'
Proverbs 27:17

My special thanks are due to
Dr David Wells, Mr William Edgar,
Mr and Mrs Joe Martin and Dr James Sire.
Nothing is more stimulating than
friends who speak the truth in love.

Part One

The Problem

I Believe in Doubt

Sometimes I almost feel on fire with the immensity of this: each of us is a person, alive, growing and relating. From the moment we wake to the moment we fall asleep we think, we feel, we choose, we speak, we act, not as isolated individuals but as persons among people.

And underneath everything lies trust. From friendships of children to agreements among nations life depends on trust. Counting on people is trust. Enjoying people is trust. Trust is the shared silence, the exchanged look, the expressive touch. Crying for help is trust, shaking hands is trust, a kiss is trust. The highest reaches of love and life depend on trust. Are there any questions more important to each of us than, Whom can I trust? How can I be sure?

This is why when trust goes and doubt comes in such a shadow is cast, such a wound is opened, such a hole is left.

God is a person too; and what is more, the person on whom personhood itself depends. That is why to know him is to trust him, and to trust him is to begin to know ourselves. That is why the chief end of man is to glorify God and enjoy him for ever. It is also why doubting God is so devastating.

Some people who are approaching faith in God doubt God because they want to believe but dare not. How would you feel if someone flew more than halfway around the world to say to you, 'I am at a loss. Life has no meaning unless God is there. There is hardly anyone left whom I can trust. Will you help me in my search?' Just recently I was talking to a man who had crossed the world to see someone for this very reason. How would you respond if you knew that after his previous failures to find answers he had cried out louder and more often, and that the scars of the razor blades were still on his wrists to show it? What would you say? How would you help him? How would you introduce him to God who would never let him down, especially since God is less certain to him than human beings who have let him down?

Other people who are backing away from faith in God doubt God because they do not want to believe but do. I will never forget a girl who sat in the living-room of our home in Switzerland. She argued, she cried, she pounded the floor. Why should she trust God? He was a monster, a hard, unyielding monarch, a Mafia boss whose power was everywhere, a merciless creditor who demanded his pound of flesh. Hadn't she tried to obey? But the more she saw God the more she feared, and the more she feared the more she became angry, and the more angry she became the more she hated, and the more she hated the more afraid of God she grew.

She knew she was caught in a vicious trap, sliding down a slippery spiral. She was young, she was loved, she was successful. But none of it made any difference. She could not trust God, and in the bitterness of doubt her spirit was like darkness at noon.

The doubts of these two people were entirely different, but they were both doubting God for the same reason: they did not know God as he really is. The man, however, knew that he did not know, while the girl thought that she did. Her picture of God (which came from experiences in the past) was so distorted that without realizing it she was believing a grotesque caricature of God which for sanity's sake she was forced at the same time to doubt.

Fortunately, she is not in that position today. She has come to know God as he is, she is able to trust him, and her whole life reflects the difference. In later chapters (such as chapter six) we will examine doubts like these in depth to see how they arise and how they can be resolved. They are only two types of doubt among many others, but they introduce us directly to the heart of our problem.

Doubt is not primarily an abstract philosophical or theological question, nor a state of morbid spiritual or psychological anguish. At its most basic, doubt is a matter of truth, trust and trustworthiness. Can we trust God? Are we sure? How can we be sure? Do we trust him enough to rely on him utterly? Are we trusting him enough to enjoy him? Is the whole of living different for that trust?

A healthy understanding

Christianity places a premium on the absolute truthfulness and trustworthiness of God, so understanding doubt is extremely important to a Christian. Of course, faith is much more than the absence of doubt, but to understand doubt is to have a key to a quiet heart and a quiet mind. Anyone who believes anything will automatically know something about doubt. But the person who knows why he believes is also in a position to discover why he doubts. The Christian should be such a person.

Not only does a Christian believe; he is a person who 'thinks in believing and believes in thinking', as Augustine expressed it. The world of Christian faith is not a fairy-tale, make-believe world, question-free and problem-proof, but a world where doubt is never far from faith's shoulder.

Consequently, a healthy understanding of doubt should go hand in hand with a healthy understanding of faith. We ourselves are called in question if we have no answer to doubt. If we constantly doubt what we believe and always believe-yet-doubt, we will be in danger of undermining our personal integrity, if not our stability. But if ours is an examined faith, we should be unafraid to doubt. If doubt is eventually justified, we were believing what clearly was not worth believing. But if doubt is answered, our faith has grown stronger still. It knows God more certainly and it can enjoy God more deeply.

Obviously then, each one of us should understand doubt for God's sake and for ours. God is to be trusted yet people are doubting: that is justification enough for trying to understand doubt. But an understanding of doubt will also bring two particular benefits to the church at large.

First, it will act as a safeguard against today's widespread and unnecessary breakdown of faith. Christians are confronted by a situation which militates openly against faith. The Christian foundations of Western culture have been torn up and discarded. Our Christian past is in disrepute, and the very basis for any faith, Christian or otherwise, is held to be discredited. Into the vacuum has sprung a bewildering variety of alternative philosophies, facing us with a post-Christian mosaic of confusing pluralism. Many of us are smarting emotionally under the sting of reactions to our belief and keenly aware of the deficiency in our response. It is hardly surprising if at times we falter as believers in a disbelieving age.

This state of affairs has aggravated the already serious problem of doubt among Christians. The loss of faith has not been staunched, and this has suggested that the Christian faith is a fragile, vulnerable belief with little intellectual integrity. This suggestion, in its turn, lends support to the common rejection of Christianity among thinking people. What is most damaging to Christianity is not that Christians doubt but that there seems to be so little open discussion and understanding of doubt. This must be changed.

Second, an understanding of doubt helps us to prepare for the years of testing which, I think, are to come. Faith at its truest is radical reliance on God. It is a conviction born of understanding, grounded solidly in the truth of who God is and what he has said and done. But what our faith 'should be' may be far removed from what our faith 'is'. In practice many of us have become Christians and are continuing to believe for less than the best reasons and clearest motives. This may have serious consequences in the critical years ahead.

For example, one person's faith may be a genuine trust in God but also a trust in certain Christian friends, while another person has truly committed himself to God and also to the care of a Christian community. Or again, someone may honestly put himself under the lordship of Christ yet at the same time adhere to a Christian lifestyle or espouse Christian values which by temperament or nationality he would be likely to appreciate anyway.

In each specific case it is impossible to determine the exact line of distinction between faith and faith plus, between our faith in God and our faith in other men. Even where faith is weak or even wrongly based, it is not necessarily illegitimate. (If our motives had to be completely pure, which of us would pass the test?) But such faith is running a risk. To the degree that other motives are also at work faith is not radical reliance on God alone.

Seen in this light, every test which shows us what we are really relying on can be constructive. If testing shows that our attachment to Christian friends or to a particular lifestyle is stronger than our attachment to God himself, we must ask whether these supports for faith are in danger of becoming substitutes. What we need, then, is to be stopped short before the process of substitution is complete.

The 'Square One Principle'

Jesus challenged the Jews of his day with a searching question: 'How can you have faith so long as you receive honour from one another, and care nothing for the honour that comes from him who alone is God?' Ostensibly their faith was solely in God, but that faith was only nominal. In reality their faith was in each other. More precisely, their nominal faith in God was supported and accredited by a closed system of mutual human honouring which made the need for any honour from God superfluous.

We should ask similar questions of ourselves, particularly those of us who are western Christians. What sort of faith do we have? How can we know how strong our faith really is so long as we are comparatively untroubled in a world of material affluence, social ease and spiritual privilege? Or to reverse it, could it be that in the deepening turbulence of our generation God is not only judging a culture which has abandoned him but also, as it were, shaking up the bag and testing the foundations to see if we Christians are as ready as we think for the critical years ahead?

The coin has two sides. Much of the breakdown of faith we are witnessing is a logical consequence, pure and simple, of the deep deficiency of faith today. On the other hand, it may also be a sign of God's hidden control and wisdom preparing us for the future.

Long-standing supports are crumbling, and many of the accepted assumptions of normal Western life are being shaken – such as social stability and a reasonable prosperity. We are forced to see the true foundations of our faith (that is, our practical rather than professed faith, our day-to-day trust, our matter-of-fact belief, our down-to-earth reliance). Far better to be tested today and have the chance to put right what is shown to be wrong than to be tested tomorrow and be found wanting.

The issues we are facing in the present crisis of faith touch on what I call the Square One Principle. Life can proceed with deceptive ease on the basis of a faith which was once vital but has become so taken for granted that it is no longer authentic. At that stage any pressure may be such a test for faith that the believer is faced with a choice: Give up or go back to square one. If we give up, then we abandon faith altogether. But if we go back to square one (and so back to the roots, back to the foundations, back to the beginning), we will find a faith which is solid and secure. The lesson of the Square One Principle is this: the person who has the courage to go back when necessary is the one who goes on in the end..

Seen this way, the collapse of Christendom is a blessing for Christianity, and the present crisis of faith may be the best opportunity in centuries, at least for Christians in the West. To use this opportunity fully we must stop the severe haemorrhaging of faith among believers, we must work towards a clearly discernible Christian mind, and we must carefully answer the questions and objections of our contemporaries. Developing a fresh understanding of the old problem of doubt will contribute to this.

Let God be God

What is faith? And what is the misunderstanding or mistreatment of faith which causes doubt, and how can it be avoided? And, above all, what does it mean to let faith be faith to such an extent that it will in turn let God be God? These are the questions we will examine and that is our goal – to let God be God.

What will be our approach in this book? In part one (chapters one to four) our objective is to examine the nature of doubt, setting it off clearly from three common misconceptions which cloud the issue today. For some people chapters one and two will be sufficient for this purpose and they may wish to pass from there directly to chapter five, missing chapters three and four which are more theoretical.

Part two (chapters five to eleven) is the heart of our discussion. The objective here is to examine the seven most common categories of doubt and to develop a framework in which we can understand and analyse all our specific doubts.

In part three (chapters twelve to fifteen) our objective is to examine what is involved in helping a person in doubt, and to see how this can be made practical and specific without being mechanical and stereotyped.

In part four (the last two chapters) we will look at two

specific types of doubt which are especially difficult and important today.

Getting to the heart of doubt is rather like peeling a chestnut: it's worthwhile in the end, but it entails getting through a prickly layer. The prickles surrounding doubt are the various layers of misunderstanding which obscure what doubt actually is. There are three basic misconceptions which are especially common: first, that doubt is wrong because it is the same thing as unbelief; second, that doubt is a problem which troubles faith but not knowledge; and third, that doubt is something to be ashamed of because it is dishonest to believe if you have doubts.

We will examine each of these misconceptions in turn, so that once we have torn away these layers of misunderstanding we can get to the kernel of doubt and see not only its dangers but its value. Then, since there is no believing without some doubting and since believing is all the stronger for understanding and resolving doubt, we can say as Christians that if we doubt in believing it is also true that we believe in doubting.

Chapter Two

In Two Minds

I once witnessed the proverbial sight of a peasant beating his donkey. The peasant was walking behind, driving his donkey on. Huge bales of firewood were strapped to its back, but the donkey forced its way up the steep little path that served as a village street. Gradually it slowed, exhausted. Spurred on again by a stream of oaths, it staggered a few paces further and sank to the ground, defeated. It was then that the peasant beat it – and beat it and beat it and beat it again.

How many Christians treat faith like that? Believe this! Believe that! Stop doubting and believe more firmly! Admonitions and warnings are piled onto faith's back until it can take no more. Cajolings then give way to threats and threats to the big stick until, undernourished and overloaded, their faith sinks to the ground and expires.

We might ask which is worse, the cruelty or the stupidity? Which sadder, the plight of faith and the donkey or the plight of the man? But this is not a book about donkeys or even about faith, at least not directly. It is a book about doubt. Yet what is doubt but faith suffering from mistreatment or malnutrition? Concern for the prevention of doubt is automatically concern for the prevention of cruelty to faith.

The way to get the best out of something – whether faith or a donkey or anything else – is to find out what it is and treat it accordingly. Mistake it for something else or push it beyond its limits and its purpose may be destroyed. Ask it to do more than it can and it may not do what it should. Donkeys have no objection to donkey work, but they cannot stand being taken for racehorses or tractors.

As soon as we ask what faith is and what sort of mistreatment of faith causes doubt, we are led to the first major misconception about doubt – the idea that doubt is the opposite of faith and the same thing as unbelief. Implied in this is a view of faith that is unrealistic and a view of doubt that is unfair.

Faith is the ass of the modern world. Like the donkey it is despised by its enemies and mistreated by its friends, but only because it is bound to be treated unfairly when it is seen unrealistically. The injustice is that the donkey is beaten until it collapses and then it is beaten *for collapsing*. In the same way many Christians drive their faith unfairly when they believe, and then they flog their faith unmercifully when they doubt. In both cases they have been led to believe that true faith is doubt-free and that doubt is the same thing (and just as sinful) as unbelief.

A divided heart

What is doubt? And how is it related to faith and unbelief? Our English word *doubt* comes from the Latin *dubitare* which is rooted in an Aryan word meaning 'two'. So we can start by defining our terms like this: to believe is to be 'in one mind' about accepting something as true; to disbelieve is to be 'in one mind' about rejecting it. To doubt is to waver between the two, to believe and disbelieve at once and so to be 'in two minds'.

This two-ness or double-ness is the heart of doubt and the deepest dilemma it represents. *The heart of doubt is a divided heart.* This is not just a metaphor. It is the essence of the Christian view of doubt, and human language and experience from all around the world also bear it out.

In English the double-ness of doubt is pictured in phrases such as 'having a foot in both camps'. There are many equivalents in other languages. The Chinese picture of irresolution is humorous as well as graphic. They speak of a person 'having a foot in two boats'. In the Peruvian Andes the Huanuco Quechuas speak of 'having two thoughts' and the Shipibos further to the east have an expression, 'thinking two things'. In Guatemala the Kekchi language describes the doubter as a man 'whose heart is made in two', while the Navajo Indians in the southwestern United States use a similar term, 'that which is two with him'.

The New Testament words which are translated into English as 'doubt' are equally fascinating. Examining root meanings is not everybody's cup of tea, but in this case it is worthwhile since it sheds so much light on the nature of doubt. Notice that in each case there is an unmistakable emphasis on the ambivalence or double-mindedness of doubt.

One Greek word (*dipsukos*) speaks of a man who is chronically doubleminded. James in his letter describes such a doubter as 'a heaving sea ruffled by the wind'. A second word (*diakrino*) is the stronger form of the word *to sever* or *to separate*. This word can convey several meanings but one of them expresses an inner state of mind so torn between various options that it cannot make up its mind. Jesus uses this word when he says to his disciples, 'Have faith in God. I tell you this: if anyone says to this mountain, "Be lifted from your place and hurled into the sea," and has no *inward doubts*, but believes that what he says is happening, it will be done for him' (Mark 11 : 23).

A third Greek word (*meteorizomai*) means 'to raise' or 'to suspend' when it is used literally (as it is in the root of our modern word meteor) or to raise a person's hopes when it is used figuratively. When it is used figuratively, it can mean to soar or to lift oneself up, and so to be arrogant in spirit. Or else, because one is lifted up in the air, to be unsettled and therefore restless, anxious, tense and doubtful.

It describes a state of mind which is the result of an awkward position. Many modern expressions capture this ambivalence, such as being 'up in the air' or being 'hung up'. When Jesus says to his disciples, 'You are not to set your mind on food or drink; you are not to worry' (Luke 12: 29 – the only New Testament use of the word), he is saying that God's care for us as Father means that food and drink are not to be a hang-up, an occasion for doubt and anxiety which constantly keeps us up in the air.

A fourth word (*dialogizomai*) is the root of our word *dialogue*. Its own root is 'thought', and from that it has come to mean the inner debate of a person who is reasoning with himself. The word is usually used in the New Testament of internal reasoning which is wrong or evil. Jesus uses it when he confronts the disciples after his resurrection: 'Why are you so perturbed?' he asks. 'Why do *questionings* arise in your minds?' (Luke 24: 38). The word opens a window into the debate raging in their hearts as they doubted. So long as there is doubt, the debate continues and the arguments fly back and forth. Only when the votes are cast is it clear whether faith's motion has been passed or defeated.

A fifth word (*distazo*) means doubt in the sense of hanging back, hesitating or faltering. It expresses what we mean when we say that we have our reservations or vacillate about something. Matthew uses the word when he records that 'Jesus at once reached out and caught hold of him, and said, "Why did you *hesitate*? How little faith you have!"' (Matthew 14:31). The same word is used of those who doubted the risen Christ: 'When they saw him, they fell prostrate before him, though some were *doubtful*' (Matthew 28:17). Genuine faith is unreserved in its commitment; doubt has reservations. Faith steps forward; doubt hangs back. Doubt holds itself open to all possibilities but is reluctant to close on any.

The combined force of all these phrases and words is surely inescapable. If a person is 'torn' between opinions, unable to 'make up' his mind, or if he is 'up in the air' over something and unsure which side he should 'come down on', or if he is furiously 'debating' with himself or 'hanging back', or weighing up his 'reservations', he is nothing if not 'in two minds'. This is the essence of doubt.

Doubt and unbelief

What follows from this is decisive for our whole discussion: doubt is not the opposite of faith, nor is it the same as unbelief. Doubt is a state of mind in suspension *between* faith and unbelief so that it is neither of them wholly and it is each only partly. This distinction is absolutely vital because it uncovers and deals with the first major misconception of doubt – the idea that in doubting a believer is betraying faith and surrendering to unbelief. No misunderstanding causes more anxiety and brings such bondage to sensitive people in doubt.

The difference between doubt and unbelief is crucial. The Bible makes a definite distinction between them, though the distinction is not hard and fast. The word *unbelief* is usually used of a wilful refusal to believe or of a deliberate decision to disobey. So, while doubt is a state of suspension between faith and unbelief, unbelief is a state of mind which is closed against God, an attitude of heart which disobeys

God as much as it disbelieves the truth. It is the consequence of a settled choice. Since it is a deliberate response to God's truth, unbelief is definitely held to be responsible.

There are times when the word *unbelief* is used to describe the doubts of those who are definitely believers but only when they are at a stage of doubting which is rationally inexcusable and well on the way to becoming fullgrown unbelief. Thus the ambiguity in the biblical use of *unbelief* is a sign of psychological astuteness and not of theological confusion.

So it is definitely possible to distinguish between faith, doubt and unbelief in theory (to believe is to be in one mind, to disbelieve is to be in another and to doubt is to be in two minds). But in practice the distinction is not always so clearcut, especially when doubt moves in the direction of unbelief and passes over that blurred transition between the open-ended uncertainty of doubt and the closed-minded certainty of unbelief.

But the over-all thrust of the biblical teaching on doubt is not ambiguous. A great variety of words are used but the essential point is the same. Doubt is a halfway stage. To be in doubt is to be in two minds, to be caught between two worlds, to be suspended between a desire to affirm and a desire to negate. So the idea of 'total' or 'complete' doubt is a contradiction in terms; doubt that is total is no longer doubt, it is unbelief.

Of course, we may call our doubt 'total doubt' or charge it with being unbelief, but only if our purpose is to stop doubt short and see that it does not become unbelief. When in Mark's gospel the father of the demented boy cried out, 'I believe; help my unbelief!', he was condemning his own doubt as unbelief. But Jesus, who never responded to real unbelief, showed by answering his prayer and healing his son that he recognized it as doubt.

The distinction between doubt and unbelief, though not hard and fast, is valid and useful. Its importance, however, is not that we know *when* doubt becomes unbelief (for only God knows this and human attempts to say so can be cruel), but that we should be clear about *where* doubt leads to as it grows into unbelief.

Soft or hard on doubt?

The healthy combination of an analysis of the nature of doubt with an awareness of where it leads is the heart of the Christian view of doubt. Curiously, it is also the reason why those who are 'soft' on doubt and those who are 'hard' on doubt can both find biblical support for their views. The former can point to the great difference between doubt and unbelief and the latter to the great similarity. Each ignores the balancing emphasis of biblical teaching.

This balance was what set apart the New Testament view from its Greco-Roman surroundings. The world of the first century was marked by a deep awareness of doubt, but usually doubt was traced back only to cultural irresolution or philosophical scepticism. In the New Testament, however, faith is synonymous with the obedience of faith, so that faith involves both the understanding and the will. Doubt is therefore tackled primarily at the point of action and not at the point of reflection.

The Old Testament had laid special stress against disobeying, rather than doubting, the Word of God. But the New Testament is strongly against doubt itself and stronger still against unbelief. Now that God has revealed himself so fully in Christ, the value of the stakes of salvation are higher, and there is less excuse for lack of faith.

This combined emphasis – that doubt is not the same as unbelief but can lead naturally to it – directs us to a mature handling of doubt that avoids the extremes of being too hard or too soft on doubt. Those who forget the first point fall into the error of being too hard. In virtually equating doubt and unbelief they make doubt the opposite of faith in a way that is true neither to the Bible nor to what we know of human knowledge. To insist that only doubt-free faith can be counted as genuine faith is to misunderstand what knowledge and faith are. The perfectionism in the demand is more destructive of genuine faith than the worst of doubts could ever be.

The true relationship of faith and doubt is closer to that of courage and fear. Fear is not the opposite of courage, cowardice is. Fear, in fact, need be no final threat to courage. What courage cannot afford is recklessness. Take a mountain climber, a Grand Prix racing-driver or a person conquering a devastating handicap. Each one has a courage which controls his fear and subdues his emotions so that risks are made responsible and commitments in the face of danger are carefully calculated.

It is the same with faith and doubt. Doubt is not the opposite of faith, unbelief is. Doubt does not necessarily or automatically mean the end of faith, for doubt is *faith in two minds*. What destroys faith is the disobedience that hardens into unbelief.

This is the second point that balances the first and safeguards it from the other extreme – being too soft on doubt. Doubt is not always fatal but it is always serious. Some people react so strongly against the morbid view of doubt that they treat doubt casually, even celebrate it. The error here is to isolate doubt from faith and unbelief and consider it strictly by itself as a mere mechanism of human knowing. The only question then asked is, *How* does doubt work? And the answer, since it is only abstract, carries little sting.

But the question is not abstract in real life, so to the interesting questions of *how* must be added the urgent question of *what*. As soon as this second question is asked (What is being doubted?), the price of doubt rises or falls immediately. It is *what* we doubt and not *how* we doubt that sets the market value of doubting.

If the object of our faith were as elusive as the Loch Ness monster or as inconsequential as whether to have a third cup of afternoon tea, then doubt makes little difference. But since the object of Christian faith is God, to believe or disbelieve is everything. Thus the market value of doubt for the Christian is extremely high. Find out how seriously a believer takes his doubts and you have the index of how seriously he takes his faith. For the Christian, doubt is not the same as unbelief, but neither is it divorced from it. Continued doubt loosens the believer's hold on the resources and privileges of faith and can be the prelude to the disasters of unbelief. So doubt is never treated as trivial.

Seven deadly doubts

Those who are interested in doubt only from a practical standpoint may want to pass from this definition of doubt as doublemindedness directly to an examination of the categories of doubt in part two. Thus they may prefer to skip the next two chapters which are more theoretical. What follows in part two is not meant to be a gloomy cataloguing of specific doubts but a look at seven of the most common 'families' of doubt.

It is not en exhaustive account of doubt. To attempt such a thing would be herculean and quixotic. What is more helpful is to gain a broad overview of some of the main types of doubt which Christians are likely to face. These broad categories can give us an over-all perspective from which to view, handle and resolve our specific doubts. But even with the field limited in this way, an exhaustive study is out of the question. It would be wise for each of us to draw up our own list and carefully think through the issues involved in each.

Nor is it a completely objective evaluation. That too is impossible. A problem, after all, is only so if it is a problem to someone. Problems strike us all differently. What is trivial to one person may raise titanic questions for someone else. Some people face doubt only if they find no answer; others trigger doubts merely by raising questions. What puzzles a philosopher and taxes his mind to distraction may look completely irrelevant or quite obvious to a businessman. The point is not to judge who is right, but to meet and resolve whatever doubt is a problem to a particular person.

At first it might appear simple to unravel a particular doubt by relating it to one of the seven broad categories, but first appearances are deceptive. There are many possible variations within each category. Some have their root causes in subjective factors, others in objective factors and others still are a mixture. Some doubts are simple in origin, others complex. Some doubts are as uncomplicated as a clean fracture of the leg – and just as damaging – while others present a tougher problem more like a compound fracture with the possible danger of gangrene.

In sickness and health

When people speak of doubt, sooner or later medical images pop up as doubt becomes seen as a sickness of faith. This analogy can be helpful, particularly if it gives a visual dimension to our thinking. But if it is pressed too far, medical imagery can lead to a sense of inevitability and passiveness which is inappropriate in resolving doubt. The image, of course, centres around the fact that faith and doubt have something of the same curious relationship as health and sickness.

As faith is the opposite of unbelief, health is the opposite of death. Both faith and health turn on the importance of wholeness, and both are much less obvious than one might imagine. In fact it is possible to enjoy them most when one is aware of them least. Since aspects of each can be understood better in the light of their absence, each may be noticed more when it is not there than when it is. In telling us what health and faith are *not*, sickness and doubt also tell us something of what health and faith should be.

Doubts are like sicknesses in that the prevalent types vary from country to country and from culture to culture. Every believer is prone to doubt, but some are more prone to one kind and some to another. This should not leave us dispirited. We all get sick, but we do not live in fear of catching every known disease. If we did, what a miserable affair life would be! Nor does leading a healthy life mean we must be vaccinated for every possible disease. Still, if we travel in an infected area, we would be foolish not to take precautions.

In the same way assurance of faith depends on our grasp of God and his faithfulness and not on a mastery of all the doubts that are ever likely to assail us. Otherwise faith could never be assured while one last doubt remained. But the alert believer should be aware of the main tendencies to doubt prevalent at the time. These will differ from generation to generation and from temperament to temperament, but it is wise to know the types of doubt to which we are most prone.

What is more, faith, like health, is best maintained by growth, nourishment and exercise and *not* by fighting sickness. Sickness may be the absence of health, but health is more than the absence of sickness, so prevention is better than cure. Equally, faith grows and flourishes when it is well nourished and exercised, so the best way to resist doubt is to build up faith rather than simply to fight against doubt.

In contrast, preoccupation with sickness is not recommended for anyone except those in the medical profession. For others preoccupation with sickness may itself become a sickness. No one would want to foster the doubter's equivalent of a hypochondriac. We must therefore resist any temptation to read a book on doubt like a medical dictionary, or before long we may convince ourselves that we are suffering from every variety of doubt.

God's part and ours

In resolving doubt, how much is God's part and how much is ours? Two things need to be emphasized with equal force. On the one hand, *God is the answer to all doubt*. Emphatically and without any question this is so. As Martin Luther said, in what must be the theological understatement of all time,' The Holy Spirit is not a sceptic.' Through the creative agency of his Word and his Spirit God is the author and giver of faith; naturally he is the prime resolver of doubt. Faith is a gracious gift of God and the resolution of doubt is a gracious gift of God.

This means that assurance of faith comes directly from knowing God and only indirectly from understanding doubt. (This is probably why there are so few books written on doubt itself.) More particularly, assurance of faith comes from knowledge of God, as objectively revealed in his Word and subjectively revealed by his Spirit. Who is it who gives us a knowledge of our adoption into God's family? Who is it that is God's seal in our hearts? Who is God's down payment on the inheritance we will receive in the future? Who is the firstfruit of a harvest of blessings to come? The answer in each case is the Holy Spirit. Without any hesitation we can say that God is the answer to all doubt and that the largest part of doubting comes simply from ignorance of what God has said and done.

On the other hand it must be emphasized that, while God is the answer to all doubt, theologically correct God-answers are not necessarily the answer. A crucial mistake has often been made here. People have forgotten that there are also spiritual, moral and especially psychological dimensions to doubt.

The plain fact of Christian experience is that many people have held a strong theology of assurance but have known no assurance themselves. Are we to say that God's assurance is no more assured than the fluctuations of our feelings? Or are we to insist that assurance of faith exists in a believer even when he is sure that such assurance does not exist?

To some the latter is paradoxical; to others it is nonsense. But much of the problem dissolves immediately once we recognize that there is a confusion of categories at its root. Some doubts are directly a matter of theology, others only indirectly, if at all.

This is a book on doubt and doubting; it is not a theology of assurance. The two are not necessarily the same. In fact, there are two types of people who in their doubt are particularly allergic to theological talk. On the one hand are those who are *insensitive* to God's truth. Their doubt is hardening into unbelief; merely to talk of God is to waste words, to pour water on a duck's back and watch it run off. Certainly they need conviction too, but of a different kind. On the other hand are those who are *over-sensitive*. They fasten on theological truths as on an armoury of big sticks, and they rain down blows on their long-suffering faith, belabouring it for being substandard and for failing to believe what it should.

Theological answers, even though correct, can be unhelpful to both of these types, though in different ways. Theological talk, as such, is only a verbal formula. Like a prescription it needs to be taken to be a cure, like a recipe it needs to be cooked to be eaten, like a cheque it needs to be cashed to be spent. To the insensitive, theological talk seems as redundant as a prescription to a man who thinks he is well or a recipe to a man who is overfed or another cheque to a billionaire. To the over-sensitive, though, what matters is the cure, the meal and the money.

This is why answering doubt is not the same as dispensing theological prescriptions. Our examination of each doubt will tell us two things: first, about the deficiency of faith which has caused the problem, and second, about the sufficiency of God which is needed as the answer. But the two need to be carefully related. God's grace can be as much misused when it is wrongly applied to those who are over-sensitive as when it is completely forgotten by those who are insensitive. So there are two reasons why we will concentrate heavily on the human side in resolving doubt. First, many books already deal with doubt in terms of a theology of assurance. Second, the deliberate stress on what we *can* and *must* do when we doubt is designed to fence off what we *cannot* and *must never* do.

All of the doubts we will discuss spring either from my own experience or from the experience of many who have shared their doubts with me. These doubts are not examined for academic purposes, nor are they treated in a critical way. Our aim is to understand doubt only in order to understand and to encourage faith. We do it in the same spirit in which in *Pilgrim's Progress* John Bunyan's Christian and Hopeful erected a sign to keep other pilgrims from the hands of Giant Despair.

> *Over this stile is the way to Doubting Castle, which is kept by Giant Despair, who despiseth the King of the Celestial Country, and seeks to destroy his holy pilgrims.* Many therefore that followed after, read what was written, and escaped the danger.

Chapter Three

Everybody's Problem

Why do some people think that faith is necessarily troubled by doubt but that knowledge is not? Or how is it that faith and uncertainty are automatically associated with each other while knowledge is regarded as certain and therefore different? These questions express the second misconception concerning doubt – the idea that doubt is a problem for faith but not for knowledge.

The word *believe* is commonly used very weakly today. If I were to ask you if you could come to dinner tonight and you replied 'Yes' or 'No', my wife and I could plan accordingly. But if you were to say 'I believe so' or 'I doubt it', we might not prepare the meal but we could hardly plan to go elsewhere until we had heard from you more definitely. Yes and No imply certainty based on knowledge and choice. But today when someone says 'I believe so', what he means is 'Yes-with-doubts'. When he says 'I doubt it', what he means is 'No-with-doubts'.

But this is the reverse of what a Christian means when he says 'I believe' in God. The difference can be seen easily if we turn the Apostles' Creed into a series of questions (Do you believe in God, the Father Almighty? etc.) and then ask what reply is appropriate. Christians are 'believers', but the appropriate Christian reply to such questions would not be 'I believe so' but 'Yes!' The modern understanding of belief suggests an uncertainty which is knowledge-minus; the Christian understanding of belief speaks of a certainty which is knowledge-plus.

Faith out in the cold
How is it that faith has been so divorced from knowledge? Picture someone being treated as an odd man out – in a family, in an office or at a party. Only rarely is such a person genuinely odd, at least in the beginning. Usually he is

merely different. The trouble is that his differences are different from other people's. But since the majority sets the standards, the differences of the majority are considered normal, those of the minority odd. In the end, the odd man out is excluded. Where he is different from the rest, his differences are exaggerated; where he is the same, his similarities are ignored.

Imagine your own examples. In a roomful of thin boys one fat boy is odd man out. What is shared in common – boyishness – would be forgotten; fatness or thinness would then be all that mattered. Or again, can the bias against left-handedness be explained apart from the fact that most people are right-handed? 'Right-hand man' is a complimentary description, whereas the Latin for left has become 'sinister', and the French for left has become 'gauche'. The suggestion is almost that since right is right, left (being the opposite of right) is wrong.

Faith is being treated in much the same way. The suggestion almost made is that, since knowledge is certain and faith is not knowledge, faith is uncertain. The way people talk about faith, you would think that rationality, inquiry, investigation, understanding and proof had all joined hands to form a circle of knowledge, leaving faith outside in the cold. Faith is treated as the odd man out, the misfit, the black sheep.

It is commonly suggested that since faith depends on assumptions, it has nothing to do with knowledge, just as knowledge has no need of faith. Faith is something which is merely believed, so it must always expect to be open to doubt. But knowledge is something which has achieved the certainty of being known and proved, and therefore need never be doubted.

The issue at stake here is vital. If faith has nothing to do with knowledge, then we Christians doubt because our faith is weaker than knowledge. In this case our doubt would be only a local problem, a sign of the inferiority of our faith. It would be solved at once if we were to abandon faith for something more solid which can be known. On the other hand, if this distinction is wrong, if faith depends on knowledge and knowledge depends on faith, then doubt would be a challenge to both knowledge and faith and not just to faith.

In fact, the latter is the case. Without faith there is no knowledge. All true faith depends on knowledge. Knowledge and faith are inseparable.

As soon as we see this our picture of doubt changes completely. Doubt is not so much our problem as everybody's problem. It is not primarily a Christian problem, but a human problem. Merely to say it does not magically dissolve the particular trouble we face as Christians who doubt. But it helps us to recognize that we are not alone in facing doubt. The root of doubt is not in our faith but in our humanness. What we doubt may undermine our faith, and even more so how we doubt or why we fail to deal with doubt. But in no way is the fact that we doubt a negative reflection on our faith.

Blood brothers, not arch-enemies

How is this so? In what sense are faith and doubt closely related to knowledge? The answer lies in the part played by assumptions or presuppositions in knowledge. Knowledge pretends it is completely different from faith and makes faith the odd man out by ignoring its own assumptions. But the fact that assumptions are necessary for knowledge shows that knowledge and faith are not arch-enemies, as often supposed, but blood brothers.

Advance in human knowledge is closely and rightly tied to how we come to know. This is why in most cases an eye-witness account is more reliable than rumour or hearsay, or why the conclusions of a scientific experiment are likely to be accepted above the claims of a spaced-out acid head. A large part of coming to know lies in discovering the best ways of coming to know. But even with the best understanding in the world some element of uncertainty is present in knowledge, for we can never know *exhaustively* how we come to know. There are some things we have to assume in order to know anything.

Fortunately for our sanity, we can say that we know something without having to delve each time into *how* we know it. If we could say 'I know' only when we could also say *exhaustively* how it is that we know, it would create just as much a problem for the sophisticated philosopher as for those of us who are simpler. The problem, though, does not lie in what we know but how we know. When we set out to know something, we do not proceed by *proving* everything we know before we know it. If we are to know anything, we must proceed on the basis of certain things which *cannot be proved but which must be presupposed.*

Could you know anything without first presupposing that *you* are there to know it and that there is *something there to be known?* Or could you prove the rules of logic without using the rules to do so? We cannot even conclude that we do not exist without presupposing that we do. Nor can we fundamentally question the rules of logic, for only when we assume them can we ask a question at all. These are obvious, though complicated-sounding, examples of the sort of indispensable presuppositions or faith-assumptions which we cannot do without.

Put very simply, in order to know anything we must assume certain things in faith. Without doing so we would know nothing at all. This means that reason is never able to guarantee itself. Rationality is part of our greatness, but it also serves to keep us humble because rationality itself must be assumed by faith. An element of faith is indispensable to all human knowledge. The situation with human knowledge is not what is often suggested – that faith begins when reason ends. Rather, if faith does not begin, reason will not do so either. *There is always more to knowing than human knowledge will ever know.*

As human beings we can choose to believe anything, but we must believe something. We can believe nothing only if this too is made into a belief. This is why all of us will doubt at some point, whatever it is that we believe. The beggar in Ingmar Bergman's film *Virgin Spring* speaks for us all. In a poignant soliloquy, watching smoke curl into the sky like an ethereal question mark, he exclaims, 'Ah, human beings – they tremble and worry like a leaf in the storm because they know and because they don't know.'

What does this mean? Simply that human beings know some things with certainty and other things with less certainty? Of course, it is true that outside the small clearing of what we know lies the unexplored forest of what we do not know. But that is not the point. The deeper reason for our doubt – and faith – is that even what we know rests only on the foundations of what we do not know.

This means that one basic source of human doubt is

located within the very foundation structures of knowledge itself. In a profound sense we doubt not only because we are ignorant of something but because we are absolutely certain of nothing. The way we know at all as human beings means not only that none of us knows everything but that none of us knows absolutely why we know anything. There is a grey area for all of us, a philosophical no-man's-land between what we know and what we do not know. In his book *Knots* R. D. Laing captures the absurdity of our pretensions to absolutely certain knowledge in one of his mental 'knots'.

> If I don't know I don't know
> > I think I know
> If I don't know I know
> > I think I don't know

This is a basic, though subtle, source of doubt, but it is not the only one. Nor, as it happens, is it the most important. But it helps to show clearly that doubt is everybody's problem. Any approach that makes doubt a problem of faith rather than a problem of knowledge is wrong.

Doubt is not primarily a question of particular faiths (Should I believe *this* one or *that* one?) or even of the strength of faith (Do I *really* believe this one or that one?). Rather doubt is bound up with knowledge and faith themselves. Martin Luther remarked, 'The art of doubting is easy, for it is an ability that is born with us.' Knowledge and doubt are inseparable to man. The sole alternative to knowledge-with-doubt is no knowledge at all. Only God and certain madmen have no doubts.

Testimony to this comes from the common agreement of many of the world's proverbs: 'Who knows nothing doubts nothing' (French), 'The wise are prone to doubt' (Greek), or 'With great doubts come great understanding; with little doubts come little understanding' (Chinese).

Self-confidence and certainty

For human knowledge to be absolutely sure of itself is a contradiction in terms. As Pascal observes in *The Pensées*, 'Nothing strengthens the case of scepticism more than the fact that there are people who are not sceptic. If they all were it would be wrong.' Since our knowledge is finite, none of us can exclude the possibility of our being wrong.

Of course, we all know people who are supremely sure of themselves. But self-confidence in the sense of psychological certitude is not the same things as absolute certainty in the philosophical sense. One man completely self-assured (in the psychological sense) is not a contradiction of what we have just said any more than what we have just said about uncertainty (in the epistemological sense) reduces all men to the level of mumbling irresolution.

Cardinal Newman wrote in his *Apologia pro vita sua*, 'From the time that I became a Catholic . . . I never have had one doubt.' But such a statement can be easily misunderstood if taken out of context. Certainly it demonstrates a virile faith, which is an excellent example to every believer. But it can also be misleading, for its strength is partly reinforced by the Cardinal's self-confidence and the place he had reached on his spiritual pilgrimage. It is a personal testimony, not a claim made for Catholicism or even for Christianity. He is not saying, 'Become a Christian and you will never doubt.' He is only saying that after a certain point in his life he himself did not doubt. This conviction may be enviable, but not everyone is able to match it, and it would be dishonest to pretend otherwise.

The Cardinal himself never pretended otherwise, but people whose doubts are depressingly real can easily forget this and become discouraged by such a standard. But their discouragement stems mainly from confusing self-confidence with certainty, so that quite unnecessarily they tend to despise their own much weaker faith. Properly speaking, the force (and also the weakness) of a personal testimony is that it tells us as much about the person who believes as about the content of what he believes. A testimony may be fascinating but at the same time quite irrelevant to the basic questions touching on faith and doubt. Self-confidence is not the same thing as intellectual certainty or moral infallibility.

For every Cardinal Newman there are hundreds for whom such words might be better described as egotism or pigheadedness. There are certainly many others who would see themselves reflected more accurately in Constantin Levin, Tolstoy's portrayal of himself in *Anna Karenina*.

'On the very morning of his wedding Constantin was filled with a radiant happiness of love, but his doubting nature suddenly cast a shadow across his joy. But do I know her thoughts, her wishes, her feelings? a voice suddenly whispered. The smile faded from his face, and he grew thoughtful. And all at once a strange sensation came over him. Fear and doubt possessed him, doubt of everything.'

The two faces of doubt

Doubt is human and universal. But if we are speaking as Christians, we must quickly add that this situation is a problem only because of the Fall. Did uncertainty play any part in man's knowledge before the Fall? It would be impossible to do more than speculate. On the one hand, before the Fall man could not have enjoyed exhaustive certainty, for he was still bound by the limitations of his finiteness, though not of his sinfulness. On the other hand, after the Fall there is a spiritual and moral dimension to doubt which transcends the mere uncertainty concerning a theory of knowing.

Doubt now is much more than a matter of uncertainty. It is an integral part of spiritual pride, moral evil, psychological alienation and intellectual confusion, each of which is a legacy of the Fall. Most probably doubt comes from the new sting given by the Fall to the lack of total epistemological certainty which was there before. At worst we can now doubt for reasons which are purely moral, spiritual or psychological, as in the case of someone who is incurably suspicious, a problem which has nothing at all to do with epistemology.

Although knowledge, faith and doubt are inseparable, there is a crucial difference in the nature of their relationship. Knowledge and faith would always have been inseparable, even if there had been no Fall (like the healthy relationship of two twins). Doubt and faith, though, are related only because of the nature of things after the Fall (like the unhealthy relationship of a leech clinging to a body).

But this does not mean that we swing to the opposite extreme and say that because doubt is a result of the Fall, all doubts are necessarily destructive, negative, even sinful. This is not so. Doubt is sometimes of great value.

The reason doubt is valuable lies in a distinctive peculiarity of reality after the Fall. We are no longer in a world where everything is perfect, but neither are we in a world where everything is evil. Instead, reality after the Fall has a curious ambiguity, a strange double-edged aspect. Reality now has two faces or two angles from which the same face can be viewed quite differently. Everything can be taken either of two ways – creatively or destructively, for God or against God.

On one side there are some things, such as human creativity, which were once completely good by virtue of God's creation. But now after the Fall, they are equivocal, ambivalent, with a potential which can be turned either way. Think of various uses to which human creativity can be put, such as humour or technology. We see immediately how easy it is to use them either positively or negatively, for beauty and life or for ugliness and death.

On the other side there are things which are now in a form which is entirely the result of the Fall. They operate in a way which runs counter to the original purpose of creation. Death is a prime example.

Yet, since they have this ambiguous, double-edged aspect too, even the latter are not totally evil but can be turned to some good. Think of situations where death, which we should usually see as outrageous and abnormal, is welcomed, as in the dying of extreme sufferers or those whose continued existence is a threat to the lives of others. (How many lives were saved by the deaths of Hitler or Stalin?) This is the other face of death. It is not our normal view of it, but it is no less real and cannot be dismissed from human experience.

Doubt is a part of this second group of double-edged realities. We might call them 'abnormal-normals', things which appear normal from one perspective and abnormal from another. Measured against the character of God and his original purposes in creation, these abnormal-normals are decidedly abnormal. But measured against the abnormal situation which has been introduced by the Fall, they have an approximate normality. This is an important qualification (that doubt is normal only in our abnormal situation), but it allows us to appreciate something of the positive side of doubt.

The value of doubt

The value of doubt is that it can be used to detect error. We live in a fallen world. All is not true, so not everything should be believed; some things ought to be doubted. Jesus was not being poetic when he described the Evil One as 'the father of lies'. The Devil's stock in trade is the world of half-truths and half-lies where the half-lie masquerades as the whole truth.

But a sword like this will cut both ways. If doubt can be turned destructively against truth so that it is dismissed as error, doubt can also be used constructively to prosecute error disguised as truth. If the surrouding web of reality which we perceive is partly true and partly false, then in order to get closer to the truth some things need to be doubted so that others can properly be believed. The original meaning of the Greek word *skeptikos* is, in fact, 'inquirer'.

The inescapable presence of doubt is a constant reminder of our responsibility to truth in a twilight world of truth and half-truth. Like a spur it challenges us to find out for ourselves. It is precisely because all is not certain that we have to make certain. Because there is always room for doubt, we are always left with room to inquire. This is what keeps open a breathing-space for the spiritual and moral dimensions to the investigation of truth in a world whose natural bent is to exclude it. Healthy scepticism is a sign of the knowing man's humility.

The constructive side to doubt has long been recognized. The essayist Francis Bacon wrote, 'If a man will begin with certainties, he shall end in doubts; but if he will be content to begin with doubts, he shall end in certainties.' Pascal, referring to doubt more specifically in relation to Christian faith, wrote, 'One must know when it is right to doubt, to affirm, to submit. Anyone who does otherwise does not understand the force of reason.' Earlier still Augustine said, 'I doubt, therefore truth is.'

Doubt may be ambiguous, an anomaly, an abnormal-normal, but the very kick-back in its double-edged nature prevents anyone from settling permanently in error. Even if someone believes the most secure and pernicious lies, he will not be able to help himself from doubting them at some time. Doubt acts as a sparring partner both to truth and error. It keeps faith trim and helps to shed the paunchiness of false ideas. Like a terrier, doubt worries at weak ideas until they escape reinvigorated or collapse exhausted. It is the nature of doubt always to be questioning, challenging, inquiring, cross-examining. Doubt is not inarticulate though its questions may lie deeper than words.

To the mind that is morally and intellectually healthy this positive value of doubt can work to its advantage. If there were no disease in the world, innoculation would be unnecessary. If there were no lies and half-truths in the world, doubt would be superfluous for everything could be believed. But just as a tiny dose of poison is sometimes the best antidote to complete poisoning (though too much kills), so a modest dose of doubt – limited, temporary and constructively used – can be an excellent preventative of unbelief (though excessive doubt is fatal here too).

This has never been better expressed, perhaps, than in the famous lines of Tennyson's *In Memoriam*:

> He fought his doubts and gather'd strength,
>   He would not make his judgement blind,
>   He faced the spectres of the mind
> And laid them: thus he came at length
> To find a stronger faith his own.

Of course, we must not exaggerate the value of doubt and forget its darker side. If doubt can conjure up images of heroism (the David of Doubt standing up to the Goliath of Lies), it can just as easily represent what is most cowardly, indecisive and dictatorial in us all. Like an amber light that changes to green or red, doubt may change to faith or to unbelief. Pascal captures the negative side when he writes, 'Doubt then is an unhappy state, but there is an indispensable duty to seek in doubt, and thus anyone who doubts and does not seek is at once unhappy and in the wrong.'

Doubt, then, is a problem for both faith and knowledge. As long as the presence of doubt is detected anywhere, neither faith nor knowledge can ever be complacent. But though doubt may be normal, it should only be temporary and it should always be resolved.. Wisely understood, resolutely faced, it need hold no fear for the Christian. To a healthy faith doubt is a healthy challenge.

Chapter Four

Hostage Unawares

What do most people do when they begin to doubt? Do they bring the doubt out into the open to examine it or silence it and pretend it never happened? Or do nothing, hoping the problem will go away? The way people react to their doubts is an excellent indication of their attitude to doubt itself.

Christians today are not normally known for their candour about doubt or for their confident ability to resolve it. Why is this? If doubt is human and universal, why do so many Christians treat it as dark and unmentionable, a problem that gnaws at the mind like the suspicion of cancer or troubles the conscience like a guilty thought? To some it is even the ultimate treason against faith, the unpardonable sin.

In this chapter we will examine a third misconception about doubt – the idea that doubt is something to be ashamed of because it is dishonest to believe if you have doubts. This is another major reason for the inadequate views of doubt among Christians. Unwittingly we have succumbed to twentieth-century views of doubt.

Particular twentieth-century objections to Christianity have certainly created doubts for some Christians. One example is Freud's view that all beliefs are the result of instinctual desires and drives. But although such objections pose serious problems for Christians, the heart of the danger lies deeper than that.

Christian thinking has been affected not so much by specific doubts as by the general concept of doubting which is entertained today. Christians have stood firm against a flood of unbelief but have failed to notice its more subtle effects. A consensus has welled up around the church and left as its high-water mark a distinctive view of doubt which is prejudicial to faith and quite illegitimate.

I am not saying that Christians subscribe openly to such a

view of doubt. Not at all. The great majority are not even aware of it, let alone able to give it a name. Yet, like most faiths in the twentieth century, Christianity has come under the hypnotic spell of this modern attitude, and Christians are beguiled into behaving as it demands.

The irony is plain. It is bad enough for a believer in any faith to have the content of his belief infiltrated by alien ideas. But it displays an astonishing degree of intellectual captivity when the entire way he doubts what he believes is infiltrated too. This is a double alienation and for the Christian a curious kind of worldliness of mind.

Reason's right-hand man

What is the modern view of doubt that does this damage? It is often described as 'critical', 'systematic', 'rational' or 'methodic' doubt. As such it is part of the legacy of a long tradition of humanist thought which stretches back to fifth-century BC Greece when the first decisive steps towards modern secularism were taken. This is not the place to attempt a critique of humanism. But the point to notice is that a key part of humanist thought, from the early Greeks down to the twentieth century, is the attempt to justify man's knowledge by his reason alone, denying the necessity of faith in general and God's revelation in particular.

This rationalism (I use the word here in a much wider sense than suggested by 'rationalism' as opposed to 'empiricism') attempts not only to use reason as a tool but to go further and make reason guarantee itself. Doubt is seen as a complement to reason, and both reason and doubt are regarded as competent tools with which to discover truth. The importance of reason in rationalism needs no further elaboration; our concern here is the equally important role assigned to doubt.

In the long, patient search for truth doubt has been slowly promoted until it is reason's junior partner or reason's right-hand man. As a reward for its services doubt is distinguished as 'critical', 'systematic' and 'rational'. Doubt therefore becomes the acid test for truth, the best solvent for error, the Geiger counter for detecting falsehood, the sieve to catch unwanted lumps of irrationality.

All 'mere beliefs' are viewed as inferior since they are only accepted on trust or via authorities or tradition. They have to be subjected to a rigorous trial by doubt, and only those considered 'indubitable' or 'certain beyond any shadow of doubt' are finally accepted as true. The purpose of this process of doubting is to strain off the dross of uncertainty and to leave behind a residue of knowledge – objective, certain, universal. Doubt everything that can be doubted is the aim of the exercise. What is left, it is claimed, will be self-evident truths which can be accepted as such by all open minds.

René Descartes, who attempted to discover truth by doubting everything he could manage to doubt, described the first principle of his method like this in *A Discourse on Method*, 'The *first* rule was never to accept anything for true which I did not clearly know to be such; that is to say ... to comprise nothing more in my judgement than what was presented to my mind so clearly and distinctly as to exclude all ground of doubt.' This method of Cartesian doubt was the process by which he reached his famous dictum: *Cogito ergo sum* ('I think, therefore I am').

The clarity and compelling power of this approach are plain. At first it sounds the same as our earlier description of the positive value of doubt. Actually, the basic differences are enormous.

Christians and humanists are not alone in agreeing that doubt can be an antidote to inauthentic faith or to error and falsehood. But while the Christian sees doubt as useful only in the preliminary stages of exposing what he should *not* believe, some humanists go much further. They almost suggest that, if applied correctly, critical doubt would rule out all answers other than their own and establish humanism as the only rational belief. Bertrand Russell, for example, claimed in his book *Sceptical Essays* that rationalism, doubt and the millennium go hand in hand: 'If only men could be brought into a tentatively agnostic frame of mind about these matters [religion and politics], nine-tenths of the evils of the modern world would be cured.... Thus rational doubt alone, if it could be generated, would suffice to introduce the millennium.'

Why stop there?

Even where it is not stated explicitly, it is often implied that the tenets of rationalism or humanism are indubitable and self-evident. But there is a glaring fallacy, an unacceptable extra step in the logic of this attitude. It is an overstatement typical of the worst type of 'leap of faith' and cannot be allowed to pass. If we listen carefully to the process of critical doubt and then examine just what it is that is pronounced indubitable, we must surely ask : but why stop here? Why should the process end at that particular point? Why is this so-called 'indubitable' itself exempted from doubt?

Take Lao-Tse's celebrated question : 'If when I was asleep I was a man dreaming I was a butterfly, how do I know when I am awake that I am not a butterfly dreaming I am a man?' Getting on with living is most people's answer to the question. But, apart from the fact that we have to live anyway, could reason alone put a stop to the dizzying effect of the question? The answer is no. Even the proofs of science would be no help for they too are founded on pre-scientific presuppositions.

If we press this and insist on doubting what the humanist holds as indubitable, we uncover a hornet's nest of assumptions and presuppositions which are far from being rationally indubitable. For example, why do we accept what we have always presupposed rather than proved? Why do we not insist that presuppositions be proved too? Why do we not query everything, even the act of querying itself?

Obviously, to take this to the end of the line is impossible and as pointless as a dog chasing its tail. But that is the point. Once we see the absurdity of doubting everything, including the tool of doubt itself, we can see the basic flaw in the use of critical doubt: *No one can doubt everything: To live meaningfully each person must assume, or believe, something.*

In fact, we can only doubt something if we believe something else. So the place at which a person stops doubting is a matter of his private preference and with many people this is entirely arbitrary. One person's point of believing may be another person's point of doubting; there is no one who does not have some faith. Doubting can help to rule out possible faiths that will not do, but by itself it cannot establish the faith that will.

The problem with critical doubt is that it is not doubtful enough: it does not subject itself to its own criteria. It is critical of others but less so of itself. A doubt that is genuinely systematic would lead its advocate to a state beyond argument, beyond language and even beyond rationality to a nirvana-like silence of nonconsciousness. As Pascal warned, 'No one can go that far, and I maintain that a perfectly genuine sceptic has never existed. Nature backs up helpless reason and stops it going so wildly astray.'

How about that rare bird, the man who professes that he is a 'complete sceptic'? Listen to him carefully and you will soon find that his scepticism is far from complete. He holds to it in a most unsceptical way – that is, with a fair degree of dogmatism. Pascal pointed out that 'sceptical arguments allow the positive to be positive. Few ... speak dubiously of scepticism'. The fact that sceptics are not sceptical about scepticism is further evidence that to doubt anything we must believe something. The person who is sceptical toward one faith or even most faiths will be the devoted adherent of another. In fact, it is a measure of his poverty both that he is unaware of it and that he can define himself only in negative terms.

Some people claim otherwise and argue vociferously for complete scepticism. But they disprove their own argument with every thought, every word, every point of logic that they use. Every moment of shared communication speaks against their total scepticism. Their very insistence of trying to make sense is eloquent testimony to assumptions that are powerful though silent.

The contradictions of this have been delightfully illustrated. Catch the 'complete sceptic' in any situation where exclamations like 'Look out for that car!' or 'Your slip is showing!' or 'Your fly is undone!' are appropriate. The most sceptical of sceptics will immediately move much faster than his scepticism should allow.

Complete scepticism is impossible. Limited scepticism is arbitrary. Each person chooses what he is sceptical about and what he believes without scepticism. To stress this is to labour the obvious, but it underlines the point that no one can know exhaustively how he knows what he knows. If the only alternatives in knowing were the Scylla and Charybdis of pure objectivism or total scepticism, our choice would be a sorry one. Pure objectivism is a myth and complete scepticism an impossibility. The answer to this impasse lies in a third way of knowing, one which is based on presuppositions. But if knowledge proceeds on what must be presupposed before it is proved, the cover is blown on the pretensions of critical doubt.

Critical doubt depends on a myth, the idea that human knowledge is totally objective and neutral. But no human knowledge is so certain that it needs no presuppositions. It is impossible to doubt anything unless there is some thing we do not doubt – our own assumptions. Even these can be criticized only upon the basis of other assumptions.

Like a man changing horses in midstream, someone can pass over in seconds from one set of assumptions to another. But even during those few seconds when he is changing he is on one horse or the other. There is no other place to be but the stream.

Presuppositions are the silent partners in thought, but their silence must not be mistaken for their absence. What the ventriloquist's voice and the puppeteer's hands are to the puppet, presuppositions are to rational thought. Without the man and the voice, there is only a limp doll. Sometimes a person may fail to see his own assumptions and sometimes he will deliberately conceal them. But systematic doubt is a handy weapon for dismissing our opponent's beliefs and establishing our own only if we ignore our own presuppositions.

It is time to identify and explode the powerful myth of critical doubt and dispel the clouds of defeatism which it lowers on Christian faith. Critical doubt is incorrect and its prestige is exaggerated. Doubt by itself is not the final test of truth. Doubt alone is not the badge of objectivity. It is not for doubt to deliver a certificate of certainty. Being constantly self-critical provides no guarantee of truth nor necessarily any immunity from prejudice and error. Doubt can have deep integrity, but it can also be lazy and dishonest.

Reduce its inflated prestige and doubt can be given its rightful place once more. The strength of scepticism is not that it can be argued consistently but that it can be used effectively against unwarranted dogmatism. The way of doubt is not itself the path to truth, but in sealing off mistaken approaches it provides an impetus to the search. It can be a prelude to inquiry just as questions are a spur to searching.

As Kierkegaard remarked, the method which doubts in order to philosophize is little more suited to its purpose than the notion of teaching a soldier to stand up straight by learning to lie down in a heap. Like an unloaded pistol held at the believer's head, critical doubt is no more than an empty threat.

Side-effects

How exactly does critical doubt affect a Christian's attitude towards doubting? Like many errors, it catches us on the two horns of a false choice. It suggests that when we have any doubts about our faith we should at once shelve our faith and doubt further. Otherwise our faith would be inauthentic for stopping short. This seems to leave us only two options: either to believe anyway (repressing our doubts and feeling guilty about those that remain) or to give up faith.

But this ignores two vital facts: first, that doubt itself is not the denial of faith, and second, that if they are pursued doubts may be resolved rather than deepened so that faith is confirmed and not denied.

We should be alert for the side-effects of critical doubt. One example is the way Christians become tongue-tied when people define themselves by what they reject in Christianity. This, the non-Christian thinks, is a sufficient rebuttal of faith. ('Well, no, I can't accept that. You see, I'm an atheist/ agnostic/sceptic'.) We should never be thrown off balance by this sort of reply, as if the discussion were ended. In fact it has only begun.

All that the other person has said is what he does *not* believe. This is important and it may be extremely interesting. But it is a red herring because it begs the question: What *does* he believe? That is where his weakness will lie. Scepticism can be a lazy belief, and we should not allow our train of thinking to be shunted off into this old siding.

A second example is the uneasy suspicion that we Christians believe only because we are less sceptical and therefore more shallow in our thinking. The truth is often the reverse. The unthinking Christian may believe his faith as unthinkingly as the unthinking pagan. But many Christians have come to believe because they were more sceptical than most. They have suffered the extreme agony of first-order doubts, so they know that their subsequent faith in God is the only answer to that question which called everything in question.

Having doubted so deeply, such Christians are only surprised that other people, whether pagan or Christian, have believed so easily. Others may play with doubt by not doubting enough. But they have gone through an experience of doubt which has purged them forever of the desire to doubt without finding an answer. This is the scepticism that rules scepticism itself out of court and clears the way for legitimate faith.

Other practical expressions of critical doubt can easily be detected. In fact, the currency of modern unbelief is largely drawn from the over inflated value of rationalism, even if unbelievers are not themselves rationalists. It lends its support to various disdainful dismissals of faith (Christian beliefs are 'nonsense', 'mere opinions', an 'illusion', 'wish-fulfilment' or an 'opiate').

In each case the damning innuendo is the same: Absolute Truth is inhibiting dogma, faith demands a high degree of auto-suggestion and repression, prayer is a sign of incompetence and irresolution, fellowship is a mark of dependency. Ralph Waldo Emerson's remark stands as a typical example: 'As men's prayers are a disease of the will, so are their creeds a disease of the intellect.'

What is suggested as the alternative to faith? Rich and powerful connotations are poured into the vocabulary describing reason and doubt. The way of doubt is the way of 'the critical question', 'the demanding investigation', 'the bold inquiry', 'the courageous challenge', 'the open mind', 'the uninhibited pursuit of truth', 'the indubitable proof', the 'self-evident conclusion'.

The 'free thinker' is the glorious ideal. By contrast, the believer is the unfortunate repository of everything that is dogmatic, inhibited, reactionary and repressive. Much of this is as amusing as it is absurd. Often it is itself only an inherited prejudice, just as G. K. Chesterton caricatured it in his little poem 'The New Free Thinker'.

> John Grubby, who was short and stout
> And troubled with religious doubt,
> Refused about the age of three
> To sit upon the curate's knee.

If the liberal humanist wishes to criticize a Christian or a Buddhist or a Marxist, that is his right. But what he must not pretend is that he was led to this solely by his 'rational doubt' when in fact he was led to it by his faith, that is, his humanism. Or let him acknowledge that while it is rational doubt for him as a liberal humanist to criticize the Buddhist, the Marxist or the Christian, it might equally be a rational doubt for the Marxist to criticize him as a humanist. If there is no faith, there can be no doubt. There is no faith which cannot choose to cast doubt on some other faith.

Hostage

The menacing threat of critical doubt is empty, though of course if the victim thinks that the pistol is loaded, the threat is real enough for him. That is precisely the explanation for the inadequate view of doubt evidenced by many Christians: they are unwittingly the hostage of surrounding intellectual ideas.

Are things really as bad as that? Or have I fallen into the trap of seeing a dozen cases of doubt and declaring a universal epidemic? Judge for yourself from your own experience. How common is it to find Christians who have thought through the problem of doubt as a whole, rather than thinking through doubt piecemeal? How common is it to find churches which encourage a person to be open and honest about his doubting?

Let me stress again that the shame is not that people have doubts, but that they are ashamed of them. Our problem is not that we have the wrong answers to particular doubts but that we do not have the right attitude to doubt in general. In talking with people in doubt I have been struck repeatedly by one thing. Sometimes it is not so much specific answers to specific doubts that bring relief but rather that doubts can be discussed at all.

There are two extremes to watch for among current attitudes to doubt. On the one hand, some Christians treat doubt as a matter of guilt and secrecy, in much the same way as the Victorians treated sex. Doubt is fenced off as taboo. It is an unmentionable subject, a terrible way of letting the side down.

On the other hand, other Christians talk constantly about their doubts. But if we listen to them carefully, it is evident that they parade their doubts not so much to resolve them as to evoke public sympathy and to gain that sense of identity which comes from subconsciously defining themselves by their problems. They disparage themselves for doubting and in the same breath defend their doubt like a treasured possession which nothing could persuade them to give up.

These two extremes are not so contradictory as they might seem. Both indicate the same unhealthy view of doubt. Only when doubt is regarded as sufficiently dire does the profession of doubt become a way for a person to define himself. So the second attitude can flourish only in a climate where the first is general.

The influence of such attitudes is wide. Even when it is near its best, the call to faith in modern preaching can often border on idealism. The Scriptures may be quoted, the heroes of Christian history may be recalled, but somehow there is a loss of biblical realism. Instead of being human and down-to-earth, faith becomes a fragrant, concentrated essence. The heroism is distilled and all the impurities of doubt, discouragement and despair are removed so the final product is exclusive – and also profoundly discouraging.

Too often we forget that the great men of faith reached the heights they did only by going through the depths. The exquisite fragrance we like to remember is a product of the ripened maturity of their faith and not of its earlier stages.

At its worst, the life of faith is portrayed in a way that it is tantamount to spiritual repression. Faith is pictured as the absence of doubt and the man of faith as the man with no doubts. If there is doubt and unbelief to be overcome, it is outside of us, and like St George we must venture out of the camp and slay the dragons for the honour of faith.

But what we are not allowed to admit is that there are dragons *inside* the camp, let alone in our hearts. 'No dragons allowed in the camp' then becomes 'There are no dragons in the camp' which is turn becomes 'Down, dragon! Down!' Why not call repression by its name?

The insight that we are what we keep secret about ourselves works out here to mean that we are our guilty secrets. The damage this does to our Christian life is incalculable. 'Do you have a doubt? Pray about it.' . . . 'Yes, that's a very terrible situation/difficult question, but if you get things right with the Lord, it will all work out.' Because of such answers and their euphemistic vocabulary doubt is called everything but doubt, and the basic dilemma is not brought into the open.

When we deny our doubts, repression takes its toll in personal integrity, faith, worship and witness. It also contributes to the leakage of faith among thinking people. Perhaps the most celebrated 'deserter by doubt' lost to Christianity in the twentieth century has been Bertrand Russell. He was better known as a spirited champion of atheism, so many people do not realize that he believed in God until he was eighteen.

There were certainly other reasons for his rejection of belief at that age. Unfortunately, for example, he believed certain things which were wrong (such as the tenets of Unitarianism), and he believed them for the wrong reasons (such as the theistic proofs). But one important reason why he turned away from belief in God was that he was forced to adopt an unhealthy attitude towards his own questions and serious doubts.

Looking back on the period when he was seriously searching as a fourteen-year-old (and for a man with a mind of Russell's breadth this was no 'mere adolescence'), he described it like this:

> I became exceedingly religious and consequently anxious to know whether there was any good ground for supposing religion to be true. For the next four years a great part of my time was spent in secret meditation upon this subject, I could not speak to anybody about it for fear of giving pain. I suffered acutely, both from the gradual loss of faith and from the necessity of silence.

The impression he was given he mistook for the truth, and his life-long opposition to the Christian faith was the consequence. Lord Russell will one day answer to God for his own choice, and our place is not to prejudge the issue. But the lesson of his tragic anti-testimony should be written on our hearts. By God's grace the church must not continue this way.

It is an old maxim that the safest way to victimize a man is to help him to victimize himself. Once he himself believes what others believe about him, he is doubly enslaved. He is not only a prisoner but is conditioned to be his own jailer too. Just as any oppressed man is most enslaved when he becomes shameful in his own eyes, so the Christian is deepest in captivity when not only in his believing but in his doubting too he dances to the tune of his culture's parody of his faith. This attitude to doubt it a part of our Christian shame today.

Part Two

Families of Doubt

Chapter Five

Forgetting to Remember
Doubt from ingratitude

Start a job badly and at once it is that much harder to finish it well. Whether it's making a bed, building a skyscraper or landing a man on the moon, the lesson is the same. Leave some initial thing undone, and it will be a handicap later, if not a factor in eventual failure. The same is true of Christian faith.

Many people doubt because they have left out something important in the way they have come to believe. Believe in God for wrong reasons or for no reason at all and you cannot expect to be free from doubt. The seven families of doubt illustrate this well. The first four are the direct result of deficiencies of faith in coming to believe and the last three the result of deficiencies of faith in continuing to believe.

We have seen that there is always more to knowing than human knowing will ever know. This should make us wary of superficial descriptions of knowledge and faith. But there are at least four levels of understanding clearly discernible in a biblical view of faith and each of the first four categories of doubt runs parallel to one of these levels.

Not everyone who becomes a Christian does so by consciously thinking through these four levels, but, consciously or unconsciously, the four levels must be built into any healthy faith. Notice that I am deliberately speaking of 'levels of understanding' in believing, rather than 'stages in believing'. The stress is not only on the idea of progression (from lower to higher) but also on unbroken continuity. Basic to the idea of a level is the implication that a higher level goes beyond a lower level by including it, gathering it up and building on it.

Just so, there are certain levels of understanding in coming to believe that Christianity is true, and these may bear no relation to the 'stages' by which we have come to faith. But a healthy faith should include them all, and it should have each of them in its proper place. To confuse the order of these levels or to omit one or more of them is dangerous – not because our faith is then invalid but because it does not rest on the strongest available foundations.

The 'once and might have been'

Becoming critically aware of one's dilemma in life without God is the first level of understanding necessary in coming to faith. For the searcher who goes on and comes to believe, this is the only possible starting point – a sense of need which may range from a mild discomfort to a deep conviction, but which spurs him to look for a solution beyond himself.

Think back to your own conversion and how you began to search for God, however vaguely. Until that point, did you ever take the gospel seriously as 'good news'? Probably not. The reason was that you had little or no awareness of what a bad situation you were in. At least that was the case with me. Only when I began to realize what my situation was really like did I see the gospel for what it was – extremely good news for people in extremely bad situations. I don't know about you, but for me that discovery was an overwhelming experience which brought tears.

This does not mean that a Christian *believes* in God because of his needs. What he does is to *dis*believe in his previous world view because of needs which his previous world view can no longer answer. This is part of what makes his eventual faith in God (which he reaches for other reasons) a radical reliance on God alone. Other points of reliance are ruled out from the start.

Christianity thus begins where all other faiths leave off. 'How blest are those who know their need of God,' Jesus exclaims in the Sermon on the Mount, and as he opened the door to the kingdom of heaven his listeners must have gasped. The lintel is so low that the only man who can enter is the man who is down on his knees. The Prodigal Son becomes the pattern for us all; he became so hungry that he was prepared to swallow his own pride. That was the point at which he took his first step towards home.

Without this first step there is no beginning, and every subsequent step in the search takes one further but always in the same direction. So when the searcher eventually believes and becomes a Christian (I am ignoring for the moment the other levels of understanding which are involved), he is nothing if not a man with a memory and a man of special gratitude. Whatever he becomes, wherever he goes, whatever he does, he should never be unaware of what once was, what might have been and what could well be again. For the believer who understands this, 'By God's grace I am what I am' is never pious rhetoric. 'There but for the grace of God go I' is as realistic a statement as any we ever make.

. This awareness of need is the first level of understanding in coming to faith, and if there is any deficiency at this fundamental level, doubt will strike later on. What happens is that we begin well as Christians as we remember our past clearly. But then time passes, the memory fades and opportunities to doubt begin to come. As we fail to remember our previous situation, a slow and subtle change of heart takes place. What emerges is an attitude of resourcefulness that eventually grows into a mood of self-sufficiency and then into independence.

The effect is that what God has done fades slowly out of the picture, and we focus increasingly on what we ourselves seem well able to do. That is, we continue to work with God, or maybe even without him, but the thought of self-sufficiency is not expressed so boldly. Finally, we reach a stage at which, whatever our external life is saying, our internal attitude is one of complete autonomy and arrogant self-sufficiency, though this may not be evident, especially to ourselves.

Press release of ingratitude

At this point there is no need of a major crisis or a profound tragedy to precipitate doubt. All that it takes is a little push, some minor inconvenience, a trifling price to pay for faith, some obligation or embarrassment involved in being a Christian, and suddenly a trail of doubts bubbles to the surface: 'Maybe after all ...', 'Perhaps I took it all a little too seriously ...', 'Surely God can hardly expect me to ...', 'Probably I was a little overwrought, but I've weathered the crisis now...' Such doubts vary in intensity but bear united witness to a complacence or a disgruntled grumbling at any need for God and for his handling of our affairs.

The magic word that justifies those doubts is 'phase' or

'period', as if a stage has been reached where God is no longer necessary. But the key motif in them all is ingratitude, a moral, spiritual and emotional insensitivity to the reality of what we once were and would be now apart from God. We become insensitive to what we might call the 'once and might have been' of faith.

The fact that this was the chosen approach of the Evil One in tempting Eve should give us a healthy respect for its subtlety and danger. 'Did God say . . . ?' he asked. His innocent-sounding questions about the facts of the case were designed to open up the deeper issue of God's goodness. Why did God say this? Could it possibly be that his knowledge is power over you? Is God really as good as you have trusted him to be? Are you really as free as you would wish? Are you sure?

The questions bore in on Eve, and a different light is shed on the picture, the first shadows on the familiar sunlit world of trust. Slowly the picture changes, and doubt is conceived at the first moment when 'thank you' is superfluous. This is always the way: the oldest temptation is also the most contemporary. Writing in his *Notes from Underground* Dostoevsky says of man, 'If he is not stupid, he is monstrously ungrateful! Phenomenally ungrateful. In fact, I believe that the best definition of man is the ungrateful biped.'

Notice that this doubt is not purely spiritual, nor purely intellectual, nor purely emotional but a question of a subtle though complete change of heart. The transformation is made up of spiritual, intellectual and emotional elements which grow together into an autonomous state of mind. Sooner or later this attitude of autonomy expresses itself in doubt. It has to in order to evade the challenge to its existence posed by the existence of God. If I am to be autonomous, God must go.

The apostle Paul in his letter to Rome described the autonomous man: 'Knowing God, they have refused to honour him as God, or to render him thanks.' His words are a sober reminder that rebellion against God does not begin with the clenched fist of atheism but with the self-satisfied heart of the one for whom 'thank you' is redundant. The bankruptcy of his previous position is forgotten, the sting of his former dilemma fad   a sense of God's conviction wears off, and his acknowledgement of God's grace becomes routine and matter-of-fact. But this process may be well under way before it becomes apparent. In fact, sometimes it is only when doubts are expressed that we have the first clue that things are no longer the same.

Doubts of this kind can be expressed in many ways, but they are usually notable for one important feature – their lack of urgency. There is no pain of loss in this doubt, no agonizing uncertainty, no straining desire for a solution. The desired goal is not recovery of faith but a respectable cover for retreat from faith. If anyone shows deep concern that he is doubting in this way, it is a sure sign that he is not. This doubt is one of unconcern. It is insensitive, not over-sensitive.

Have you ever heard a husband on the verge of asking for a divorce finding fault with his wife, picking a quarrel or blackening her name to others? What he is doing is laying the groundwork for the decisive moment and preparing his getaway. Hate, like love, picks up every shred of evidence to justify itself. Listen to the doubts of ingratitude in its terminal stage. It is not what it pretends to be. It is a back-handed note of dismissal, an explanation that is really an excuse. But not for ever. At a certain point there is no need for an alias or disguise. The ingratitude comes out into the open and sets as hard as marble. Not only is 'thank you' superfluous, God is dismissed altogether.

A computer would do better

Failure to remember is much more serious, of course, than a simple lapse of memory. The human mind is more than a computer. Computers have dull and exact memories – what went in can come out again, exactly as it went in. But the human mind selects as well as stores. It not only receives, it picks and chooses and processes all it receives. So its own spiritual, moral and psychological characteristics affect what it remembers.

Forgetfulness proves deadly because it strikes deep into the delicate area where conscience registers sin and where each person is most attuned to the nuances of relationship. With this area desensitized, it is only a matter of time before the sensitivity of faith's communication is also numbed. A spiritual movement of independence gathers force underground and comes out into the open, using doubt as its prime organ of propaganda.

The theme of remembering, with its twin truth of giving thanks, has tremendous emphasis in the Bible. The man or woman of faith is the one who remembers, and the one who remembers is the one who gives thanks. Unbelief, on the other hand, has a short and ungrateful memory. This is true for whole nations as well as for individuals, as Israel's history proved.

Again and again as the nation prepared to cross the River Jordan and enter the Promised Land, Moses solemnly charged them: 'Remember!' No one knew better than he their stubbornness and volatile fickleness, demonstrated repeatedly after the Exodus from Egypt. When the people were in Egypt, they cried out for freedom, but when they were free, they cried out to go back. If there was a lack of water, they complained, and if there was water, they complained that there was no meat. There was always something else, the next thing, always 'if only....'

At the root of all their recalcitrance lay ingratitude and a failure to remember. So, to prevent the disastrous consequences he foresaw, Moses drove home the lesson: 'Remember!' They were to remember where they came from: 'Remember that you were slaves in Egypt and the Lord your God brought you out with a strong hand and an outstretched arm.' They were to remember how they had come: 'You must remember all that road by which the Lord your God has led you these forty years in the wilderness.' And they were warned that even in prosperity and success they were not to forget: 'When you eat your fill there, be careful not to forget the Lord who brought you out of Egypt.' Their festivals were to be a commemoration of God's acts and even some of their clothes were to carry a reminder: 'Into this tassel you shall work a violet thread, and whenever you see this in the tassel, you shall remember all the Lord's commands and obey them.'

But the lesson was not learned, and the chequered pattern of independence and ingratitude was repeated. In the dark days during and after the Exile the lesson was reiterated with the added weight of still more history. 'Our fathers in Egypt took no account of thy marvels, they did not remember thy many acts of faithful love,' wrote the Psalmist. 'They quickly forgot all he had done.' Or, as Nehemiah vividly expressed it, 'They ate and were satisfied and grew fat and found delight in thy great goodness. But they were defiant and rebelled against thee.' This ingratitude in 'forgetting to remember' is the key to the tragic failure of the chosen people. Speaking through Hosea, God himself sums up the lesson of Israel's failure: 'They were filled, and, being filled, grew proud; and so they forgot me.'

What was possible for the nation under the Old Covenant is no less possible for the church under the New. 'What do you possess that was not given you?' Paul asked the Corinthians, and the unanswerable logic of his question was designed to cut decisively at the root of ingratitude. When this was remembered, one mark of the exuberant joy of the early Christians and a secret of their costly praise was an overwhelming sense of God's grace behind the whole of life.

Focusing more particularly on forgiveness, Jesus defended the woman who had poured myrrh over his feet by pointing to the same reason: 'Her great love proves that her many sins have been forgiven; where little has been forgiven, little love is shown.' The point is not that some have been forgiven a greater number of sins than others or that some are 'worse sinners' than others but that some see their need of forgiveness and others do not. The point also is that some, more than others, remember the sins they have been forgiven and are therefore more consciously grateful. Where it is forgotten that we have been forgiven, little love is shown.

This possibility is never far away. Ten lepers were healed by Jesus; only one returned to express his thanks. When the Prodigal came home and the elder brother became jealous and self-righteous, the antidote for his sour-grapes was a refresher course for his memory: 'My boy,' said the father, 'you are always with me, and everything I have is yours.' In the parable, the King's servant, forgiven a crippling debt of millions, refused to forgive his fellow servant the debt of a few coins. By demanding payment on a trifling amount, he is remembering what he should have forgotten and forgetting what he should have remembered – that he himself has just been forgiven. Only such forgetfulness could allow such unforgivingness.

The same lesson has been appreciated through the history

of the church. Augustine recognized that Paul's words touched everything: there was nothing he had which he had not received. If this was so, then all was of grace. His description of the Christian as 'a hallelujah from head to foot', is a thumb-nail sketch of the joy and gratitude of a redeemed memory. 'Let me not tire of thanking you,' he wrote, 'for your mercy in rescuing me from all my wicked ways.'

The same grace was a marvel to John Newton centuries later. He was a Christian for many years but quite unable to forget that he had once been 'an infidel and libertine, a servant of slaves in Africa'. Out of this deep sense of the 'once and might have been', which threw the wonder of salvation into sharp relief, he wrote the hymn, 'Amazing Grace'.

Keeping the lines open

Clearly, memory for a Christian is far more profound than merely having a mental skill or a better-than-average ability to recall. The redeemed memory, as it works under God's Spirit, keeps the living awareness of the present in line with a living awareness of the past. Thus our thanksgiving, which is spurred by a knowledge of the past, is linked to our faith and hope, which engage the present and look towards the future. This gives continuity and wholeness to the life of faith which are indispensable to its growth and maturity.

Titian has captured this in his painting 'An allegory of Prudence', which is in the National Gallery, London. Prudence has three heads, a youth's which looks towards the future, a mature man's which looks at the present, and an old man's which looks back on the past with the wisdom of experience. Titian has written over their heads *Ex Praeterito Praesens Prudenter Agit Ni Futura Actione Deturpit* ('From the [example of] the past the man of the present acts prudently so as not to imperil the future').

The Christian life turns carefully on the interface between the present and the past. Faith is thoroughly existential, but the moment-by-moment experience is never autonomous, nor is it awash in time, for memory serves to link it to the past. But faith is also reflective, though mere memories are never allowed to become nostalgia or remorse. The good past is joyfully remembered and the bad past is freely forgiven.

An old Russian proverb runs, 'Dwell in the past and you'll lose an eye. Forget the past and you'll lose both eyes.' When we lose this balance, each of us has a tendency to consider the present moment not only as unique but as autonomous. It therefore becomes a little universe of independent reality in revolt from God and the rest of time, and able to fence itself off from the lessons of the past and the demands of the future.

The redeemed memory, closely allied with truth, does not allow this to happen. Rather, it acts to keep open a line of communication right through the vital terrain of the past, an important sector of the battlefield for faith. If this line is not kept open, rebellion against God is much easier. Both self-sufficiency and its chief agent of propaganda – doubt – depend on a strictly censored, closely monitored view of reality. Wider reality would threaten their existence. A dull memory is their ally and a keen memory is disastrous to their cause. In keeping open the lines with the past, the redeemed memory carries encouragement and conveys warnings and lessons to faith as faith is engaged in fighting at that front line of the battle which is the present moment.

A peculiarly Protestant doubt

This first variety of doubt is a rationalization. Contrary to what it is saying the problem is not in the belief but in the believer, not in the insufficiency of truth but in the self-sufficiency of the truster. In essence this doubt holds nothing against truth except that it is inconvenient. It may express itself extremely vocally and raise a wide range of objections to the truth, but these are not genuine doubts. They are part of the propaganda exercise of doubt itself. The real bone of contention is that truth is unnecessary and unwelcome rather than untrustworthy.

Whenever a Christian community becomes a cocoon or Christian education becomes a well-insulated pipeline from the cradle to the grave, a special danger arises. Christians escape not only the world but the healthy tension of living within it. Without the constant' reminder of the 'once and might have been', a blasé attitude of complacency is harder to resist.

Many students in Christian colleges have an idea of the difference which God makes that is little more than verbal.

The world beyond is a matter of hearsay. This is not entirely their fault. But it means that when they doubt what they often need is not another sermon but more experience, not another answer but deeper questions. Their doubt is a result of too little involvement in the world rather than too much.

In a way this first category is a peculiarly Protestant doubt which is best understood as a misrepresentation and abuse of freedom. The genius of the Reformation lay in the fact that man was made free under God. Justification 'by faith alone' cut away the bureaucratic jungle of human authorities and subservience. But where this liberty was not balanced by responsibility the Reformation made man so free *under* God that it was only a short step to his being free *from* God. We might say that the despair of existentialism is simply the logic of atheism, but this is true only in so far as atheism itself is the logic of ungrateful Protestantism.

By rejecting the excessive 'form' of the medieval church, the Reformation provided a strong impetus to liberty. But in swinging almost immediately towards the opposite pole, the heirs of the Reformation indulged the West in an excessive 'freedom' from which its culture has yet to recover. Only a Christian discipleship of biblical calibre can be expected to handle spiritual freedom with responsibility. An indispensable secret of such maturity is the willingness to remember.

Not that the leaders of the Reformation were blind to this. Instinctively, Martin Luther laid stress on the old Latin proverb, 'Nothing ages more quickly than gratitude.' At times he would brood gloomily as he thought of the future course of the Reformation. 'The ingratitude and the irreverence of the world terrify me. Therefore I fear that this light will not long endure.' Fortunately for us the spiritual and cultural vitality of the Reformation outlived his pessimistic estimate, but his point should not be ignored. Why is it that no movement of spiritual renewal has ever lasted longer than the third generation? Is it not partly because men forget so soon? Can it be that without the accompanying 'form' of the lessons of the past, of which memory is a vital part, 'freedom' can never be more than a fragile short-lived luxury?

Remembering to remember

At first the remedy for this doubt may seem all too simple. The doubt may be a result of forgetting, but is the remedy only a matter of remembering? In terms of *what* happens, yes, it is just that simple. Remember honestly, remember fully and the present moment will be so vividly contrasted with the 'once and might have been' that a hard heart will be melted and sealed lips broken open by praise. But in terms of *how* it happens, it is not that simple. For doubt, full grown, is not a lapse of memory but a wilful refusal to remember. How can it be made to do what it will not do?

When a person's doubt is well-developed, it needs a special confrontation, one that is designed to disturb complacency and strike a blow at self-sufficiency. Doubts of this type are a form of games-playing which must stop. The person in doubt can choose, but his choice must be made in the full light of knowing what he is doing – disbelieving, not doubting. Gently and skilfully he must be challenged to think back and think deeply. Who is God and what difference does it make if God is not there? Where was he before he believed in God? Where would he be now apart from God? Is he merely discarding a belief or is he grieving a person?

The burden of this challenge is heavy, but the style must not be. If doubt is a moral refusal to remember, 'mere reminders' will be tiresome. The doubter will never remember unless God works in his heart bringing a conviction of sin. So pray for him as much as you talk to him; raise questions rather than make statements; use the rapier and not the sledgehammer; care for him rather than judge him. If you lecture someone with a series of reminders, his defences will be in place. But if you jog his memory, he will see your point before he can help it.

This is an example of where theological answers may be unwise because the doubter is *in*sensitive. But whose ministry is it to bring things to mind and to convict? The Holy Spirit's, of course. But it is one thing for us to know that a person needs God's conviction and another thing to say so to him. Praying and saying little is just as much a way of counting on God as preaching and saying too much.

When doubt is less developed, remembering comes as prevention rather than cure. Keeping alive a grateful memory is a spiritual art. Leave it to those moments which are spontaneous and it will tend to be as transient as it is spontaneous. But structure it too heavily and the gain in increased remembering will be at the expense of a diminishing sense of personal involvement at any particular moment when we do remember. Ideally the ministry of remembering should be a bright thread running through all our Christian living – individually, corporately, publicly, privately; in the quiet moment of intimate prayer as well as in the open statements of public thanksgiving; for single people, for couples, for families, for churches, for communities and for nations.

A lively memory is not the same thing as a colourful re-telling of spiritual experiences. The latter can become a point of pride and end in denying what it set out to affirm. The redeemed memory loses all value if it is only a formal, public rehearsal. What matters is the heart and its secret whispers before God. King David shows us the way when he says, 'It is good to give thanks to the Lord . . . and make thy praise our pride.' So long as 'God's praise . . . our pride' is the attitude of our hearts, there will be no place for this kind of doubt. But as soon as we forget, just as soon as 'no praise' describes the situation in our hearts, 'No praise . . . self pride' will be the result. The doubt that inevitably follows will be the 'press release' of self-sufficiency taking over and settling in.

Part of the moulding-power of the modern world is its ability to leave us all blasé. It makes us accustomed to the efficient, the routine and the expected. It encourages in us an arrogance which takes everything for granted. This is true of the world of science and technology where the spirit of secularism has triumphed, and it is no different in the area of faith.

We would do well today to see that times to remember are consciously worked into the pattern of our lives. Do you take stock at the end of a day, a week or a year? Do you keep some record of God's goodness to help you commemorate and celebrate? Not necessarily a diary, but perhaps a note of particular answers to prayer, special acts of guidance, amazing experiences of provision? Do you fully enter into festivals and services for remembering – the Lord's Supper, Harvest Festival, New Year's Eve? Do you pause from time to time to thank God for the hundred and one tiny joys that make up each day?

There must be endless possibilities for specific ways and moments of remembering, for lifting our hearts in praise to God. Have you considered it carefully? The prophet Samuel raised a monument to God in the hour of Israel's victory and publicly declared, 'to this point the Lord has helped us'. In the same way the moment of remembering, the time taken out for thanks, the pause for praise, will stand before God and man as a statement of declared trust, of radical reliance, of faith that will admit no turning back, in short, a decisive no to self-sufficiency and doubt, and an emphatic yes to God.

Chapter Six

Faith Out of Focus

Doubt from a faulty view of God

Have you ever had the experience of being met at an airport or a station by someone who didn't know you? Usually it is not too hard to spot the person by his broad welcoming smile or the eager, slightly nervous way he scans the arriving passengers. But once when I arrived in Boston I was at a loss. No one stepped forward, no one seemed to be on the look-out for a stranger and the other passengers quickly dispersed. Then, just when I was wondering if there had been some mistake, a man came up full of apologies, 'I'm so sorry,' he said. 'I completely missed you. I was expecting someone quite different!'

Pictures and presuppositions

The idea we have of people always affects the way we see them. Sometimes our pictures are so inaccurate that we see a person wrongly or miss him altogether. Imagine, for a moment, a rather different ending to my experience. What if the official welcomer had stuck to his preconceptions to the point of concluding that I had not arrived? In one sense he would be right – the person he had in mind had not arrived. But in a more important sense he would be wrong, for there is no such person as he had in mind and I would have been there all the time.

When we speak of 'the idea we have of people', we are referring to a kind of picture of them we carry in our minds. When this picture is true, the picture and the person are one, and we are hardly conscious of the picture as something separate from him. The picture does its job by 'introducing' us to the person and helping us relate to him. But when an idea or the picture is false, we are more conscious of it as a separate thing, for we can clearly see it as a preconception or a prejudice. Since the picture comes between us and the person, false ideas hinder relationships rather than help them.

The pictures we have of people act as assumptions. We expect the people to be like them and presuppose it in dealing with the people themselves. This means that our pictures can affect the relationships. To an important degree our assumptions can even determine our relationships, just as our relationships may demonstrate our assumptions. For example, if I assume a man is honest when in fact he is a rogue, he may cheat me when I trust him. But if I assume he is a rogue when in fact he is honest, I cheat myself when I do not trust him. Trust is betrayed in each case. While the two reasons may sound opposite, they both come from the same cause – a faulty assumption. The person is different from my picture of him.

The second category of doubt is just like this. For some reason or other a believer gets into his head such a wrong idea of God that it comes between him and God or between him and his trusting God. Since he does not recognize what he is doing, he blames God rather than his faulty picture, little realizing that God is not like that at all. Unable to see God as he is, he cannot trust him as he should, and doubt is the result.

Doubt of this variety stems from a deficiency at the second level of understanding, the level at which Christian presuppositions enter for the first time. The first level is reached when a person becomes aware of his need. That is when searching properly begins. From then on life is marked by the search for an answer which will meet the need and prove trustworthy.

Knowing his need, the searcher asks two basic questions of anyone or anything which claims to be 'an answer'. Does it really provide the answer? And if it does, how can it be known to be true? A searcher reaches the second level of understanding when he is satisfied that Christianity answers the first of these questions. Having examined Christianity, he recognizes that *if* it is true (as it claims to be and as the third level promises to show how it can be seen to be), *it does provide the necessary answer*.

Obviously I am not thinking of 'answers' as something necessarily conceptual or purely verbal, as if a Christian answer was a string of words beginning 'Christianity says that. . . .' A nineteenth-century drunkard sobbing at the penitents' bench found no less an 'answer' in the cross of Christ than the twentieth-century philosopher with his carefully articulated questions. Whether the need is articulated clearly and the answer given is conceptual is not our concern here. What matters at this level is that the searcher clearly understands that *if* Christianity is true, his need, whatever it is, is met.

Do you see how presuppositions come in? A searcher is like a man going to buy a suit. He doesn't buy the suit and then ask later if it fits and if it is what he wants. First he looks for the one that he likes or that matches his needs, then he sees if it fits. Last of all he pays for it.

In the same way Christianity is presupposed by a searcher *before* it is proved. In fact it is presupposed to see if it is worth proving. The searcher says to himself, '*If* Christianity is true, what difference would it make?' And when he asks that question he is presupposing it provisionally. Not until the third level of understanding is reached are Christian presuppositions seen as certain (the suit 'fits'); and not until the fourth level are they accepted as final and chosen as personal (the suit is paid for; it belongs).

Christian presuppositions are simply Christian-truths-presupposed. We could insert 'Christian truths' (or doctrines or promises) for 'Christian presuppositions', but I prefer to speak this way to focus attention on what a presupposition does rather than on what it is. If we said 'truths', it would be easy to think of their content only. But when we say 'presuppositions', the stress is not on truth's content but on truth being counted on. But, of course, they must never remain purely abstract. Christian presuppositions are nothing less than the whole truth of who God is and what he has done for us. We are speaking here of presuppositions, but just as easily we could spell them out in terms of specific things, such as God's holiness or justice or love, or simply that 'Jesus loves me'.

From this second level onwards, the element of presupposing will always be a part of faith. This means that presuppositions are not just a part of coming to believe but the heart of continuing to believe. A man may try on a suit in the fitting-room, but a suit is bought to be worn. So when presuppositions are seen to fit, they are to be 'assumed', that is, to be put on and worn. What matters is not the shop but the street outside.

To change the picture; presuppositions are not a booster rocket to get faith off the ground – to be jettisoned as soon as faith is in orbit – but are as vital to faith as an engine to an aeroplane. What falls away when we believe, which distinguishes coming to faith from continuing to believe, is the 'if-ness' or trial-run quality of the early use of presuppositions. Knowledge is always presuppositional, but at a certain point it is no longer provisional. Once presuppositions have been tested, found to be true and adopted, they can be counted on.

Our picture of God

To believe in God is to 'let God be God'. This is the chief business of faith. As we believe, we are allowing God to be in our lives what he already is in himself. In trusting God we are living out our assumptions, putting into practice all that we say he is in theory, so that who God is and what he has done can make the difference in every part of our lives.

This means that the accuracy of our picture of God is not shown in the orthodoxy of our creeds or testimonies but in the truths which we assume and count on in the concrete situation; those moments when the heat is on, the chips are down and reality seems to be breathing down our necks. What we presuppose then is the real picture we have of God, and this may be very different from what we profess to believe about God.

Presuppositions, therefore, are vital to faith. They affect the picture of reality we hold in our minds, and if they are sharply or poorly focussed, reality will be correspondingly clear, blurred or distorted. As with a pair of glasses, presuppositions determine what we see and how we see it, but they do not necessarily determine what there is to be seen.

The same is true of faith in God. If we presuppose in practice what is true in fact, then our faith in God is focussed clearly and our picture of God is true – that is, it allows God to be God. But if our picture of God is wrong, then our whole presupposition of what it is possible for God to be or do is correspondingly altered. When the presuppositions are wrong, the picture is wrong. Faith is out of focus, God is not seen as he is, and in this field of badly focussed vision, with its dangerous loss of clarity or completeness, doubt is encouraged to grow. Such doubts are directly the result of a faulty picture of God.

Notice exactly where the problem lies. This doubt is not a matter of doubting the right presuppositions but of believing the wrong ones. This is an important difference. If our presuppositions were right but we could not believe them, the problem would lie elsewhere (as we will see in chapters eight and eleven). The problem arises here when we still believe our presuppositions even though they are wrong.

Give yourself a simple test. Think back to some crisis (a moment of shock or time of stress or failure). What did your attitudes then show you of your real view of God? Or think back over some deep personal concern and the way it was brought to God in prayer. In situations like those we see our real views of God. What faith is asking always reveals what it is assuming. What faith says in a situation is an expression of what it sees behind the situation. If it asks confidently, it is because it assumes correctly. Other motivations may pull out of line this relationship between assuming and asking; but at its purest, faith is strong or weak, advances or retreats in direct proportion to what it assumes.

If we say we believe God is there and that he loves us but live as if he were dead or couldn't care less about us, then the beliefs we presuppose in practice are out of line with the beliefs we profess in theory, and we are bound to doubt God eventually. This is why living faith is better tested in crisis than in creeds. Sometimes the way we act shows up our beliefs as little better than the hazy notions of an unbeliever. One minute we are reciting the most orthodox creed and the next minute we are practising a pathetic view of God which would do no credit to a pagan.

A Trojan horse

There are two main ways in which a Christian's mind can be affected by faulty presuppositions. The first is by allowing pre-Christian presuppositions to remain. Instead of rooting them out and replacing them, we can leave them undisturbed until they are intermingled with the new presuppositions of Christian truth which should be the sole foundation of the Christian's mind. Often this passes unnoticed because changes in other areas, such as lifestyle, seem so drastic and appear so obvious. A new broom has swept through everything, but the basic furnishings of the old pre-suppostions go untouched. The result is a sorry compromise in which the old assumptions neutralize the new ones and act as a Trojan horse in the mind. Finally the point is reached where our minds are not renewed so much as patched up. Or worse, the old presuppositions completely usurp the place of the new.

No army would advance into enemy territory and care-lessly leave behind it important pockets of resistance. If it did, it would find that temporary gain in speed of advance would be more than offset by eventual loss. Likewise, the Christian mind will make little progress in any direction un-less its presuppositions are completely and consistently re-newed by being brought into line with the whole of God's truth.

God's warning to the Israelites as they embarked on their conquest of the Promised Land can be applied easily to the renewal of mind which each of us should experience. 'If you do not drive out the inhabitants of the land as you advance, any whom you leave in possession will become like a barbed hook in your eye and a thorn in your side. They shall con-tinually dispute your possession of the land.' The renewed mind is nothing less than the mind of Christ in the believer, a mind so under his authority that its presuppositions are entirely influenced and informed by the truth of God. Any-thing less or anything other than this is not only untrue but alien and unhelpful, and if it is not dealt with it will in-evitably create doubts.

The second main way in which a Christian's mind can be affected is by allowing alien presuppositions to enter and dominate afterwards. Usually infiltration of this sort is not too obvious, or the mind would instinctively reject it. (A frog dropped into hot water will jump out instantly in a reflex action of escape.) But if the alien premises are as subtle as they are pervasive, they can filter in and overpower the mind before it is even aware of their presence, let alone their danger. (A frog can be boiled alive in water that is brought to boil slowly.)

A good example of this is the way that some Christians have all but taken over, or perhaps been taken in by, the complete relativism in the modern concept of truth.

Whether this comes from the apparent tolerance in the Eastern religions or from the Western dismissal of absolutes, the relativism of modern truth has a strongly corrosive effect on historic Christian conviction.

On one side of the church we have the pull of a misguided liberalism which dissipates the truth, and on the other side the pull of an equally misguided conservatism which stifles it. The one reduces theology to the Christian's 'way of looking at things', makes evangelism just an open-ended dialogue and articulates faith in a way which previous generations would have seen as a denial of the faith, in need of an answer itself. The other, instinctively realizing the danger, swiftly retreats in a reflex movement of social and theological withdrawal, but all that it does from then on is marked by a deepening social and intellectual insecurity. One leads to an alienated theology and the other to an alienated lifestyle.

Historic Christianity is thus shorn of its unique strength – the conviction of its claim to be the truth. The result is a significant number of Christians, as bewildered as they are faithful, who are left to struggle bravely with the doubts which the situation creates. Considering the relativism eating into faith today, it is hard to know which is more surprising – that so many people lose their faith or that more people do not.

Perhaps the reason why more do not is that most people are protected by their lifestyles from the uncomfortable logic of the deficiency in their faith. But this is dangerous. The subtlety of the wrap-around influence of alien presuppositions is that they do their work before they are noticed. Whether it is a Christian student surrounded by relativism on a university campus or a Christian family surrounded by the influence of the mass media, too few are awake to the danger. And when they do wake up to the situation, they find that the combat against relativism is not a clean, hand-to-hand fight but a wearing war of nerves against an enemy who is everywhere and nowhere, friendly but deadly at the same time.

Whether the problem is the result of old presuppositions which have not been rooted out or of alien presuppositions which have filtered in, the effect is the same. The presuppositions are wrong, so the picture of God is wrong too. Faith is out of focus, not seeing God as he is, and temptation to doubt is inevitable. When such temptation comes, it should be seen as an amber light to warn of the worldliness of mind into which we are slipping.

Notice that if God *really were* like our picture of him, then the doubt would be valid. But it is our picture of God, not God, which is at fault, and the doubt is fuelled solely by misunderstanding. Sometimes when I listen to people who say they have lost their faith, it strikes me as less surprising than they suggest. If their view of God is what they say, then it is more surprising that they did not reject it much earlier.

Other people have a concept of God so fundamentally false that it would be better for them to doubt than to remain devout. The more devout they are, the uglier their faith will become since it is based on a lie. Doubt in such a case is not only highly understandable, it is even a mark of spiritual and intellectual sensitivity to error; for their picture is not of God but an idol.

This second variety of doubt indicates that faith is suffering from a confusion of systems, a mixture of Christian and non-Christian presuppositions which have produced a disintegrated frame of mind. Doubts like this crystallize at one or two points, either where the presuppositions are so mixed and unsatisfactory that they are inaccurate, or where the presuppositions are true as far as they go but do not go far enough and so are incomplete. Although true, in the sense that they are not in error, the latter are not the whole truth and this is their problem. In the first instance the picture of God is at fault because it is all wrong, and in the second because it is too small.

A God all wrong

A biblical example of the first problem can be seen in the hopeless compromise of faith which resulted from religious syncretism in the ninth century B.C. On entering the Promised Land, the Israelites found that every piece of the land had its own deity, its own 'Baal' (meaning 'lord' or 'possessor'). Probably in all innocence they began to use the word *Baal* to describe the Lord God. But by the ninth century this had degenerated into gross confusion, under cover of which the worship of Baal-Melqart, the official god of Tyre, had crept in and was widely corrupting faith in God.

The prophet Elijah's approach to this was direct: Confront the people and clarify the issues. Was he, Elijah, the cause of the problem or was Ahab? Was Baal truly sovereign or was the Lord? The people were commanded to assemble and were faced with a simple choice: 'Elijah stepped forward and said to the people, "How long will you sit on the fence? If the Lord is God, follow him; but if Baal, then follow him."' There was to be no limping between two opinions. They were not to serve two masters. They were not to be in two minds. They were to choose and they were to live with the consequences of their choice.

A parallel situation exists today, though with different details. Faith is a drab and joyless affair to many Christians because what they presuppose is a sorry mixture of Christian and non-Christian ideas. They are half-hearted because they are double-minded. They want the best of both worlds, but they find the best of neither and the worst of each. If they are less than complete in rejecting Christianity, they are less than complete in believing it. One person is a Christian but carries over his previous attitude to race and wealth. Another person believes in God but still subscribes to his naturalistic view of science. With some the problem of premises is theoretical; with others it is practical. None of us, for example, would subscribe to belief in strict materialism in theory, but a searching look at our homes and our lifestyles might tell a different story.

In each case the foreign presuppositions bring their own problems with them. Believe in naturalism and you weaken your view of prayer. Believe in relativism and you won't see Christian truth as unique. Believe in dialectical materialism and the class struggle will be more important to you than the kingdom of God. Carry over the assumptions of psychological determinism and the new nature of the Christian will be reduced to a figure of speech. Carry over the assumptions of philosophical positivism and the basic notions of revelation will become nonsense. Carry over any presupposition which is not in accord with Christian truth and doubts are bound to arise.

What is the answer to this? We must see how this doubt develops and be careful to presuppose only what we know to be true and to commit ourselves consciously to the consequences of these suppositions. Once it is decided that certain assumptions are true, it only makes sense to demonstrate this by counting on them in practice. Equally, if we conclude that other presuppositions are not true, we can be sure that in the long run they will not prove satisfactory either, and we should root them out. Centuries before Elijah, Joshua glimpsed the same syncretistic tendencies in Israel and delivered an ultimatum to the people: 'If it does not please you to worship the Lord, choose here and now whom you will worship: the gods whom your forefathers worshiped beside the Euphrates, or the gods of the Amorites in whose land you are living. But I and my family, we will worship the Lord.'

Once it has developed, the best way to deal with this doubt is to bring it to a head. At the point where the Christian and the non-Christian premises are intermingled the issues are often confused. But to clarify things locate the questionable premises and follow them through to their logical conclusion so that the person in doubt can see it himself. Don't be sidetracked into answering a surface problem or comforting the person in doubt if the alien presuppositions are left unchallenged. The way this kind of doubt is expressed is only a symptom of the deeper problem of premises, and there is no final remedy unless the root cause is dealt with.

Pascal's approach shows us the way: 'The hypothesis that the apostles were knaves is quite absurd. Follow it out to the end.' This is the thinking believer's equivalent of Christ's statement, 'You will recognize them by their fruits.' What the seed is to the fruit, the premise is to the conclusion. Many of us might never be able to distinguish one variety of seed from another, but we have no trouble in telling an apple from a pear, or a cauliflower from a cabbage.

The same is true of presuppositions and conclusions. Find out what the person in doubt is believing wrongly and help him to follow the logic of these presuppositions to their necessary conclusion. Challenge him to check the full-blown consequences of his ideas to see where they lead. He will then see that his views are both wrong and unchristian. Nothing is more nourishing to doubt than hazy mists of vagueness; but clear thinking disperses them and leaves a clear-cut choice either to believe or to disbelieve.

A God too small

The second problem of having inadequate – as distinct from inaccurate – presuppositions is a little different though just as dangerous. The weakness here is not that the assumptions are incorrect but that they are incomplete. But the effect is the same. In the long run they are incorrect to the degree that they are incomplete.

Part of the purpose of presuppositions is to provide a coherent explanation of the whole circle of life and reality which we perceive. So if we adopt presuppositions which are too small to handle the range of reality we are facing, their rationality and coherence will be severely limited and any conceptions they give rise to may be equally confined and distorted.

If we believe in God yet at the same time presuppose a picture of God which is less than he really is, our faith is bound to suffer. Our conception of God will be pinched and uncomfortable. The false idea of God will act like a tight collar on faith, cramping its style, confining its movements, throttling the full freedom of the wider truth. Could some-one expect to be comfortable if he is wearing a belt two inches too tight or a pair of shoes two sizes too small? Is it different for faith? Confronted with a shrunken picture of God, faith has no room to be itself and doubt is the expression of its discomfort.

In Genesis, Sarah's reaction to the news that she would give birth to a son in her old age is a good example. She knew that her husband was well past it and that she herself was beyond the age of childbearing, so her first reaction was to laugh. But God confronted her about that laugh – not because she laughed in God's presence but because her laughter expressed a limiting view of God which was a denial of his power and an incitement to doubt. 'The Lord said to Abraham, "Why did Sarah laugh and say 'Shall I indeed bear a child when I am old?' Is anything impossible for the Lord?".' She laughed at the very thought of it because she doubted it was possible because her conception of God was too small.

The same problem of faith that sees God as too small shows up in the attitudes of those who approached Jesus for help. Very few came to him with a complete understanding of who he was and what he had come to do, so their faith was correspondingly weak.

A leper begged Jesus for help: 'If only you will,' said the man, 'you can cleanse me.' The father of the demented son pleaded, 'But if it is at all possible for you, take pity upon us and help us.' Notice the difference in each appeal. The leper saw no problem in trusting the power of Jesus – it was the compassion of Jesus he was unsure of. His appeal could be expressed, 'I know you could if you would, but you probably won't.' The father, on the other hand, was unsure of the power of Jesus, and it is almost as if he says, 'I know you would if you could, but you probably can't.'

The response of Jesus to each of them is fascinating. To the leper, who sensed his power but not his love, 'Jesus stretched out his hand [and] touched him.' But to the father who had little sense of his divine power, he replied, 'If it is possible! ... Everything is possible to one who has faith.' Each had an incomplete faith because the aspect of truth he sensed was only a part of the full truth of who Jesus is. So Jesus concentrated on that part which needed filling out if faith was to have a chance of being itself.

. What is the answer to this second error in this type of doubt? Simply to correct the presuppositions. They need stretching and filling out so that they reflect the fullness and adequacy of who God is. This is not a theoretical or mechanical exercise. It must be personal and it must be specific. *We* must do the work, and we must do it *where it is needed*. If I see God's power clearly but not his wisdom, then it is no use my finding out about his justice or faithfulness. What I need to know is his wisdom, and this means wrestling with the truth of it until I can count on it myself.

This is not our work alone. God has revealed himself through his Spirit in his Word, and he continues to do so. Moreover, God is bigger to us than our small ideas of him, and more gracious to us than our mean views of who he is. He is more eager and able to expand our faith than we are to have it done. We are all more shortsighted than we realize, so there is no one who need not count on the illuminating, mind-expanding power of the Holy Spirit.

Putting it this simply does not make light of the doubt but takes it very seriously. It shows that on these given presuppositions it is little wonder that there is some doubt, and this is only the beginning of it. *But again, the presuppositions which produce such doubts do not describe who God is for the god they describe is not God.* How often we confine faith and insult God by entertaining puny conceptions of him! How many times God must be saying to us what he said in anticipating Israel's doubts after the exile: 'Even if it may seem impossible to the survivors of this nation on that day, will it also seem impossible to me?'

Simple and compound

This is a useful place to illustrate two things which are also true of many of the other categories of doubt. First, notice that this type of doubt can easily be part of a 'compound' doubt. The cause most immediately apparent may be presuppositions which are inaccurate or inadequate, but this is not necessarily the root of the problem. How did these faulty presuppositions get there in the first place? Trace the answer to that and it may lead into much deeper waters.

Take, for example, two people who have a problem in realizing that God really loves them – so that mention of God's holiness inspires only terror or guilt. For both of them their doubt has become a protective reflex against the unhealthy responses they feel forced to make to such a God. But *why* do they see God like that? That is the real question. For one of them the reason may lie no deeper than an ignorance of who God is, with all his Father's love as the Bible and Jesus reveal him. Whereas for the other his faulty picture may go back to badly tangled family relationships which have left him unable to see any authority as good or loving.

Both of them carry over this faulty picture into their relationship with God, though for different reasons. The first because he has been wrongly taught and the second because he has been wrongly treated. This means that for the first one the doubt is 'simple' and can be cleared up in a straightforward way, but for the second it is 'compound' and needs much greater care. Any help which tackles only the surface expression of the doubt lacks compassion and is bound to fail.

Second, notice that as with the remedy for most doubts, there are two parts to approaching it. The short-term need is to deal with the roots of the doubt – in this case a matter of incompleteness of the picture of God – while the long-term need is to train a habit of faith which will close the door to this type of doubt in the future.

In terms of the doubt we are discussing, the long-term habit of faith is particularly necessary because the constant drive of our fallen natures is toward idolatry. The principle of sin leads to the perspective of sin. The claim to the right to myself leads to an insistence on viewing all reality from my viewpoint alone. Sin therefore reduces God to man's image, scales him down to man's size and substitutes man's view of God for God himself. Once this happens, it is no longer God who is over us, judging us by his Word, but we who are over God, using our god-concepts to justify what we are doing and to make judgements on what he should be doing.

'Let God be God' and we find ourselves on the path of discipleship. But let smaller pictures of God satisfy us and squeeze him out, and we are back on the easier road to cheap grace and nominal faith. The latter is the respectable man's introduction to idolatry. We love our idols because we made them. God's truth, however, is much less comfortable, and the habit of being stretched by its demands is challenging. But the rewards are incomparable, for we have the joy of getting to know God for himself, with the attached strings of lesser motives cut away.

What picture of God do you show in your beliefs? Is it sharp and clear or blurred and ill-defined? Is it something you have dreamed up? Or stuck together from various descriptions like an identikit picture? Or is it the picture God has given us of himself? Is it complete and whole? Or is part of it missing so that you trust what you know but wonder what the rest is like?

If we make sure of the right answer to these questions we will develop the full, clear picture of God that he himself has given us in his revelation. If we content ourselves with anything less, we can only expect to doubt.

Chapter Seven

No Reason Why Not

Doubt from weak foundations

I remember a student who dropped into our home two years ago on his way around Europe. Almost immediately he began to share with us the intense enthusiasm of his Christian faith. After listening for some time, I began to grow uneasy, feeling increasingly suspicious that his faith, though enthusiastic, was almost entirely groundless. Eventually I asked him how he had become a Christian and why he had believed, and then asked him how he would answer some of the questions that his visit to a French university was bound to raise.

Finally, with considerable reluctance, I suggested that his faith seemed to have very little foundation and that without more understanding to match his enthusiasm he was in danger of being tripped by the questions of life – let alone by those of his fellow students. He listened politely, and if he showed no concern at least he took no offence and we parted on good terms.

Just over a week later I received a letter, short and to the point. 'I am writing to tell you that I no longer believe in God or consider myself a Christian.' And then after a brief explanation, 'The only reason I write to you is that you warned me this would happen.'

This is a clear example of the third basic kind of doubt, a kind so common that it qualifies as the twentieth-century doubt *par excellence*. For every person who experiences what this student did (and this experience is far from rare) countless others are potentially as vulnerable. It is only their sheltered lives which keep them from facing the same problem.

Faith and reason

The third type of doubt stems from a simple but basic deficiency in understanding why Christianity is true. This is the issue which is at stake in the third level of understanding. The importance of this level can hardly be exaggerated today. As we have stressed repeatedly, the understanding Christian knows not only *what* he believes but *why* he believes. He is able to say that what he believes is true, and behind such a statement he has sure and sufficient reasons of which he is fully persuaded.

So as soon as someone has faced the critical nature of his dilemma without God (the first level) and has come to recognize that *if* God's revelation is true he does have a meaningful answer to his dilemma (the second level), then, logically, the next urgent question is, But how may I know that God's revelation is *true*?

If no answer is given or if the question is not encouraged (or still worse, not allowed), then the searcher may become a believer, but he will be constantly at the mercy of the potential doubt that his faith is only make-believe. He will never be certain that it is not a form of psychological wish-fulfilment and that his belief in God is not purely a result of his need for God.

This doubt is far from new, but today's intellectual climate provides an ideal breeding-ground and it has come into its own again. It is a very damaging doubt and needs to be blocked firmly by a decisive reaffirmation of what it means for Christianity to be true.

Christianity is not true because it works. It works because it is true. No issue is so fundamental both to the searcher and to the believer as the question of truth. The uniqueness and trustworthiness of Christianity rest entirely on its claim to be the truth. God, who is the Father of Jesus Christ, is either there or he is not there. Either he has spoken or he has not spoken. What his revelation claims is either true or false. There are no two ways about it.

This stubborn insistence on truth is the only thing which lifts Christianity out of the common pool of completely personal, relativistic, subjective beliefs. As a young Christian exclaimed to me on realizing for the first time the titanic implications of this claim, 'I always knew Christianity was true, but I never realized it was *this* true!'

Naturally the stronger the claims to truth which are made for Christianity, the stronger the substantiation must be. Christianity is not true because it makes its claims more boldly or more loudly than anything else (or belief would be

taken over by bravado). If it claims to be true, it must be
willing to show the areas in which the evidence for its claims
can be examined and found to be true. At this point Christianity is not only willing, it is eager. Nonetheless, exactly
how this is done is a question which would take us beyond
our immediate purpose. What matters at this point is to see
the importance for faith and doubt which this claim implies.

This much should be clear: Christianity invites people to
an examined faith. Although a Christian should believe
simply, he should not 'simply believe'. The pale brand of
modern faith which lapses into 'easy believism' has little in
common with the virile attitude of understanding plus commitment which is the biblical notion of faith.

Part of the Christian's responsibility is to understand and
be able to express what and why he believes or, as the apostle
Peter expressed it, 'Be always ready with your defence whenever you are called to account for the hope that is in you.'
If you hear someone claiming to believe something but even
after listening carefully it never becomes clear exactly what
he believes or why, you are surely entitled to wonder if his
belief is valid at all. Unless a Christian's faith includes this
level of understanding, he is short-changing himself.

Two qualifications should be quickly added. I am not
saying that someone who does not understand his faith has
no faith. Large numbers of people become Christians for all
sorts of reasons other than the fact that they fully understand
why Christianity is true. Undeniably their faith is genuine,
but the weakness is that their faith is developed at the expense of their understanding. This may be preferable to the
opposite mistake (where someone's understanding is far
stronger than his faith), but a better way is to develop both
faith and understanding together.

A person can become a Christian for all sorts of reasons,
but it is vital for Christianity if it *is* true, that he think
through his faith afterwards to the point where he understands why he believes – at least to the level at which his
mind demands satisfaction in understanding other areas of
life.

A second qualification must be added. A person may have
sure and sufficient reasons for coming to believe, but he will
not always have similar substantiation in every field at every
moment. Christianity is rational partly because it is a faith

with a foundation of sure and sufficient reasons. But it is one thing to have sufficient understanding in coming to believe and another to have it in every area of continuing to believe.

Some people misunderstand what the rationality of faith means. They imagine that they have believed in God because faith is rational – which it is – but they then expect every aspect of faith to be equally open to rational investigation – which it isn't. So when they come across the first element of mystery which they cannot understand, they conclude that Christianity is not rational after all. God has led them to believe it was rational, but now apparently he has cheated them by unfairly slipping in a mystery.

What they forget is that rationality is opposed to absurdity, not to mystery. The rationality of faith goes hand in hand with the mystery of faith. It isn't that God has hoodwinked us into believing, as if rationality were the bait and mystery the hook. Far from it. The fact is that the greatest mystery of all – the Incarnation – comes at the very beginning and is the central reason why we believe in God. We cannot explain it: there is the beginning of the mystery of faith. But because of the evidence neither can we explain it away: there is the beginning of the rationality of faith.

So there are times (as we shall see in chapter sixteen) when the rationality of faith must go hand in hand with the mystery of faith. But the person with sufficient reason for his faith can avoid the otherwise powerful down-tow toward nonsense and absurdity.

Again, rationality is the alternative to absurdity, but it has no quarrel with mystery. Mystery is beyond human reason, but it is not against reason. It is a mystery only to man and not to God. Where God has spoken and spoken clearly, rationality comes into its own; where God has not spoken, or for his own reasons has not spoken clearly, there is the area of mystery. An area of mystery is rational to God, but faith must suspend judgement and not press human reason to answer questions when it has insufficient information.

In parenthesis I should say that I am passing quickly over the significance of these four levels of understanding. What matters here are their implications for doubt. But if you are reflecting more deeply on them, you will see how the second and third levels, which centre on presuppositions and evidences, are closely related. They can be distinguished logically, as we are doing here, but they should never be separated in practice.

The mutual relationship between presuppositions and evidences could be expressed like this. Premises without evidences are unsupported and weak; evidences without premises are meaningless. The premises provide the framework of thought and so satisfy creative reason; the evidences provide the facts within the framework and so satisfy critical reason. The role of premises is to throw light on a subject; the role of evidences is to give weight to it. It is the purpose of premises to make sense of something and the purpose of evidences to make solid sense of it.

Thus their relationship is reciprocal: each one not only presupposes the other, it accredits the other. Life is not long enough for a faith without meaning. Nor is it stable enough for a faith without foundations. These are questions to which premises and evidences speak.

An uneasy limbo

This third category of doubt strikes just at the point where the Christian is strong in faith but weak in faith's foundations. What his faith assumes may be correct, but it is unsupported. He believes all the right things but for no reasons at all or even for the wrong reasons. What happens then is that faith runs up against an awkward question or a scornful dismissal, and suddenly everything that had seemed so unmistakably certain, meaningful, true, collapses like a balloon leaving the remnants of faith limp and deflated.

The cause is easy to see – faith had no sure and sufficient reasons. The believer is not at all certain why he believed. If there is 'no reason why' in terms of faith, there will certainly be 'no reason why not' in terms of doubt. Here precisely is the rub. As the flaw is exposed and the doubt sweeps in with its impressive academic credentials and powerful, emotional threat, the doubt is unanswerable, because there is *no reason why not*.

This doubt is especially prevalent today since religious faith is often viewed as anything but a matter of truth. In the discussion of more faith the question of truth is not even on the agenda. It is the forgotten issue. Instead of presenting a strong, clear answer to this misconception, many Christians show that their defences are down at the very place where modern unbelief is most devastating. Failure to understand the significance of truth is the Achilles' heel of many Christians. The real wonder is not that some who profess to believe fall away after continuing so long but that some last as long as they do with as little as they have.

Any Christian who is in touch with thinking people outside Christian circles must surely be deeply saddened by the large numbers of people who were once professing Christians but who now claim to have 'lost their faith'. In my experience a great number of these are people who lacked little in terms of orthodox belief or depth of experience but who have never understood why their faith is true. Caught with neither a foundation, nor a thought-through framework for their faith, they find university-level questions puncturing their Sunday-school-level faith. Overtaxed by questions they are discouraged from facing, they escape the impossible tension by 'graduating' from such a faith.

For many Christians the world of faith is suspended in an uneasy limbo between complete ignorance (which is no longer possible) and sufficient understanding (which is not yet attained). If there are those on the fringes of the church who do not really believe but have no idea why they disbelieve, there are others inside the church who do not really disbelieve but have no idea why they believe. When not pressed too hard, the former prefer to disbelieve rather than believe and the latter to believe rather than disbelieve; but both feel extremely uncomfortable if their position is severely tested. Tolstoy's Levin in *Anna Karenina* is a perfect example of the former:

> Like the majority of his contemporaries, Levin found himself in the vaguest position in regard to religion. Believe he could not, and at the same time he had no firm conviction that all was untrue. And so, unable either to believe in the significance of what he was doing or to regard it with indifference as an empty formality, all the time he was preparing for the sacrament he was conscious of a feeling of discomfort and shame in taking part in something he did not understand, which was therefore, an inner voice told him, deceitful and wrong of him.

Many Christians are examples of the latter. In each case it

is the lack of understanding which constitutes the inauthenticity of either the faith or the doubt.

Each of us should examine the foundations of our own faith. Why do we believe God is there? Why do we believe God is good? How do we know Jesus ever lived? How do we know Jesus rose from the dead? Why do we trust the authority of the Bible? How do we understand that Christianity is true? How would we answer a modern philosopher, a Freudian psychologist, a follower of Guru Maharaj Ji, each of whom denies the truth of Christianity in a different way? Answers to such questions are no substitute for faith. But without the answers to such questions faith may be no match for doubt.

Different aspects of basic understanding are needed in different areas of the world. People in Western Europe, for example, rarely dispute that Jesus lived, but in Eastern Europe the denial of his historical existence is almost a canon of Marxist dogma. Different stages of our lives need different levels of comprehension to match our growth and maturity. How sad it is when a believer in his forties or fifties is merely an absentee landlord, living idly off the intellectual rent from the thinking of his student days! The challenges to faith will go on and must go on being answered. As we face the issues and questions which are before each of us *now*, do we know why we believe? Are we able to relate and apply faith to life without suppressing questions and without unnerving our security?

Flying blind

This sense of knowing for sure is a central element of biblical faith. It has been an unmistakable part of the testimony of Christian believers throughout history. But the same cannot be said of twentieth-century Christianity, which is why the type of doubt we are now considering is so prevalent. Modern faith suffers from a severe shortage of understanding in its basic diet, a deficiency which can be detected at many points.

One example is the place given to irrationality in faith. Take a sampling of modern preaching, for example a minister who is culturally aware or an evangelist in the classic nineteenth-century tradition. Both in their different ways will give impressive witness to the importance of faith, but both may have a careless disregard for the foundations of faith. Faith's value, some even suggest, grows in direct proportion to its lack of a rational basis. Whether it is one side's cry of the 'radical uncertainty' of authentic faith or the other side's reiteration of the 'leap of faith', we are offered an imposing edifice of faith with little or no mention of foundations.

A whole armoury of biblical interpretation accompanies this mentality – one side often majoring on the sacrifice of Isaac in Genesis 22 and the other side of Thomas's doubt in John 20. But the best answer to the unwarranted interpretations wrested from these texts is a closer look at the very biblical passages in question.

Abraham's story is widely used to justify the irrationality of faith. Certainly his trust in God despite the opposing evidence of immediate reality was such that his faith was 'counted ... to him as righteousness'. But to conclude from this that the quality of his faith lay in the fact that he trusted God for no reason whatever is quite illegitimate. Certainly, as Abraham set out to offer Isaac as a sacrifice in the way God had commanded him, his faith was flying blind in its implicit obedience, just as it had when he set out from Ur for a country which he had never seen. But as to why he knew God and obeyed him at all, his faith was not the least blind. Quite the contrary.

It is precisely because he knew who God was that he knew he could trust God in the dark. More precisely still, it was because he was not in the dark about God that he could walk in the dark about Isaac. Faith was against sight, but it was not against reason. In terms of the immediate situation he did not know why, but in terms of the ultimate context of his life *he knew why he trusted God who knew why*. Knowing God as he did, his faith was a trust in the face of mystery but not in the face of absurdity.

Significantly, after the mention that his faith had been counted by God as righteousness, Abraham's first recorded words were 'O Lord God, how can I be sure?' God answers this question without any hint of rebuke in a covenant promise which speaks to this question directly: 'Know this for certain....' Abraham's faith went far beyond the reach of understanding, but it is a travesty of the facts to ignore the elements of understanding which enabled him to do so.

Another passage which is often misrepresented is the account of Christ's rebuke to Thomas: 'Because you have seen me you have found faith. Happy are they who never saw me and yet have found faith.' Certainly Thomas was rebuked, but the question is why. He was not rebuked because he refused to believe without enough reasons but because he refused to believe with more than enough reasons. For three years he had been with Jesus and heard his teaching – that he was bound to suffer, to die and to be raised from the dead. So his lack of faith was not a matter of failing to straddle an impossible credibility gap, but of baulking at a simple step of trust on the evidence of inescapable reasons.

For him to demand repeated empirical evidence at that stage was doubly unnecessary, for not only had he heard the words of Christ, he had listened to the eye-witness accounts of his fellow disciples. Yet still he refused to believe. Those who misinterpret this in the interests of encouraging a 'leap of faith' also ignore the fact that Jesus still invited him to touch and see, unnecessary as it was. If this was what it would take for Thomas to believe, then even this was possible. Fortunately for Thomas' self-respect the sheer excess of grace as well as evidence made further proof unnecessary.

The biblical view of knowledge has many dimensions, some of which go far beyond a knowing which is solely related to reasons, but 'reason-able' knowledge is a basic part of knowing in the Bible. Biblically, much of what is knowable can be checked, verified, substantiated and confirmed.

The Gospel of John tells of the royal officer who returns home to discover that his son has recovered: 'The father noted [knew] that this was the exact time when Jesus had said to him, "Your son will live", and he and all his household became believers.' He believed in Jesus, and an essential part of his coming to faith rested on the exact correspondence he observed between what Jesus had said and what in fact had happened.

In Acts, when he describes the reaction of the Jews at Berea as they heard the gospel for the first time, Luke brings out this same point. 'They received the message with great eagerness, studying the scriptures every day to see whether it was as they said. Many of them therefore became believers. And the same point is put beyond dispute in the careful declaration of purpose in John's Gospel, expressly written about the evidence of Christ's signs: 'There were indeed many other signs that Jesus performed in the presence of his disciples, which are not recorded in this book. Those here written have been recorded in order that you may hold the faith [or, that you may come to believe] that Jesus is the Christ, the Son of God.'

The force of this evidence should be plain. Faith is an act of the whole man, not of his understanding alone. But it is precisely because it is an act of the whole man that it includes the understanding. As we go on in our faith, we may be led into areas 'beyond reason', but what we mean by this is beyond *humanly discernible* reasons and not in any sense *against* reason. So the Christian who glories in a non-rational basis for his faith leaves himself vulnerable to a particularly lethal blow which strikes at the very foundation of faith. The only comfort is to remember that it is usually foreseeable and quite unnecessary.

A second place where today's deficiency of understanding can be witnessed is in the improper place given to experience at the expense of understanding. Many Christians are afraid of rationalism and rightly suspicious of a purely intellectual faith. What they forget, though, is that if knowledge-without-experience is a product of rationalism, so also is experience-without-knowledge. Yet they reject the first and welcome the second. Knowledge-without-experience is only the reverse side of the coin of experience-without-knowledge. Both are born of rationalism, and both are equally wrong and finally destructive of true faith. To come to faith on the basis of experience alone is unwise, though not so foolish as to reject faith altogether because of lack of experience.

The biblical relationship of understanding to experience is quite different. Knowledge and experience are not opposed but related, and there is a profound spiritual logic in the relationship. Experience does not generate itself. Nor is it self-justifying and self-sustaining. Instead, the quality of a Christian's experience depends on the quality of his faith, just as the quality of his faith depends in turn on the quality of his understanding of God's truth.

Genuine understanding generates genuine faith, and genuine faith in turn generates genuine experience. Without genuine faith, experience can be easily counterfeited by emotionalism. Without genuine understanding, what passes for faith can be a counterfeit confidence of purely human origins (such as the power of positive thinking). So understanding is integral to faith, just as faith and understanding are both integral to experience.

In short, to deny and stifle the understanding unnecessarily is to sow a crop of future doubts. We may efface the intellect in our teaching or in our practice, but we cannot escape the uneasy conscience of a good mind trying to adapt to a bad faith. Such a mind may become so restless and frustrated with repression that sooner or later it will tear itself on some nail of its own making.

Where God has given us sure and sufficient reasons for believing or the possibility of profound understanding in our believing, it is perverse to insist on having less than what he offers. It is one thing to realize that our faith will always be weaker than we would like it to be, but it is quite another to insist that our faith must be weaker than it can afford to be.

Reasons for faith

What is the remedy for this type of doubt? First, to diagnose it correctly, second to locate exactly where the weakness in understanding is and third to do the necessary homework on it – that is to examine the matter to see what the truth of the situation is.

Are the foundations of faith so shaky that nothing of any weight can be built on them? Or is it that because of ignorance and haste crucial parts of the foundations have been left out? This is the crux of it: Are there good and sufficient reasons to believe what we need to believe or is faith on shaky ground? This straightforward approach is the natural response to a situation of uncertainty, and it is also the biblical one. The attitude of the Bereans is a pattern for us all. They studied 'to see whether it was as they said'. When we are not sure, it is time to make sure – to see if the things which we believe are in fact true.

When the disciples first heard from the women that Jesus had risen, they were incredulous: 'The story appeared to them to be nonsense, and they would not believe them.' But they did not stop there. Doubt was only their first reaction. It is characteristic of faith that it cannot remain in two minds; it cannot leave things in the air. Luke's next words are typical of faith's inherent drive for resolution: 'Peter, however, got up and ran to the tomb, and, peering in, saw the wrappings.' Faith may not always know, but it always wants to know what it may. It cannot be sure of everything, but it will always be as sure as it can be. Where it is not certain, it will always seek to ascertain.

Faith does not feed on thin air but on facts. Its instinct is to root itself in truth, to earth itself in reality, and it is this which distinguishes faith from fantasy, the object of faith from a figment of the imagination. In those places where there is a delay in substantiation, faith is prepared to wait for a long time at the bar of history. But the verdict it looks for is always the judgement of truth, the verdict handed down by reality.

Luke writes of the natural hesitancy of the Jewish believers over the unprecedented inclusion of Gentiles in the early church. But he points out that what decided the issue was Peter's laying the irrefutable facts of the matter before them so that 'when they heard this their doubts were silenced'. This is always the way. This type of doubt is silenced by facts, answered by truth and reassured by understanding.

This insistence on knowing for sure and examining the facts of the matter is particularly important in dealing with the doubts which arise because of the many misrepresentations of Christianity today. Every generation is apt to see Christ in its own image and produce its own 'plastic Christ', a picture of Jesus pressed through the sieve of its own assumptions and set solidly in the mould of its own values. But it is ironic that a generation that is so impatient with the cultural adaptations of other generations has been so adept at setting up its own.

Our generation dismisses the penitential Jesus of the Middle Ages or the gentlemanly Jesus of the Victorian drawing-rooms, but the selection of 'Christs' which is offered today is worthy of the supermarket age – Jesus the Liberator, Jesus the Soul Man, Jesus the Blessed Master, Jesus the revolutionary, Jesus the archetypal poor man, Jesus the Great Prophet.

The array is bewildering and the effect is numbing. After all, how do we know that our own picture of Jesus is necessarily right, especially when we realize that we too bring

assumptions to faith? Perhaps we are more shortsighted than
we think? Perhaps what we believe today is no better than
the Sunday-school notions we were forced to discard yesterday and is different to us only because we are believing it
today? Will today's faith look as embarrassing if we look
back on it tomorrow?

The train of thought that begins like this is as slippery as
an eel, and the only effective way to catch it is to examine
the truth of the matter. This is the only test – to unleash
doubt on doubts, to examine the matter and to see where the
truth lies. The trouble with most of the 'modern Christs'
is not that they are anti-Christian but that they are un-
historical. Our basic quarrel with them is not that they are
unappealing (for unquestionably, some of them are) but that
they are untrue.

Do the Dead Sea Scrolls explain away the uniqueness of
Jesus? Was Jesus really only a psychedelic mushroom? Is
Pasolini's *The Gospel According to St Matthew* closer to
the original than the Jesus of Christianity? Was Jesus speaking of the *Tat Tvam Asi* (Thou art That) of the Hindus
when he said, 'The kingdom of God is within you'? Why is it
that *Jesus Christ Superstar* leaves a Christian feeling so sad
and angry?

Truth is the only sufficient answer faith can give doubt,
for it is the truth of the matter, the facts of the case which
give faith its solid foundation. If it is caught without the
credentials which truth alone supplies, faith knows it will be
mistaken for fantasy or for wish-fulfillment. It may even be
tempted to wonder itself.

Some people think that having reasons for faith is an insult to God, as if we were desperately grubbing around for
make-shift reasons to believe in him. But the opposite is the
case. Verification is only one aspect of Christian truth. Verification itself depends on the unchanging authority and stability of the Word of God. We are not insulting God but
bringing glory to him by taking his Word as the stable,
authoritative truth it is.

Theological answers are necessary and entirely appropriate to this doubt. But they must be specific. If someone is
doubting the resurrection, it is irrelevant to assure him of
Christ's promise never to leave him – Christ never was with
him if he has not risen. Equally, if someone has lost his sense

of Christ's presence, he will need more than bare historical facts with which to rediscover it. The assurance and inner witness of the Holy Spirit are what he needs.

Here then is the third category; doubt that is caused by an unnecessary lack of understanding of what our faith is grounded on. If there is 'no reason why' for faith, the time may come when there is 'no reason why not' for doubt. And the best remedy for this doubt is to know the sure and sufficient reasons God has given us, to know why we can know God is there, to know why we can trust his revelation as true, to know why we can be sure of his love and his goodness, and to stand firm in our understanding of these truths.

Notice two things in conclusion. First, just as with the previous two categories, a doubt of this kind may well be simple or compound. For example, someone can have a specific doubt about God which is caused by an unnecessary lack of understanding. If the doubt is simple, it can be cleared up, as I have suggested, by supplying the necessary understanding. But if the doubt is compound, you will find that although a doubter can understand the answer, he may be reluctant to accept it. (We will deal with this in chapter eleven.) He may even refuse to search for any answer at all, though expressing the deepest need for one. This indicates a far deeper problem and the surface doubts are only a symptom of this.

I think of some people who keenly desire a rational faith. You can almost see them hold their breath when it dawns on them that they understand that Christianity is true. But then they hesitate in doubt, not because they spot a new snag about believing but because they remember a previous experience. Once before they went ahead and believed, but it was a leap of faith with no questions asked and they fell and were hurt. This time around it is a case of 'once bitten, twice shy' and their doubt is not simple but compound.

A compound doubt must be approached with special sensitivity. To the person with a simple doubt, a helpful discussion, a suggested book or a more detailed explanation may be enough to show him the way along which he can eagerly search for himself. But to the person with the compound doubt, an answer which would satisfy his surface doubt alone may put even more pressure on the deeper problem and twist the knife in his hidden wound. Providing an answer only for the surface doubt answers neither doubt in the long run.

Second, of all the families of doubt this is probably the one best helped by reading. Not all doubts are helped in this way. Some are made worse. But there is nothing like a carefully chosen book to stimulate the examination and reflection which deals with this doubt. The question 'Have you thought through the basis of your faith?' is for many people almost inseparable from the best books they have read dealing with the heart of faith and understanding.

Are you building up a small library of essential books? Do you read as widely in the great classics of the faith as among modern authors? Naturally your selection will reflect your own pilgrimage, your own struggles and interests. But this will make it richer and more real when you recommend books to others who are questioning and searching.

I need add little recommendation to some of the books in my own library. Their well-thumbed, much-handled appearance says it all. Scores of people have been through them and their marginal jottings and exclamations are reminders of those who searched and those who found. Like the faith for which they argue, the best books are there not to collect dust but to stretch minds and to shed light.

Chapter Eight

An Unsigned Contract

Doubt from lack of commitment

Is it possible for a person to move smoothly through the first three levels of understanding and still leave out something essential? In other words, is it possible for a person to know his need, to know that if Christianity is true it provides an answer, to know on the basis of sufficient evidence that it is in fact true, and yet believe inadequately?

A friend told me recently that she no longer called herself a Christian. She wasn't at all defensive. She had no quarrel with Christianity or the church, and she expressed no particular doubts except that Christian things generally were rather unreal to her. After a while she shrugged her shoulders and said, 'You know, I don't think I ever was really committed to Christianity.' My reply was simple: 'But do you think you have ever been really committed to anything?' In this case my comment was not a stab in the back or a shot in the dark; I knew her well. If there is a recurring weakness in her life it centres on her fear to commit herself. Because of this she rarely enjoys anything in depth or sticks at anything for very long.

This is an example of doubt which comes from a deficiency at the fourth level of understanding, the only one which actually overlaps with the experience of becoming a Christian. This level centres on the question of commitment. A searcher becomes a believer when he chooses and commits himself to the consequences of his choice. This commitment is not a separate, independent stage but a higher level which builds logically on the implications of the previous levels. Like cement an understanding commitment transforms mere beliefs into solid convictions. By *conviction* I am not suggesting the idea of 'conviction of sin' but of 'the courage of one's convictions'.

The goal of this chapter is to examine the importance of commitment and conviction and to analyse the doubt which grows out of a deficiency at the threshold of conversion. Christian conversion is rich in multi-dimensional truths and can be viewed from many angles. The modern tendency to reduce it to simplistic, stereotyped formulas is an insult to the creativity of God and the integrity of man. Christ is the only way to God, but there are as many ways to Christ as there are people who come to him. Conversion may be gradual or sudden, quiet or dramatic, unmistakably evident to others or almost unnoticed. The variations are infinite.

Nonetheless, certain things are always required in an adequate understanding of conversion, and it is in ignoring these that we leave openings for later doubts. The individual's responsibility in conversion is to repent and believe; God's initiative and response are his gift of forgiveness and his gift of the Holy Spirit; and the church's role is to welcome the new believer into fellowship, symbolizing this publicly in the act of baptism.

Each of these aspects has its place as a foundation for faith, though the church's part is not so much essential to faith as an expression of faith. A weakness in any of them does not mean that faith is illegitimate but that it is an easy prey for doubt, as later testing may show.

A contract and a signature

The good news of the Christian gospel is a covenant agreement, a contract which God offers to us. The gift of the Holy Spirit is the seal of his part of the contract; by committing ourselves to him we put our name to it too. It is not enough for us only to see the need of the contract (the essence of level one) or even the attractiveness and reliability of the terms (levels two and three). What is needed to make the contract binding and valid is our signature, a commitment of faith. Without this signature, however excellent the terms are, the contract is only a piece of paper.

Personal knowledge always implies some degree of personal commitment to truth. Human thinking and language would dissolve into a topsy-turvy jumble of uncertainty if we were to use the word *know* as if it were interchangeable with words like *guess* or *dream*, or if we were to say *right* when we really meant *wrong*. The reason that knowing is different from guessing or dreaming is that knowledge implies an unspoken submission to what is real or thought to be real. I can legitimately say, 'I know', and add in the same breath, 'but I am open to being shown I am wrong'. But if knowledge is to have any substantial meaning, what I must never say is, 'I know', and then add, 'but I am sure I am wrong'.

If we say we know something, a personal and responsible commitment to what we know is assumed in our claim. It is not that once we know something we commit ourselves to it but that knowing something is itself a commitment. Knowledge is an acknowledgement of what is true. Knowing is a response to something beyond us, so it is more than subjective. But it is also *our* response to something beyond us, so it is more than objective too.

When you say, 'I know this is true', you are really saying, 'This is what *I* am convinced is the truth of the matter.' What is true for all personal knowledge is also true for the knowledge assumed in faith. Hence, there is no true knowledge of God without some personal conviction, and the idea of a healthy faith that has no personal commitment is a contradiction in terms.

This means that, however objectively true something may or may not be, if I am not personally convinced of it, then for me personally it is not true. That is, objectively it may be true, but subjectively I refuse to accept it.

This shows the important difference between subjectivism in faith and in doubt. The former says that because something is true for me it is necessarily true, while the latter says that because something is not true for me it is not true. Both notions are mistaken, but their respective dangers lead in opposite directions. Subjectivism in faith makes something out of nothing and turns fiction into fact. Subjectivism in doubt, on the other hand, turns something into nothing and makes fact into fiction.

Notice again: this type of doubt has nothing whatever to do with the truth. The weakness is not in truth as the object of belief; the weakness is in the believer since he is failing to enter into the essential obligations of believing. When a person suffers from this lack of personal commitment, the problem is not that he cannot genuinely believe *something* but that he will not genuinely believe *anything*. If he appears to believe, it is only because his underlying lack of conviction is covered by other supports for faith, such as the encouragement of fellow believers, so that the weakness is not exposed.

But take away the healthy assurance which grows from personal conviction and every pressure is likely to bear down on the weakened commitment and raise tremors of uncertainty which grow into doubt. Without commitment faith seems to cost more than we bargained for. Apart from conviction each new voice of authority appears to have the same weight as the one we believe, and every moment of unreality calls in question the reality of all past experience. We are then inclined to think, 'Perhaps it isn't true after all.' But in all honesty that should be translated, 'I never really believed this anyway.' For what has been lacking is not the terms of the contract but the signature of the believer.

Seen from a purely theoretical standpoint, the leap of faith which produces this kind of doubt completely by-passes the question of truth. Someone believes because he needs to believe, and that is that. He doesn't ask for reasons to believe and he doesn't inquire into what is involved. So when he experiences doubt, it is he, not his belief, that has been weighed and found wanting.

From a practical standpoint, however, this distinction makes little difference. The person who no longer believes will blame what he believed rather than the way he believed, and the rationalization this involves means that the chances of his reconsidering belief in the future are greatly diminished. His mind and heart are burnt-over ground.

Fashion and change

Two features of the present cultural climate make this element of conviction all the more necessary. First, there is the prevailing relativism, the unchallenged assumption of much modern thought. It cuts the ground from under conviction and precipitates a crisis of authority. The basic consideration 'Is it true?' has been replaced by 'Does it work?' or 'How will it sell?' And the effect has been to reduce truth to timeliness, morality to usefulness and personal faith to a matter of what is fashionable.

On the one hand, the loss of conviction means that minds are unsettled, directions are changed and loyalties are switched, all as if convictions were nothing but custom or fashion. The problem is not that people change but the ease and rapidity with which they change.

On the other hand, where there is commitment, it is often only for its own sake, and conviction has been replaced by passionate intensity. So a dangerous tolerance of error and a specious attitude of humility towards truth has arisen. Since nothing is a matter of conviction, everything can be taken with equal seriousness or lack of seriousness. All is allowed because little can be done. G. K. Chesterton gave an early warning: 'What we suffer from today is humility in the wrong place. Modesty has moved from the organ of ambition. Modesty has settled on the organ of conviction; where it was never meant to be. A man was meant to be doubtful about himself but undoubting about the truth. This has been exactly reversed.'

The second feature which makes personal conviction more necessary than ever is the tendency towards group thinking. For both good and bad reasons the emphasis on man's individuality which has dominated the West since the close of the Middle Ages is now being discouraged in favour of emphasizing community. Man's individuality is now viewed against wider frames of unity such as the state, the balance of nature, the progress of evolution and the historical process. The merits of individuality are being lumped together with the dangers and both are being dismissed as 'individualism'. The advantages of unity over diversity, or collectivism over individualism, are assumed to be self-evident and the obvious totalitarian overtones are ignored.

People in groups are now apt to think in ways that a more independently-minded age would have rejected. The obvious checks to this are a sense of individual identity, a willingness to assume responsibility, a mature morality and a developed sense of integrity. But these have been so badly eroded that the controlling guards of critical thought are down. Large groups of people are unthinkingly accepting what is sometimes harmless nonsense but can just as easily be fraudulent propaganda or dangerous ideological evil. In its most obvious form, this is the problem that silent majorities pose for democracy, but the same pressures operate in groups and whole subcultures at many lower and less obvious levels.

The problem for many people today is not that it is too difficult to believe but that it is too easy. It is hard for them not to believe, for they slip in and out of belief caressed by the changing breezes of cultural fashion. Almost anything goes in the permissive climate, anything, that is, except those beliefs (like Christianity) which take truth and personal conviction seriously.

The problem this creates for Christianity is that a part of the turning to faith in our generation may be only a reflection of the psychological and sociological undercurrents of our time. One person may become a Christian because to believe in Jesus is 'where it's at'. Another may refuse because in his circles it is not 'where it's at'. Neither asks if it is true. Both simply reflect what is fashionable for them. When the group or the fashion changes, such people change too.

Without the anchor of personal conviction they are at the mercy of every ebb and flow of opinion. This throws a more realistic light on the spectacular statistics and glowing reports of widespread conversions, and it should make us wary of the forced professions and the hot-house wonders of superficial evangelistic movements. There is no iron in the new faith because it lacks personal conviction.

Commitment and responsibility

Choice is one of the root ideas in the word *believe*, and this element of responsibility and commitment is the key to the 'obedience of faith' which is the heart of Christian discipleship. Stress obedience apart from faith and you produce legalism. Stress faith apart from obedience and you produce cheap grace. For the person who becomes a Christian the moment of comprehension leads to one conclusion only – commitment. At that point the cost has been counted, a shoulder has been put to the yoke, a hand to the plough, and a contract for discipleship has been signed. The decision is irreversible. It is not faith going a second mile; it is faith making its first full step and there is no going back.

The responsible commitment which is assumed in a small way in all personal knowledge comes into its own in the Christian faith. In Christianity it is not only assumed, it is required. Faith is 'obedience to the truth'. Discipleship is an undertaking which grows out of an understanding. What faith has seen, obedience is prepared to sign. This is the obedience of faith to which personal conviction leads.

A conviction is nothing if it is not our own. Other things may play their part in helping us to understand, but nothing can take its place. Unless each of us wrestles with the truth for ourselves, we will end up with opinions rather than convictions. Pascal warned that 'hearsay is so far from being a criterion of belief that you should not believe anything until you have put yourself into the same state as if you had never heard it.' No conviction is truly our own unless we are prepared to hold it even if all men are against it.

A very elementary test of whether we have thought something through in this way and are ready to speak of being convinced of it is to see whether we can express it. A good argument can usually be expressed in a sentence or two. It provides a healthy challenge to the virility of a believer's conviction to see if he can say succinctly just why it is that he believes Christianity is true.

The note of conviction is evident in biblical faith. 'Choose here and now whom you will worship,' Joshua challenged the people of Israel but did not pause for a reply: 'But I and my family, we will worship the Lord.' 'We have no need to answer you on this matter,' is the calm response of Shadrach, Mesach and Abed-nego to Nebuchadnezzar's threat. 'If there is a god who is able to save us from the blazing furnace, it is our God whom we serve, and he will save us from your power, O king; but if not, be it known to your majesty that we will neither serve your god nor worship the golden image that you have set up.' 'I know the one whom I have trusted,' writes Paul from his prison cell, 'and am confident of his power to keep safe what he has put into my charge until the great day.'

The same note is equally clear in the testimony of Christian history. Polycarp, the second-century Christian leader in Smyrna, faced a hostile mob and quietly refused to go back on his faith in Christ: 'Eighty and six years have I served him, and he hath done me no wrong; how then can I blaspheme my King who saved me?' Martin Luther, excommunicated by the Pope and defending himself before the Emperor, closes his statement with the celebrated words: 'My conscience is taken captive by God's word, I cannot and will not recant anything. On this I take my stand. I can do no other. So help me God.' 'The witness of history is as stirring as it is unmistakable. The examples that we know are but the heroic and visible tip of the great hidden iceberg of faith which is Christian conviction through the centuries.

Certain opponents of Christianity have disliked it. 'Their pertinacity and inflexible obstinacy should certainly be punished,' wrote the Younger Pliny to the Emperor Trajan, about AD 112. Others, like the modern thinker, Alan Watts, have grudgingly admired it: 'Without any disrespect it must be said that Christianity is pre-eminently the gamblers' religion. In no other religion are the stakes so high and the choice so momentous.' But both the ancient emperor and the modern mystic observe the same thing – the obedience of faith and the stamp of personal conviction which are hallmarks of Christian discipleship. Without such commitment there is no real faith.

Speaking personally

Let me be personal here, for coming to grips with this has been an important milestone in my own life as a Christian. I can see this now, yet it was not until nearly ten years after I became a Christian that I finally faced the issue that whatever other influences had been involved in my conversion (such as my family and friends and the work of God in my life) there was a sense in which the decision to believe was entirely my responsibility. I am not saying that my trusting God was 'all up to me', but that I had to see that all of me was involved in trusting God. The decision to believe was one for which I at least was fully responsible.

Up until then I had found that when difficulties came or doubts arose in my Christian life, I could always escape their force by not holding myself answerable for my own faith. This meant I could blame the problems on other people or on situations outside myself. The irresponsibility of this helped me to escape the force of the problems, but at the same time I was constantly troubled by suspicion. I had entered fully into the shared joys of Christian experience, but I had never quite gained the satisfaction that other Christians seemed to have. I was on the inside of Christian faith, yet in my mind I was also on the outside looking in. I was not prepared to commit myself completely in every situation, as I found myself as the actor and the spectator at the same time.

At times, in fact, there was a sense of hollowness about much of my faith. This came home to me when I was travelling alone in the Far East for some months. I knew almost no one, and because of the language barrier I could speak freely with few people. The surrounding culture was fascinating but not my own. Slowly the pressures of its differences bore down on my thinking and decisions, prying open my defences and forcing me to face questions I had not been conscious of before.

Why did I do things this way rather than that? How did I know that such-and-such a principle was right, especially when no one there shared it? How did I really know? And how had I chosen what was 'right' and what was 'wrong'? Were my beliefs my own or were they merely the product of my culture, my country, my education or a legacy from my parents?

When I was separated from all these early influences, my choices became simple. For once in my life there was no need to believe as I did or act as I chose for any reasons other than that I was personally convinced it was right. Familiar people and influences were distant. They would never know or be affected. Existentially, they did not touch me at that moment. If I was to believe something or to choose to do something, the decision was one which I had to make *myself* and make *before God alone*.

It wasn't that I was doubting my faith or denying the reality of my becoming a Christian, but rather that, though I had genuinely believed ten years earlier, my commitment had been intertwined with the emotional comfort of sharing the beliefs and way of life of my family and certain friends. I had not only come to faith. I had also, as it were, 'fallen in line' again, so that although I believed, my faith had been marked by a continuing lack of personal conviction.

I was convinced of it, but I was not staked on it. Partly I had believed for reasons which were extraneous, and I had used the emotional commitment I had found in this to cover for a lack of genuine commitment. I had been both committed and non-committal. It was only after the resolution which this experience brought that I could say with a new reality, 'This God is *my* God.' The decisiveness and fresh conviction it brought made no difference to my theology and very little difference to my choices and values seen from the outside. The difference it made was internal. Now the choices and values are not only what I trust are right choices and correct beliefs; they are *my* choices, *my* beliefs, *my* convictions. Of course they are always more than my choice, but they are never less than my choice.

A cancer of unreality

The type of doubt which is generated by a weak sense of personal conviction is not always immediately apparent. It is not in the nature of this doubt to cry out in pain or groan in anguish. It has little intellectual sharpness, and its theology is often impeccable. It appears baffling because it seems to call no attention to itself. It is not so much doubtful about Christianity as diffident about itself, and at first sight this looks appealing. Its defining feature is that it has none except, as time goes on, a growing sense of unreality.

Here is the heart of it. While a person in this situation professes to believe the truth, he nonetheless has no serious engagement with truth, and without this the doubt is allowed to act like a cancer of unreality on faith. Or, to change the metaphor, a weak conviction acts on faith like a slipping clutch. The driver is experienced, the car is powerful, the engine is tuned, but the clutch will not engage. It can be the same with faith. A good mind and a warm heart can be made impotent if there is no commitment.

This sense of unreality marks only the opening stage of this doubt. It is quickly followed by a second stage, chiefly characterized by guilt. The doubter knows that his beliefs are true, but they are still unreal to him. So he grows ashamed of harbouring a doubt to which he knows the answer himself, and he keeps it to himself, a fugitive thought, locked away from the light of open discussion. This is doubt's incubation period, and the dark aura of guilty secrecy is an ideal womb. Finally it bursts out in a different form in its third stage of development.

Here it is most true to itself. Weak all along in terms of commitment, doubt now shows its colours and acts true to form by refusing to shoulder any responsibility for the unreality it has caused. It shifts the blame to belief. This is the moment when bad theology enters, not – notice this carefully – as a reason for doubt but as a rationale for the doubting which has already been going on. The doubt which was originally a result of an uncommitted belief becomes a rationale for committed unbelief. Through a clever about-turn, the evasion of responsibility is concealed. Though the doubt is really an expression of not-being-committed, it passes itself off as an excuse for not-committing.

Stages of doubt

The remedy for this doubt must begin with a careful discernment of which stage the doubt is in and what the root of the lack of conviction is. Only when the cause of the doubt has been understood and dealt with can faith be re-engaged and personal conviction encouraged.

There are many reasons why people have a diminished sense of personal conviction. On a level which is not hard to discern or to deal with, there are some who have almost 'grown into faith' through their family or their church) so that they have never become aware of the need for their own convictions. This is a common feature of faith in countries where there is an established or state church – faith is almost inherited. Others have become Christians at a particular moment in their lives but have believed for good reasons which have had mixed in with them other less solid motives for believing, so that their faith was never based on a strong, established conviction.

With these people the remedy lies in pointing out the responsibility that faith requires. Their problem is not that they could not take on this responsibility before but that they were not asked to. There might be some question now as to whether they will, but there is no question that they can if they want to.

But there are still others who have no sense of conviction because of problems on a far deeper level, such as a crisis of identity. It takes some*one* to know something. If conviction in belief is like the authorizing signature on a contract or a cheque, then the person who has no sense of himself will have no 'name' to sign to what he believes. The contract may be good or the cheque generous, but it lacks the binding authorization of a signature.

Imagine a millionaire who has decided to donate to a charity. He writes out a generous cheque and sends it off. Later he has second thoughts. He gets cold feet and phones his bank manager asking him to stop the cheque. But then, just as he is halfway through explaining it, the secretary of the charity organization is shown in, wreathed in smiles and eager to thank him for his generosity. So he is caught between the two of them, embarrassed to welcome his guest and unable to say more on the phone.

There are doubters who are like this. Their weakness is not that they will not commit themselves to God but that they do not commit themselves to anything. Nothing terrifies them more than the responsibility of choosing. They do anything to avoid choosing, and if events force them to make a choice, they question it by raking over the ashes of the decision until it is dead and cold. Even when they make the right choice, they don't let the choice go through. They write out a cheque but it never gets cashed for it's taken back at once. They are paralyzed and embarrassed by the dilemmas they create for themselves. As a Spanish proverb puts it, 'Among the safest of courses, the safest of all is to doubt.'

The remedy for these people begins when they see where the problem lies – with them, not with God. It isn't that God is unreal; lack of commitment has made everything unreal. The shadow is not over God more than it is over anything else. What they must do is relearn to choose and commit themselves to the consequences of their choice. As they do this, trusting in God's help, inching forward like a baby taking its first steps, a sense of reality will return to their faith as well as their lives. The early choices will be painful, of course, but in much the same way that 'pins and needles' are painful when your leg has gone to sleep. Pins and needles can even hurt so much that we would almost prefer to let the leg sleep on. But not really. Better pins and needles than no leg at all.

This type of doubt is already aggravated by the contemporary crisis of identity, but it may grow even more serious wherever there is a hardening of society's attitudes towards Christianity. It takes conviction to stand firm when there is a price to pay, when a strong authority is openly hostile or when the surrounding consensus considers belief ridiculous, harmful or unpatriotic. This is already the position of many Christians in the world today, and those of us with more freedom now may well experience it before the end of this century. If this is the case, the ones most likely to buckle under the heat of the pressure will be those Christians who lack personal conviction. The difference between an enduring faith and a nominal faith is largely at this point.

It is none too soon to be aware of the tests we may face,

but our defence will not lie in brilliant, far-sighted anticipation of specific pressures and persecutions. For one thing it is for the Holy Spirit to tell us in that hour what we are to say, and for another thing the people we prove to be in that hour will be determined, not by our thinking about that hour, but by our thinking and living in this hour. We will measure up to tomorrow's requirements only by measuring up to today's. Five minutes of limelight may win a reputation, but character is built in the unseen succession of little obediences and little acts of faith.

'As now, so then' applies also to conviction. Examine yourself honestly to see whether your convictions are truly your own or merely inherited beliefs or shared opinions. It is not that God is testing us to see whether we believe or not. God does not need to find out whether we will stand or fall. He knows that already. It is we who do not know, and like Peter we can be too sure of ourselves for our own good.

As C. S. Lewis warned in his book *A Grief Observed*, 'Your bid will not be serious if nothing much is staked on it. And you will never discover how serious it was until the stakes are raised horribly high; until you find that you are playing not for counters or sixpences but for every penny you have in the world. Nothing less will shake a man – or at any rate a man like me – out of his merely verbal thinking and his merely notional beliefs. He has to be knocked silly before he comes to his senses. Only torture will bring out the truth.'

C. S. Lewis was writing after a deep personal crisis in his own life, but his words apply equally soberly to the crises of faith which persecution would mean for Christians. As the apostle John was told by the third angel who described the pressure of crises on faith, during his vision recounted in the book of Revelation, 'This is where the fortitude of God's people has its place – in keeping God's commands and re maining loyal to Jesus.' Martin Luther, whose own convictions had been tempered and proved like the finest steel, knew well that in the hour of trial each man must have his own convictions, or he will find himself with none. His warning should put the importance of conviction in faith beyond all question: 'Bear in mind, then, that when you face death or persecution, I cannot be with you, or you with me. Every man must then fight for himself.'

Chapter Nine

No Sign of Life
Doubt from lack of growth

Sometimes it is easy to be so taken up with learning to start something that the question of what comes next never crosses our minds. I remember feeling like this on a beginners' ski slope. Like everyone else I was concentrating desperately on standing up and staying up. Suddenly, after all the effort, I was off! And that's when it hit me. What do I do next? How do I keep going? How do I stop? In our desire to get started in something we often forget that starting is not an end in itself. We are getting started to go somewhere or to do something.

Becoming a Christian can be the same. It is easy to forget that becoming a Christian is only the beginning. The journey of a thousand miles begins with the first step, but the purpose of the first step is the whole journey. It is not the other way round.

The first four varieties of doubt stem from a deficiency of understanding in becoming a Christian. They are all common but unnecessary in the sense that, if we enter into the full biblical understanding of faith, there is no room for any of these doubts to grow. We can go on in the Christian life with confidence, even at these potentially dangerous points. But these are not the end of possible doubts for the believer. They are only the end of doubts at faith's beginning. We must now examine some of the other basic varieties of doubt which the Christian faces as he goes on in his new life.

The next doubt comes right there, when the Christian does *not* go on, when he does not grow, when he fails to experience and express his new life, when he simply fails to practise the truth. This is the doubt we will examine in this chapter, and our goal will be to see how it grows from a deficiency of faith and how this can be remedied. What moves and grows and bears fruit shows life. What is inert or barren may be dead. This does not mean, of course, that everything that is not growing, moving or bearing fruit is dead. But it does mean there may be *no way to tell* if it is alive or not. Movement, growth and fruit are unmistakable signs of life.

The Christian life is new life, the life of Jesus Christ implanted in the Christian believer, transforming him and bearing fruit through him. Like all life, this life is nothing if it is not lived out. Christian thinking, Christian choices, Christian action do not bring life into a Christian. They are expressions of life which is already there. Without this prior life, they are barren, mechanical and dead.

So a special challenge to faith comes here: if faith is not being practised, how is anyone to know it is real? If there are no signs of growth or fruit, how are we to know it is alive? If we are unable to answer these questions, it does not necessarily mean that there is no life but that at the moment there is no way to tell. This is what opens the door to doubt.

Putting it like this can be very unhelpful, for it may suggest the misleading picture of the Christian life as a plant that must be pulled up by the roots periodically to see whether it is growing. The problem with this is not only that it is bad for the plant, but that it is impossible for the Christian.

A more helpful angle must be found, from which we can examine growth and fruitfulness as a test for signs of life. One possibility is to think in terms of world views. Just as a plant grows or withers, so a world view must be developed and practised and produce results or it will be discarded as impractical. Of course, being a Christian means much more than just having and using a particular world view. But to examine faith's growth from this viewpoint is extremely useful in understanding this doubt.

A working philosophy

The testing of faith, on which this doubt centres, is not as dramatic as it is with many other doubts. Each human being has his own world view, but few people are consciously aware of it and this is as it should be. What health is to the body, a working philosophy is to the mind. The mind may be at its healthiest when its owner is least aware of his world view.

But even if a person is unconscious of his philosophy of life, he is not uncritical of it. Throughout his life, down below the surface of his conscious thoughts, emotions and choices, he is constantly testing and trying out his world view. For a world view the process of living is a non-stop examination by experience in which only the practicable is preserved.

Man is driven by a deep desire for meaning. He can live meaningfully only if he can make sense of his situation at some level. Part of being human is the need to find a framework through which life can be interpreted. so that the bare facts and raw experiences of life are given coherence and meaning. All our views and values are a close-knit series of beliefs which are rooted in our basic assumptions. Deeper even than a value system there lies in each of our minds a meaning system. Thus our judgements, our decisions, our principles and our opinions are not arbitrary or unconnected but have a hidden logic and inter-dependence which is rooted in our basic world view and presuppositions.

The usefulness of a person's world view depends on how well it can order and handle experience for him. Once a person makes a world view his own by believing it, it will either be proved in practice or disproved by being impracticable. At this level what he believes either works or it is non-existent – theory is quite irrelevant. Here faith is not what a man says he believes but what he shows he believes. His faith is what he functions on. It has nothing to do with profession, everything to do with practice.

Living is faith's reality test. Every moment and each new experience challenge faith for an interpretation. Can faith order the new experience, cope with it, handle it, assimilate it? Or will the new experience undermine faith, proving too much for it to understand and assimilate? If faith is to continue supplying a person's world view, it must answer this challenge constantly and completely. Equally its answer must be practical, not theoretical, and it must be fresh and contemporary, not yesterday's answer to today's challenge. This constant challenge demands that faith be existential. Either it will rise to the occasion, and if so it will grow in the process, or else it will fall and retreat, losing authority, imperceptibly growing weaker and to that extent becoming unreal.

It is at the point of moment-by-moment choice that doubt waits in the wings. If faith plays its part, faith grows stronger and more assured, dominating the stage so that doubt can make no entry. But if faith hesitates only slightly or shows the slightest sign of retreat, doubt takes its cue and slips on stage. A part of life, an area of experience has proved too much for faith to handle, and this unmanaged situation calls in question faith's authority and makes room for doubt. This, of course, is not a process of which we are aware, but it is no less dangerous for being unconscious. The doubt generated begins as a tiny crack in faith's authority, and it may take a while before it widens. But left unchecked it will only be a matter of time before it breaks through into the conscious mind.

There is no one without a world view, so this testing of faith is common to all men and not just Christians. The difference for us as Christians is that our world view operates on a conscious as well as unconscious level, and therefore we become sensitive to unreality much sooner. We are not unique in this. Rather, like the world views of Hindus or humanists, our world view can be developed explicitly and formally and not just left at implicit and informal levels.

If we view growth in terms of putting a world view to work, we can see that there is nothing mysterious about the loss of growth and vitality which leads to this type of doubt. It has nothing to do with God's displeasure or any projected sense of abandonment or supposed spiritual withdrawal. Doubt arises naturally because truth which is un-practised will soon be taken to be impracticable. And, since practicability is an absolute essential for a world view, truth which is impracticable will soon be discarded as untrue. Christianity is not true because it works, but if it is not put to work a severe doubt is cast over its truthfulness.

Little by little and choice by choice

The key to this kind of doubt is simple. People do not so much lose their faith as cease to use their faith. This doubt is characterized by standing still, by indecision and drift. The French novelist, Georges Bernanos, describes this in the words of a young country priest writing in his private journal:

No. I have not lost my faith. The expression 'to lose one's faith', as one might a purse or a ring of keys has always seemed to me rather foolish. It must be one of those sayings of bourgeois piety, a legacy of those wretched priests of the eighteenth century who talked so much.

Faith is not a thing which one 'loses', we merely cease to shape our lives by it. That is why old-fashioned confessors are not far wrong in showing a certain amount of scepticism when dealing with 'intellectual crises', doubtless far more rare than people imagine. An educated man may come by degrees to tuck away his faith in some back corner of his brain, where he can find it again on reflection, by an effort of memory: yet even if he feels a tender regret for what no longer exists and might have been, the term 'faith' would nevertheless be inapplicable to such an abstraction.

This type of doubt is very gentlemanly. One might almost say that it is a very English way of doubting, as if a slow choice to disbelieve was no choice at all. Personal responsibility is sidestepped so that faith can eventually be laid aside with a kind of courteous and chivalrous regret. The manner is deceiving, but, stripped to its essentials, the complaint against faith is quite blunt: faith does not work; it must be discarded.

The question left unasked is whether the faith was really useless or simply not used. What would you think of a man who gave up learning to ride a bicycle, complaining that he hurt himself because his bicycle stopped moving so he had no choice but to fall off? If he wanted to sit comfortably while remaining stationary, he should not have chosen a bicycle but a chair. Similarly faith must be in use, or it is useless.

A celebrated description of such a slow erosion of faith is given us by Charles Darwin in his autobiography: 'I gradually came to disbelieve in Christianity as a divine revelation. ... Disbelief crept over me at a very slow rate, but was at last complete. The rate was so slow that I felt no distress, and have never since doubted even for a single second that my conclusion was correct.'

This is the way that many people doubt, little by little, choice by choice, thought by thought. Faith is not torn up, it is merely frayed. It is not eaten away suddenly but nibbled at the corners. It is not hit by a bolt of lightning, it is the victim of the slow erosion of many winters. In a time of cultural and religious decline like our own, the incidence of this doubt is more common than ever. As C. S. Lewis observed, 'If you examined a hundred people who had lost their faith in Christianity, I wonder how many of them would turn out to have been reasoned out of it by honest argument? Do not most people simply drift away?'

We have a graphic biblical example of this in the state of the late first century church in Sardis, in Asia Minor, to which Jesus said, 'Though you have a name for being alive, you are dead. Wake up, and put some strength into what is left, which must otherwise die!' Under the penetrating gaze of Christ the difference between the actual and the apparent, the reality and the reputation, was all too obvious. He knew that the seeming peace was a sleep that would end in death.

In a curious way the state of the church mirrored the celebrated history of the great city in which it was. Built by the fabled Croesus in the sixth century BC, the citadel of Sardis had been constructed on a promontory of rock and was regarded as impregnable. But twice in its long history the citadel had fallen, not because of the strategy of superior armies but simply because the garrison had been so overconfident that there had been no vigilance and it had been caught off guard with its defences unmanned. Spiritually speaking, the Sardis church was in the same danger. Self-confident in the reputation they enjoyed, they were careless about putting their faith to work, and the drift towards death was well under way.

A living faith is a relationship, and like any relationship it must be cherished, nurtured, fostered and prized for itself. Think of any special friendship you enjoy. Was it all there when you first met each other? Or is its richness many-splendoured, a mosaic of all the moments of shared experience?

Like an art or a skill, faith must not only be learned but kept in practice and developed. Just as a concert pianist practises for eight hours a day or a marathon runner covers twenty or thirty miles in road-training, so faith grows strong in believing but atrophies if out of use. Nothing is more pathetic than the sight of a Christian of forty or fifty attempting to get by on the faith which he had when he was twenty, especially since the intervening years have seen development and maturity in every other area. Such faith is little more than a memory.

Putting faith to work

What is the antidote to this variety of doubt? To put faith to work. To stretch it, to put it on the line, to prove it in the crucible of experience and so let it deepen and grow with the testing of life. This doubt is not in need of comfort but challenge. The problem is not that faith is untrue but that it is untried. As Martin Luther pointed out, 'The true, living faith, which the Holy Spirit instils into the heart, simply cannot be idle.' Or as George Whitefield, the great eighteenth-century evangelist whose life was a blazing torch in God's hand, wrote in his diary, 'I am never better than when I am on the full stretch for God.'

This is the challenge which we all face. Faith must go on being exercised. Faith must mean everything today or in some tomorrow it may mean nothing. Yesterday's experiences, insights, answers to prayer, ways of putting things were completely legitimate and satisfying yesterday, but today is another day. God's truth and God's love will always be fresh, but will the same be said of our response? Will our faith and our love for him be as fresh? Paul's question to the Christians in Corinth is a question for us all: 'Examine yourselves: are you living the life of faith? Put yourselves to the test.'

Doubt from an unused faith is widespread. We could point to several factors to explain it. The continuation of state churches in post-Christian cultures, the equation of Christian values and cultural norms, the presence of Christian ghettos, the concentration on faith in conversion rather than faith in living, the preoccupation with evangelism at the expense of ethics – these are all features of modern Christianity which discourage faith from being stretched and applied and which therefore foster doubt.

The anaemia of modern faith can be detected in surprising places, for instance in attitudes to Bible reading. Would you expect it in those who recognize the Scriptures as their authority and read and study them carefully? Judging from the place of the Bible in their theology and the sales that are reported by publishing houses, we might conclude that such segments of Christianity are indeed alert, virile and biblical.

But in many areas it is becoming clear that this situation is not as healthy as it seems. What passes for a deeply biblical spirit can become an unimaginative, if faithful, traditionalism. In principle it holds that no authority is higher or more powerful than the Bible, but in practice it may deny this, confine the authority of the Bible within narrow traditions and reveal its true estimate of the power of the Bible by its styles of insecure defence.

Again the issue is not theological so much as practical. The correct theology is there, but where is the consistent and courageous practice of it? This is what will make the world sit up. We are people of One Book, but we have failed to read other books in the light of that One Book. Instead we have kept it in quarantine, isolated in a religious world of its own, and we wonder why it has lost its power and significance.

Instead of bringing the demanding reality of life to our reading of the Bible, we tend to turn away from life to read the Bible and keep the two worlds apart. Instead of bringing the questions and issues of life to the Bible and the answers and demands of the Bible to life, we have censored the two-way conversation and in a manoeuvre of shortsighted piety we have allowed the Bible to talk only to itself.

Instead of sitting under its judgement, stretching ourselves to understand it, laying ourselves on the line to obey it, searching it for a knowledge of God and his will, we limit the Bible to a shrinking circle of reality outside which more and more of life is separate and secular. We exclude it from reality and wonder why it is unreal. We make it flat, stale and one-dimensional, and wonder why it is no longer dynamic and alive.

The drive of our fallen nature is to tone down the volume of the Word of God, to make it less insistent, less pressing, less precise and to turn it into a kind of sacred Muzak. What we need, when we read God's Word, is to take our fingers off the control and let it speak to us and search us as it will. One of two things is bound to happen. Either we will be under the Word of God or the Word of God will be under us. The first is the way of discipleship, whereby all that we are and all that we do is truly judged by the Word of God (including science, politics and so forth). The second is the way of nominal faith and cheap grace, whereby all that we would do anyway is falsely justified through the Word of God. That is, the Bible is interpreted to sanction whatever we do (including science, politics and so forth).

Could any well-meaning person ever fall into the second category? It might seem unlikely. But how does collective evil ever arise? How was it that Christians supported the Crusades, slavery, racism or other forms of evil? The problem does not arise because evil-intentioned people deliberately set out to abuse the Bible by exploiting it to their own ends, but because well-meaning people do not practise the full truth revealed in the Bible. In not consciously choosing to sit under the judgement of God's Word, we unconsciously slide in the opposite direction. God's Word is no longer the judge of what we do but the justification for whatever we do.

The same is often true of our defence of the Bible. Defend it in a manner which undermines what you are out to defend and eventually you tear it down yourself. Defend its authority by limiting its authority and you reject its authority. We may protect faith from science (or politics and psychology), but to the degree that life includes scientific (or political or psychological) questions faith is not so much preserved as hamstrung. We do the Bible a great disservice through our well-meaning but unfortunate defensiveness.

Strengthening muscles

What is true of faith's attitude to the Bible is true of faith in every area. Like a sportsman in training, faith must keep itself fit. It must be trim and in good shape. It must keep its hand in, and never be out of practice. It will have its limits, but it will know them and do its best to extend them. What it fears above all is the test which shows that its training has gone to seed, its muscles have grown soft, its confidence has been misplaced. In short, it will practise.

Not surprisingly, many of the biblical pictures of faith are strenuous, active and energetic. Faith is the athlete straining for the finishing line, the boxer kept in superb condition by his training, the soldier stripped to his essential equipment. There is no place for the poorly-trained runner, the overweight boxer moving sluggishly round the ring, the reluctant soldier distracted by civilian pursuits and preoccupations. Faith presses forward or is pushed back. Faith trains or grows slack.

In his classic, *Pilgrim's Progress*, Bunyan depicted the danger of inaction in his charming but vacuous character, Mr Talkative, whose companionship was so beguilling to Christian and Faithful. Faithful was the first to remember something of his reputation. 'I have heard of you that you are a man whose religion lies in talk, and that your conversation [way of life] gives this your mouth-profession the lie.' But Christian sees through Mr Talkative too and warns his friend,

> He thinks that learning and saying will make a good Christian and thus he deceiveth his own soul. Hearing is but as the sowing of the seed; talking is not sufficient to prove that the fruit is indeed in the heart and life and let us assure ourselves, that at the day of doom, men shall be judged according to their fruits. It will not be said then, 'Did you believe?' but 'Were you doers or talkers only?', and accordingly shall they be judged. The end of the world is compared to our harvest, and you know men at harvest regard nothing but fruit.'

Is Bunyan's character only one type of believer or is he a part of every believer? Is he the nominal Christian who sits near us in church, or is he the other person in our hearts? It is to the Mr Talkative in us all that Jesus often addressed his sternest warnings. The sermon on the Mount closes with unrelenting severity, directing warning after warning against an empty profession of faith, making it clear beyond question that the only faith which counts is faith that obeys.

> A good tree cannot bear bad fruit, or a poor tree good fruit. And when a tree does not yield good fruit it is cut down and burnt. That is why I say you will recognize them by their fruits.
>
> Not everyone who calls me 'Lord, Lord' will enter the kingdom of Heaven, but only those who do the will of my heavenly Father. . . .
>
> What then of the man who hears these words of mine and acts upon them? He is like a man who had the sense to build his house on rock. . . . But what of the man who hears these words of mine and does not act upon them? He is like a man who was foolish enough to build his house on sand.

In an incident in Mark's Gospel Jesus asks the question:
' "Who is my mother? Who are my brothers?" And looking
round at those who were sitting in the circle about him he
said, "Here are my mother and my brothers. Whoever does
the will of God is my brother, my sister, my mother." ' The
practice of truth and the obedience of faith could easily be
construed merely as external marks of discipleship. But Jesus
restores them to their proper place at the heart of faith.
Each at its highest is a part of the intimate family relationship which is the fellowship of faith. For faith to obey is for
faith to come into its own. For faith to practise the truth is
for faith to be most itself. Obedience is the blood-tie of the
new community. This is the style of faith which makes life a
rich experience and effectively rules out the possibility of
this doubt.

Chapter Ten

Coup d'Etat from Within
Doubt from unruly emotions

I know someone who is frankly afraid of flying. Several times I have heard well-meaning people trying to persuade her that it is much safer to fly in an aircraft than to drive in a car. Perhaps one day someone might convince her, either by marshalling an impressive array of statistics and well-documented evidence, or by appealing to factors which are essentially emotional if not manipulative. Their case might be convincing, even irrefutable. But I know she would still prefer to drive in a car.

The strength of the rational argument would be no match for the power of the emotions. It's one thing to think rationally in an airport lounge and another thing to feel rational on the runway. When the seat belts are fastened and the engines are revving, the voice of reason can hardly be heard above the roar of the emotions. The problem is not that reason attacks faith but that the emotions overwhelm reason as well as faith, and it is impossible for reason to dissuade them.

The sixth variety of doubt comes just at the point where the believer's emotions (vivid imagination, changing moods, erratic feelings, intense reactions) rise up and overpower the understanding of faith. Out-voted, out-gunned, faith is pressed back and hemmed in by the unruly mob of raging emotions which only a while earlier were quiet, orderly citizens of the personality. Reason is cut down, obedience is thrown out, and for a while the rule of the emotions is as sovereign as it is violent. The coup d'état is complete.

The place of the emotions
The basic issue of faith is the question of credibility. Is what I believe true? Is the person whom I trust trustworthy? Coming to faith is a question of grappling with the truth of the

matter and the trustworthiness of the person. Is there compelling evidence or not?

Subjective elements play their part in the decision to believe. But if faith is not to be make-believe, objective considerations must finally determine whether faith is true or misplaced. Understanding and choice are both essential to genuine belief, and they are always more important than the emotions in conversion.

Because conversion is a complete change involving the whole person, it may be profoundly emotional. But however emotional it is, the emotions alone do not affect conversion. This is not because Christianity is unemotional but because this is how human knowing works anyway. Christianity, in fact, provides a basis for the highest place for the emotions, but in coming to believe the place for understanding and choosing truth is primary and the place for the emotions is secondary.

This may be fine in theory, but the fact is that even if we come to faith with our emotions playing their proper part, it is quite another thing to keep that balance in continuing to believe. And, of course, not all of us started with it anyway. Perhaps the greatest single human factor in explaining why faith does not go on as it began is the explosive power of the emotions subsequent to conversion.

If we were not marked by the results of the Fall, we would experience an unconscious natural harmony between our understanding, will and feeling. All our actions and reactions would be whole. But none of us enjoy that perfect balance now, and the alienation of sin means that we are alienated not only from God and each other but also from ourselves. The deep harmony within each personality has been lost. For some people the alienation is so extreme that it leads to severe emotional disorder. But for the great majority of us the hassle of living with our contradictory 'selves' and struggling with our conflicting emotions is a run-of-the-mill aspect of living. We are so used to putting up with the brokenness of our fallen human nature that we tend to accept it as normal and take it for granted.

The alienation of sin can play equal havoc in our understanding, our choosing or our feeling. It is not that one of them has 'fallen further' than the other two. But the emotions are distinctive for one important reason. They are that part of us which is most vulnerable to outside influences, and in this sense they are the part of us which is most easily manipulated. For some people even the body is more immune to sickness than the emotions are to 'catching' whatever is around. Our understanding can be persuaded not to believe, and our conviction can be broken. But when we are under pressure our emotions throw in the towel long before our understandings or our will.

This gives the impression that the emotions are a problem because they are weak. But it is just the reverse: The real problem is that they are too strong. Not only are they easily influenced; they are highly influential. Once persuaded, they become the powerful persuaders, and here is their danger.

The emotions and the imagination may sometimes be under the control of reason and understanding, but they are seldom effectively tamed. Just as often the emotions will rise up against reason in their own special kind of 'palace coup' within the personality. Then they carry everything before them in a flood of feeling which overwhelms logic and reason. At such times the frailty of rationality is all too apparent. Gossamer-thin, feather-light, glass-brittle, reason seems to stand no chance against the elemental power of fear, anger, hatred, jealousy or desire.

Elijah and the kingdom of despair
Here is yet another doubt that has no intrinsic link with the Christian faith. The situation is not that Christians have emotional doubts while all other men enjoy certainty, but that all men have emotional doubts and, naturally, the Christian experiences his in the context of his Christian faith. This cannot be stressed too strongly.

A defining feature of this emotional uncertainty is that it has little to do with the content of belief and everything to do with the believer. Pascal wryly noted, 'Put the world's greatest philosopher on a plank that is wider than need be: if there is a precipice below, although his reason may convince him that he is safe, his imagination will prevail.' James Thurber made the same point: 'Every man is occasionally visited by the suspicion that the planet on which he is riding is not really going anywhere. These black doubts creep up on a man just before thunderstorms, or at six in the morning when the steam begins to knock solemnly in the pipes, or during his confused wanderings in the forest beyond Euphoria after a long night of drinking.'

The classical biblical example is the deep depression and suicidal longings of Elijah, the ninth-century BC prophet in Israel. 'He came upon a broom-bush, and sat down under it and prayed for death: "It is enough," he said; "now, Lord, take my life, for I am no better than my fathers before me."' Viewed from one angle this despairing collapse of will and indulgent self-pity seem incomprehensible. Here is Elijah at the high point of his ministry, recognized, vindicated and successful. Everything seems to be his for the taking. The crowds were behind him, the royal power was humbled, his enemies were largely wiped out, his cause was vindicated, and then suddenly at the threat from one woman – Jezebel – his courage crumples and he runs for his life. Nothing appears more unreasonable.

But looked at from another angle it becomes understandable. Under the strain of the emotional intensity, he has snapped. The gruelling demands of public confrontation have summoned up and exhausted his reserves of strength. The lonely years in the desert followed by the dramatic road-race to Jezreel must have stretched his emotions that at a simple threat he folds. It was not God who had let him down but his emotions which had overpowered his faith and reason, and plunged him into a trough of despair. Writing of a harrowing period in his ministry in the seventh century BC, the prophet Jeremiah expressed the same emotion. Physically drained and emotionally exhausted, his faith had weakened too: 'Then I cry out that my strength has gone and so has my hope in the Lord.'

However firm our understanding in faith and however strong our wills, there is no absolute guarantee against doubt making inroads into faith through our emotions. Exhaustion, loneliness, a long drawn out illness, an accident, bereavement, overwhelming tiredness or a flash of anger or jealousy or even being undernourished – any of these give the emotions opportunity to usher in doubt. Battered emotions can produce a crop of doubts just as devastating as the militant atheist's toughest questions.

Since these doubts are coloured by the imagination, what they lack in logic is more than made up for in drama. The facts of the matter are the same, but when the imagination speaks it magically creates its own reality, and a different perspective is put on everything. What was real before is only a shadow now. What was nothing before has become everything.

As Christian and Hopeful languished in the dungeons of Doubting Castle, a dark night of distress settled over Christian, and he forgot the certainties, joys and triumphs of his pilgrimage up to that point. Hopeful prods him to recall the past: 'Rememberest thou not how valiant thou has been heretofore; Apollyon could not crush thee, nor could all that thou did hear, or feel, or see in the Valley of the Shadow of Death; what hardship, terror, and amazement hast thou already gone through, and art thou now nothing but fear?'

Clearly the entry point for such a doubt need not be a lofty problem. Far more effective is some little pin-prick discomfort, an issue completely removed from God and theology, perhaps just an opinion of a fellow Christian. Granted even the strongest faith, doubt can usually be guaranteed a good run here. God's truth is as unshakeable as before, faith is as firm in its convictions, but with the sudden fleeting thought of a Christian who is even the slightest bit ridiculous, distasteful or different, the clear certainty of faith can become strangely muddied by emotions of embarrassment, hostility or superiority.

Is there anything to equal the frustration we can feel with our fellow believers? No doubt this is partly a projection of the frustration we feel with ourselves, and it probably means that others have the same problem with us. One moment the sheer diversity of Christians seems a many-splendoured thing of joy and wonder, while the next moment the same diversity is all individualism, oddness and peculiarity. It isn't our theology which has changed, only our emotions.

Pascal, musing on the weakness of reason, concluded: 'It is the same with knowledge, for illness removes it.' Later in a similar vein he spoke of how imagination can toy with reason: 'Reason may object in vain, it cannot fix the price of things.'

C. S. Lewis in *Mere Christianity* made the same point in a helpful warning for newly-converted Christians.

Supposing a man's reason once decides that the weight of evidence is for it. I can tell that man what is going to happen to him in the next few weeks. There will come a moment when there is bad news, or he is in trouble or is living among a lot of other people who do not believe it, and all at once his emotions will rise up and carry out a sort of blitz on his belief. Now faith, in the sense in which I am using the word, is the art of holding onto things your reason has once accepted, in spite of our change of moods.

Heart and mind

There are several reasons why this type of doubt is particularly dangerous today. For one thing, much contemporary Christianity puts an emphasis on emotions which is exaggerated and unbalanced by biblical standards. Often understanding is then decried, and the pride of place given to the emotions is justified by appealing to a correct-sounding division between 'head' and 'heart'.

Certa nly it is man's heart to which God constantly speaks in the Bible, but the vital question is whether the biblical understanding of *heart* and our modern understanding of *heart* are the same. The Bible's understanding is, in fact, almost the opposite of modern usage. In the Bible *heart* can be translated as emotions in only a fraction of its many hundreds of uses. In the overwhelming majority of cases it makes nonsense of the passage to translate it this way. Understood biblically, *heart* refers to the seat of man's whole personality, his true self. In most cases it refers to man's understanding and not his emotions.

Mistaken teaching like this spawns a view of faith which is not only unbiblical and weak, but completely ineffective in combating the doubts which come from an emotional source. The battle is lost before it begins. The understanding was not in control in time of faith, so it is too much to expect it to be in control in time of doubt. The emotions were everything when faith was there, and now that doubt is there they are still everything. All that is different is that they have changed sides.

If the emotions are really all that matters, then neither faith nor doubt have anything to do with truth; they are simply the names which the emotions give to their changing moods.

Strangers in a strange land

Another reason why this doubt is common today is the effect of social isolation on many Christians. This is less true of Christians in the West, although we too are in a curious situation in a society that is pluralistic and post-Christian at the same time. The pluralism in society means that all are free to believe as they like, but the fact that society is post-Christian means that some are less free than others. For in a mass society the effect of the media is to create a shared world of reference, corralling society into subtle general attitudes with the whip of the constantly repeated word and message (the power of the shared joke, the shared value-system, the shared ideology). Wider differences are encouraged but only within definite, if unmentioned, limits, and tolerance itself can be highly selective. There is no official pecking order of philosophies and beliefs, let alone a party line. Rather the latest and most novel are usually at the top of the ladder, and what is thought of as 'yesterday's way of thinking' defines the bottom rung.

Being a Christian in such a society means swimming upstream. Ignorance of Christianity, not to speak of prejudice and caricature, is as common as understanding. The courage of one's convictions must be a fact to the Christian and not a figure of speech. A certain inescapable loneliness is felt in this situation, and it tends to demoralize the emotions.

Think of a new student in a philosophy class where the case against Christianity is a continuing trial by scorn. Imagine a Christian professor of anthropology, misunderstood by his fellow believers as much as by his secular colleagues ('How could a Christian be in that field?'). Put yourself into some of the situations which believers daily face alone – the army canteen, the factory floor, the hospital ward, the office. You do not have to imagine a situation which is particularly difficult, hostile or 'pagan'. That might almost be easier. What is hard for a believer among no fellow-believers is the constant burden of being different, of being the 'odd man out' or of living in two worlds at once. The pressure of such loneliness can lead to doubt.

A close friend wrote to us recently from Eastern Europe. Living under a Marxist state in a country where the vast majority of people are of a different religious faith, he finds that the Christian groups he comes from are retreating from today's world, rigid in their ways of thinking. They are groups, as he puts it, 'with whom I will never have a common language. So I am pretty alone with the religious struggling that still goes on in me, and I very much feel like giving up.'

His loneliness is made more painful by the fact that he is a sensitive Christian thinker, and I would venture to say that the agonized doubts he went on to raise were inspired by isolation as much as by purely intellectual dilemmas. In replying I could have entered into long philosophical and theological discussions, but I sensed that what was wanted to silence those doubts was not laboriously written solutions to laboriously written dilemmas but expressions of love and human friendship – as in times when the mind runs deep, on an autumn walk, in a conversation over a glass of wine, during a time of prayer, those times in fact which he was most missing.

Whenever anyone becomes a Christian he may face something of this in his family or among his friends if only in a small way. His 'new belief' separates him from his friends with their 'old beliefs', and it is dangerously easy to relate as a new believer to unbelievers and not as a person to people. Urged to witness at all costs, young Christians do so, but sometimes their motivation is tinged with insecurity as much as it is fired by enthusiasm. As a result they unwittingly tend to focus on the differences between believer and unbeliever rather than on the difference that belief makes. The new faith is therefore seen as a threat, and a family or a group of friends reacts by closing its ranks in a protective wall of scorn or indifference. 'Silence is the worst form of persecution,' wrote Pascal.

This leaves the young Christian dejected, with a heavy sense of failure and rejection, of having 'blown it', and this may be the occasion of his first doubts. In reality it is not his faith he is doubting, it is himself. Still, if he has to face much more of this, he may blame it on his faith. What is really to blame is a style of witnessing, high in emotional pressure, and sometimes low in content and sensitivity, which urged him to say too much too soon and in quite the wrong manner.

All of us have our 'moments', those times when our emotions are likely to run away with our trust in God – a student under the pressure of exams, a father hearing that he is redundant, a business executive in a lonely hotel room, a mother worried about breast cancer, an author with his rejection slips, a minister struggling with jealousy over a neighbour's success, a teenager with few friends.

Seek to know yourself well enough to recognize those special times and the pressures they bring. The important thing to see in each case that it will not be Christian truth which is under fire but your faith. When faith is in danger of being cut off by an insurgent army of emotions, it panics and loses effective contact with the faithfulness of God. This loss of contact leads to doubt.

Down to earth spirituality

What is the remedy for this variety of doubt? As with some of the other doubts it is twofold. The immediate and short-term remedy, once the particular root of the doubt has been diagnosed, is to give the appropriate practical solution. Beware of being side-tracked at this point. This type of doubt is not important for what it says theologically (however wrong that may be) but for what it shows emotionally. Since the doubt is not a statement so much as a symptom, it is no use correcting what the emotions are saying. What needs to be changed is what the emotions are showing, the practical root of the problem of which both the emotions and the doubt are only a result.

Interestingly, the remedy which God prescribed for Elijah's depression was not a refresher course in theology but simply food and sleep. 'An angel touched him and said, "Rise and eat." He looked, and there at his head was a cake baked on hot stones, and a pitcher of water. He ate and drank and lay down again.' Before God spoke to him at all, Elijah was fed twice and given a good chance to sleep. Only then, and very gently, did God confront him with his error.

This is always God's way. Having made us as human beings, he respects our humanness and treats us with integrity. That is, he treats us true to the truth of who we are. It is man and not God who has made spirituality impractical. God, the Father of Jesus Christ, numbers the hairs on our heads. Our driving concern for food in our stomachs, for a roof over our heads, and for love and friendship are cares to which he is no stranger. Jesus meets us and teaches us to pray: 'Give us today our daily bread.' And he fleshes out his own words. He feeds the crowds which others would dismiss, and after bringing Jairus's daughter back from the dead, he first reminds her parents 'to give her something to eat'.

It is man who has made spirituality impractical. The Fall has appeared to drive a wedge between the human and the spiritual. When we say something is 'all too human', we are usually referring to the weaker, darker side of man, to that which is anything but spiritual. By contrast the spiritual has been made to be an escape from the real. Thus man who is bound to the earth struggles to escape the animal and aspires to become the angel, but ends by being either practical at the expense of being spiritual or spritual at the expense of being practical. Paradoxically, it is God who becomes the most down-to-earth (in the incarnation), it is the divine who is most truly human (in Jesus), and it is the one most truly spiritual who is most practical.

The temptation is to keep spirituality and practicality in conflict – or to make them mutually exclusive. Christians have demonstrated both extremes. Some have been too 'worldly' and others too 'other worldly'. But the lesson of both is the same. The person who is spiritual without being practical ends in being unspiritual, and the person who is practical without being spiritual ends in being impractical. It is certainly so today. A grave weakness of current super-spirituality is its inability to be practical. In this area, for example, doubts with practical roots are often given other explanations which are sometimes simply rationalizations to cover failure to get to the practical root of the matter.

If someone is doubting because he is tired, the best remedy is not for him to pray but to sleep. If a person is plagued with doubt because he is exhausted from overwork, what he might need is not spiritual heart-searching but a day off in the country or three weeks in the sun. If someone is feeling 'down', maybe what he most needs is some stiff exercise or a better diet or an evening with some friends at a hilariously funny film.

Some people are affected by weather or by a seasonal change, others by the emotional associations of a certain memory or a certain date. If there is a month in the year in which I am more 'down', it is June, but this has nothing to do with horoscopes; it is simply because it is my month for hay fever. In each case our emotions are affected by a very practical cause which needs an appropriately practical solution.

Of course, we cannot always remove the root of the problem. The anniversary date with its memories still comes round, the pollen still blows, a particular task is still daunting, but we can defuse the potential blast against faith. Obviously the discouraged Christian who is the only believer in his office cannot wave a wand and see all his colleagues converted. Nor is it usually the best answer simply to quit. But what a person can do is to recognize the emotional pressures that create the loneliness and doubt, and counterbalance this by deliberately seeking encouragement and fellowship outside work situations.

In the long run the most practical remedy is also the most spiritual. Whatever deals with doubt is the most helpful contribution to faith. But a solution must be appropriate as well as practical. If two people are depressed and full of doubts, perhaps only for one is the best solution a little more sleep; for the other the solution might be a little less sleep and a little more discipline in tackling the pile of letters on his desk.

In other cases still the doubt may be compound. If so, no exclusively spiritual or practical remedy will do. Both roots must be dealt with at once. Nehemiah's reaction, facing the twin threat of an enemy attack and discouragement on his own side, illustrates this. 'So we prayed to our God, and posted a guard.' It is not that prayer is spiritual and posting a guard is practical (though this is how we tend to talk about it), but that each is thoroughly practical and appropriate, and neither of them is sufficient without the other.

A good talking to

The second part of the remedy lies in the long-term discipline of training faith so that it is not overwhelmed by moods and emotions. If we ignore this second part of the remedy and concentrate only on meeting the immediate practical need, it is easy to give the impression of pandering to indulgence. Are we to expect a day-off every time we doubt?

But the long-term remedy balances this and makes us less vulnerable at the short-term level by building up our faith where it was too weak in the first place. This is the real problem. It may be comforting to think of doubt being resolved by a few nights of sleep, but it is challenging to think of faith being so weak that it could be dissolved by lack of sleep. Our faith should dictate to our emotions, not the other way around.

Martyn Lloyd-Jones raises a key question: 'Have you realized that most of your unhappiness in life is due to the fact that you are listening to yourself instead of talking to yourself? We must talk to ourselves instead of allowing "ourselves" to talk to us!' In listening to our emotions rather than talking to them, we fall prey to the same temptation which caught Adam and Eve off guard. The order of creation is stood on its head when man is dictated to by the animal world (in the form of a serpent). The same thing happens when the emotions dictate to faith. The control each of us is called to exercise over nature is the same control we are to exercise over our own nature. Such control comes only from a disciplined faith. Pascal suggests, 'We must resort to habit once the mind has seen where the truth lies. In order to steep and stain ourselves in that belief which constantly eludes us.'

Habits are much maligned in a spontaneity-loving age like our own; but a habit need not be a rut. Habit is built-in second nature, and what is built in, whether it is a good habit or a bad habit, a dull rut or a positive strength of character, depends entirely on what we choose. Repeat an active habit and you grow strong; repeat a passive habit and you grow weak. In this case the habit we are building is the practice of trusting God so that in every situation it becomes 'second nature' to us. Faith will then be the controlling principle of our lives and not the victim of our fluctuating emotions.

The quality of our emotions depends upon the quality of our faith, just as the quality of our faith depends on the quality of our understanding. 'Feeling must follow; but faith, apart from all feeling, must be there first.' This is Martin Luther's understanding of the relationship of faith and emotions, but he also makes clear that this is not our first nature, and it will be our second only if we carefully and patiently learn it. 'The lesson of faith is a lesson that must constantly be practised and rehearsed.'

Lloyd-Jones expresses this even more strongly in his book *Spiritual Depression*:

> The main art in the matter of spiritual living is to know how to handle yourself. You have to take yourself in hand. You have to address yourself, preach to yourself, question yourself. The essence of this matter is to understand that this self of ours, this other man within us, has got to be handled. Do not listen to him; turn on him; speak to him; condemn him; upbraid him; exhort him; encourage him; remind him of what you know instead of placidly listening to him and allowing him to drag you down and depress you.

Mastering our emotions has nothing to do with asceticism, or repression, for the purpose is not to break the emotions or deny them but to 'break in' the emotions, making them teachable because they are tamed.

The apostle Paul's example underlines again how insipid our understanding of the obedience of faith often is. Speaking of himself he writes to the Corinthians, 'For my part, I run with a clear goal before me; I am like a boxer who does not beat the air; I bruise my own body and make it know its master.' And in case someone excuses himself from submitting to Paul's rigorous standards, he adds in a letter to Thessalonica, 'Each one of you must learn to gain mastery over his body.'

Unless we do this our emotions will lead us around by the nose, and we will be captives to every passing impulse or reaction. But once faith is trained to control the emotions and knows how to lean resolutely against weaknesses of character, another gateway of doubt is blocked and sealed shut for ever.

Chapter Eleven

Scars from an Old Wound

Doubt from fearing to believe

Have you ever seen a small boy woefully anticipating a visit to the dentist? Or a student entering an examination insisting to everyone that he has no chance whatever of passing? Neither is being hopelessly pessimistic, the psychological ploy they are using is much more subtle. They are trying to cushion themselves against the worst that could possibly come so that however bad it turns out to be, it will always be better than they feared.

The next variety of doubt is like this in having purely psychological origins. This type of doubt is so closely related to the previous one that some would make no distinction between them. But a separate look is worthwhile, for it operates at a far deeper level than emotional doubt and is inevitably more painful. Moreover, there are marked differences in the manner in which it works.

Every generation has the tendency to major in its own special insight, its own favourite discipline, its own chosen frame of reference, and to reinterpret all previous thinking in the light of this framework. For our own generation the discipline of psychology is the leading contender for this dubious honour, and its predominance creates a situation with two equal, though opposite, dangers. Either everything is interpreted in terms of the psychological or no interpretation in terms of the psychological is admitted. Some people, for example, see doubt only as a psychological reality. They deny that faith has any objective basis and locate doubt in a believer's subjective ability or inability to believe. Thus they make doubt as well as belief purely a matter of psychology. But others emphasize the element of sin, choice and responsibility so strongly that any suggestion that psychological factors are also involved is swiftly brushed aside as an attempt to evade responsibility. The former is the psychologizing tendency and the latter the spiritualizing tendency.

A balanced understanding is both more accurate and more helpful. It is as mistaken to account for objective causes of doubt by subjective explanations as to account for subjective causes by objective explanations. The doubt we are dealing with in this chapter is indeed primarily psychological, and it cannot be explained without understanding the subjective makeup of the person who is doubting.

They 'disbelieved for joy'

Healthy faith can be pictured as the firm, solid grip of a person who is able to reach out and grasp whatever he wants to hold. Imagine what it would be like, though, to grasp something firmly if you had a bad wound in the palm of your hand. The object you want to hold is still available, your muscular strength is as powerful as ever, but the pain resulting from pressure on the wound would mean that you could not comfortably exert the same strength. This is what happens in a case of this seventh type of doubt. The person knows he needs the truth in question, he can see the difference it would make, he can even see that it is true, and he is quite able to believe it. The problem is that the very process of believing puts painful pressure on an old psychological wound that is still too sensitive to bear it or that he thinks is too sensitive to test. When this happens, doubt is the process and the excuse for drawing back from such a risk.

A vivid example is found in Luke's description of the evening of the Sunday of the resurrection. Without warning Jesus suddenly entered the room where his disciples were assembled and confronted them with the living reality of his risen presence. Momentarily they were taken aback, caught in two minds over whether to believe, and Luke captures the curious suspension of that moment: 'And while they still disbelieved for joy...'

What a distinctive and intriguing variety of doubt this is! The average doubt is more like those mentioned earlier in the story where the disciples refused to believe that Jesus had risen when they heard the first accounts that the tomb was empty. They had no first-hand evidence, so they dismissed the initial report as an idle tale. But in doubt or not, at least they hurried to find out the truth for themselves. It was not that they believed and then doubted, but that they refused to believe without sufficient evidence. They wanted to make sure for themselves.

This later doubt, however, is quite different, and there was not the same excuse. More than half a day had gone by, and the evidence to confirm the first accounts had been flowing in from all sides. They heard it from the women, from the two disciples on the road to Emmaus and from Simon Peter. Before Jesus appeared, they had already come to a conclusion: 'It is true: the Lord has risen.' But suddenly, now that Jesus was actually right in front of them and their faith was not just a tacit agreement but a demanding reality, they disbelieved for joy. That is the uniqueness of this doubt: they disbelieved *for joy*. What they were seeing was the one thing in the world they wanted most. That was precisely the trouble. They wanted it so much that to believe it and then discover it was false would have been profoundly disillusioning. So, instead, they preferred the safety of doubt to the risk of disappointment.

Can you explain this 'disbelieving for joy' any other way? There was no denying that Jesus was alive. He was there as large as life, and it was quite impossible to pass it off any longer as an idle tale or an early morning fantasy. It is not as if these men were deep-dyed sceptics or modern philosophers trained in the rigorous procedures of critical doubt. They were down-to-earth men accustomed to dealing in the hard currency of 'the facts of life', men who lived naturally in a world where 'seeing is believing'. Yet for some reason they rejected the evidence of their own eyes and ears, and insisted on disbelieving. By doubting they were taking out an insurance policy to cover the possible pain of any eventual disappointment.

They were grown men whose lives had been far from sheltered and reserved, yet the experience of the crucifixion had been more harrowing than any of them cared to face again. Any hopes they might have tried to salvage from the wreckage of those fateful days must have looked forlorn. All around them lay the debris of shattered dreams. Hour after hour, over and over again, they must have rerun the events in their minds. But at the end of every possible train of thought was the stark finality of a bloody cross. And then, at last, the gaping wound which was their memory must have slowly begun to heal; their thoughts must have started to turn naturally towards resuming their lives.

It was then that Jesus appeared, and he caught them on the raw before the sedative of passing time had dulled the pain. He stood before them, the sum of all they wanted, but for the sheer joy of what it would mean if true, they refused to believe in case it might not be. What they were saying in their doubt is that it was too good to be true, and this way they adroitly protected the wound and refused to risk reopening it. The one fact that they wanted became the one fact too much, so they disbelieved for joy.

This doubt comes from the fear of being hurt where we have the scars from an old psychological wound. It is one to which many of us are prone. Are not most of us wounded at some point? It is not necessarily that we have scars which stand out publicly – livid and unhealed – but that even if our wounds are not visible, we know they are there and we know the pain and discomfort which pressure on them brings.

Sometimes even the memory of previous pain at a particular point is enough to summon up the pain again. This means that though we have come to believe in Christ and have grown into a deep conviction of faith, there is still one place sealed off, one place where healing is not allowed, one place where we shy away from complete openness. So if to trust involves opening up, if to believe means laying ourselves open, if to love is to make ourselves vulnerable, then rather than taking the risk of faith, we choose to doubt.

Polite but self-defeating

There are two interesting features of this type of doubt. The first is its style of argument and tone of voice. Here, there is no discontented grumbling or sharp intellectual criticism, such as is common in the other doubts that also are rationalizations. Initially in fact this doubt can look so appealing and sound so polite that it is hardly recognizable as doubt. The heart of its case is the claim that God's word is too good to be true. Indeed the New English Bible translates Luke 24:41 as, 'They were still unconvinced, still wondering, for it seemed too good to be true.' But this is put forward with such unassuming deference that it sounds more like a compliment, and it seems churlish to consider it even a veiled criticism.

The suggestion of doubt can be expressed in a gloomy, unbudging melancholy or in an excited, trembling joy, as if the person was longing to reach out his hand and take for himself but does not yet dare to do so. But the effect is the same. While the doubter rarely hesitates to see that someone else might benefit, he says in effect, 'It is too good to be true *for me*.' The doubter sounds humble when he suggests he is unworthy of such a wonderful truth, but this humility is only a smokescreen to conceal the deeper problem: He is not so much unworthy as unwilling.

In almost every instance of this doubt a person is challenged to believe at the very point where he most needs and most wants to believe. This is not a coincidence. The psychological hurt of the doubt comes from the clash between the desire to believe and the fear to believe as they meet head-on right over the old wound. The doubter claims that the trouble with God's truth is that it is more desirable than credible. But neither the desirability nor the credibility of the matter are the cause of the issue. All that really matters to the doubter is that the wound remains covered and protected. So what would otherwise be eminently desirable and entirely credible must be dismissed. It is done with a show of reluctance, but the dismissal is no less decisive.

A second feature of this doubt is that it is self-defeating. Here lies its special sadness; no one is hurt more than the doubter. Afraid to believe what he wants to believe, he fails to believe what he needs to believe, and he alone is the loser. With some doubts the issue rises at points which are not central to faith. They are taken seriously at once only because it is the style and integrity of faith-with-understanding to do so. But this doubt is different. The issue raised does not lie on the circumference of life but at its very centre. Whether it is solved is not a matter of indifference to faith but a matter of life and death.

Most other rationalizing doubts are self-serving. The issues they raise are viewed as welcome excuses. If doubt is pressed, faith can be thrown over for what looks like freedom. But if this type of doubt is a rationalization, it is not a glib one, and its outcome is not more freedom but more frustration. The doubter is doubtful where he would most like to be certain. He hangs back at the one moment he would most like to step forward. He shrugs his shoulders when he longs to embrace. He rejects what he is dying to accept.

What has happened to create this doubt is that a problem (such as a particular weakness of character or a bad experience) has been allowed to usurp God's place and become the controlling principle of life. Instead of viewing the problem from the vantage-point of faith, the doubter views faith from the vantage point of the problem. Instead of faith 'sizing up' the problem, the situation ends with the problem 'scaling down' faith. The world of faith is upside down, and in the topsy-turvy reality of doubt a problem has 'become god' and God has 'become a problem'.

This is exactly why the doubt is self-defeating, for whatever takes God's place must be taken with ultimate seriousness. And if we think about it, we can see that the only problem which can be taken with ultimate seriousness is an 'unanswerable problem', an enduring problem to which no answer can ever, or perhaps must ever, be found. Only the unanswerable problem is big enough to 'play god' for us psychologically. As soon as a problem is answered, it is reduced to size and can no longer be taken with ultimate seriousness.

This is why people who are apt to define themselves in terms of their problems will do so only in terms of large problems (or small problems which have assumed large proportions). If a problem is small, then psychologically speaking I can say, 'I have a problem.' But the greater the problem becomes, the more it is likely to reach the point where psychologically speaking I should say, 'The problem has me.'

'I am the Lord your God ... You shall have no other gods to set against me' is not only a principle of correct theology but of sound psychology. Whatever assumes in our lives a practical importance that is greater than God will 'become god' to us. And since we become like what we worship, to let an unanswerable problem 'become god' to us is the surest way to guarantee that life will be characterized at its heart by defeat. When we listen to this doubt we are wheeling a Trojan horse into our camp. Doubt claims to offer the best protection against pain, but in fact it becomes the sole barrier to healing. It introduces itself as the best insurance agent to cover the risk of faith, but it protects faith at the cost of smothering it. As Shakespeare put it in *Measure for Measure*:

> Our doubts are traitors
> And make us lose the good we oft might win
> By fearing to attempt.

At worst such doubts do more. Not only is it in their power to fear, but in their insistence on their supremacy they create the facts they fear.

This particular doubt works out this way because experience has been made into an absolute, and bad experience at that. So the working absolute for life is not God but a bad experience which colours the rest of life. 'It is often the case,' writes Augustine, 'that a man who has had experience of a bad doctor is afraid to trust himself even to a good one.' After an experience with a bad doctor, it would be reasonable to check the credentials of every subsequent doctor but ridiculous to reject all doctors completely. Cheated once with a counterfeit bank note, it is only sensible to keep an eye open for future fraud, but to refuse to use any money at all would be plain silly. Yet this, in effect, is the self-defeating logic of this doubt.

Puddleglum and his kin

With some people such doubt is almost a matter of temperament – whether this is a result of heredity or environment or the outcome of their own brooding reflections. With others it is a characteristic which appears from time to time. Like A. A. Milne's 'Eeyore' or C. S. Lewis's incomparably gloomy but loyal 'Puddleglum', they can always be relied on to see the dark side of everything. After a week with six days of sunshine, they will remember the one day of rain. Life has its pleasures, its joys and its success, but somehow they seem to happen to everyone but them.

It is not that they are killjoys, unhappy because others are happy, for they are genuinely happy for others. But sometimes they seem to be happy for others mainly because it proves that things like that don't happen to them. The happiness of their unhappiness is its reliability. The unhappiness of happiness is its risk. If they are ever offered what they want, the strength of their desire can be gauged by the speed with which they spot the snag. If this person says that something is too good to be true, you can take it that they see it as both good and true but, for some hidden reason, not allowed to be so for them.

What would you think of a man who won the football pools after a lifetime of trying but who took the letter to his next door neighbour saying he is sure it must have been sent to the wrong address? It is exactly what he wants. After all, he has been attempting to win the pools for forty odd years, but when it finally happens it's too good to be true. 'Better not get too excited. Better not dwell on it. There's always the pleasure of trying again.' Finally he settles for the fun of hoping to win rather than the fun of winning. We would shake our heads in amazement if we knew someone who acted like this. But the logic of the doubt we are discussing is no less silly, though far more understandable.

With other people this doubt is not a question of temperament but the result of a particular experience in their lives. Ours is a violent generation – wounded and wounding – and there are few people whom life has given no injury capable of producing such a doubt. I know a man whose whole life cries out for God's love as father but whose desire for God's love as father is checkmated by an overriding fear of God's love. And the root of this lies not only in his experience of the cruelly twisted relationship which was his father's 'love' but also in his adamant refusal to consider forgiving his father. So God's love continues to be 'too good to be true' for him, and what was once a winsome, entirely understandable doubt has degenerated into a self-pitying rationalization, a poorly-constructed façade to cover a festering wound. The trouble is not that God's trustworthiness is the least bit undesirable or incredible but that to trust God is to risk an openness that would prise loose his right to his grievance and so remove his right to self-pity.

Such doubt is even more common at less serious levels. Many examples spring to mind. A philosophically minded person trembles on the verge of faith, keenly desiring to believe God's truth, which is the goal of his life's search, but considers it too good to be true. It is not because it is any less good or true than he might wish but because his experience of Christians to this point has shown a 'leap of faith' so suicidal to his mind that his integrity shudders at the thought. There is no doubt which of the two he wants, and the point is not really which of the two is true. He disbelieves for joy because he is afraid to run the risk.

Most of us know something of this in ourselves. With one person the wound is a childhood experience. With another the memory of a previous marriage. With yet another the result of an experience of particular shame or fear or hurt. All of us have our painful memories, and it is when the call to faith puts pressure on an unhealed memory that we balk, preferring the comfort of doubt to the risky business of trusting.

Don't imagine that people like this are particularly gloomy, as if the whole of their lives were overcast like a leaden sky. Far from it. Quite often they are not the slightest bit gloomy or hesitant about anything – except at the particular point where the old wound still festers or the scar is still tender. In all other points they are only too glad to respond readily in faith to any challenge or promise which God gives.

This is perhaps why stumbling on 'the one point' is often such a surprise. It is so different from what one might imagine, so totally against the grain of what one was led to expect. Why is it that an apparently placid searcher can pass through violent cynicism and rejection just before he believes? Why is it that a girl who obviously wants to get married can become most negative just after a proposal? The reason is that each is struggling intensely as the desire to believe and the fear to believe clash like a psychological implosion right over the old wound. What each is doing in that vivid moment of internal violence is 'disbelieving for joy'.

Healing

Is there a remedy for this subtle form of doubt? At first we might wonder, for any obvious solution might be as circular and therefore as self-defeating as the doubt itself. To be told to 'believe' when we doubt is as unhelpful as being told to 'cheer up' when we are depressed, or to 'join in' when we are feeling alienated from everyone around us. The doubt may look ridiculous to faith, since from faith's point of view doubt is refusing what faith most wants to believe. But the solution looks equally ridiculous to doubt, for from doubt's point of view it is having to believe what it least wants to believe. So another way must be found, a way that by-passes altogether the essential circularity of this type of doubt.

This doubt, like others, must be solved on its own terms. If someone is doubting because he is no longer thankful to God and has quite ignored the 'once and might have been' (as we saw in chapter five), then no amount of intellectual discussion will touch his problem. Equally, if someone is doubting because he has no basis for faith, then no amount of stirring reminders or encouragements will be a substitute for the necessary intellectual understanding. Basically, though, psychologically-rooted doubts can be understood in a similar way to the emotionally-rooted doubts, for their cause too is subjective. The initial wound was objective and real, of course, yet the doubt is caused, not by the wound itself but by the way it was regarded and the place it was given. These are a matter of subjective choice, so the remedy must be directed accordingly. Moreover, both types of doubt can be best helped with long-term and short-term remedies.

The long-term problem is unhealed wounds, and these wounds need healing so that faith is able to come into its own. It is not a sign of weakness to have wounds; but to keep wounds from being healed is sheer stupidity.

The best long-term remedy lies in remembering that God is light and that we are called to 'walk in the light as if he himself is in the light'. We should practice a style of openness in our relationships that will mean constant forgiveness for our sins, healing for our wounds, comfort in our sorrow. If this is our practice, if we make this the disciplined set of our mind, then we will be letting God be God over our sins, over our wounds and over our sorrows – in short, over all our problems.

A problem is no less a problem for having been brought before God – at least, not *before* he solves it. But to have a problem solved is not the only point of bringing it to God, or God would not be fully God but merely a divine panacea and problem-solver. The point is not that a problem is less a problem when brought to God (though eventually it is) but that a problem brought before God never becomes *more* than a problem. It is kept under his Lordship.

A problem we will not bring to God is a problem that we

are saying is too big for God. Such a problem may grow to mean almost everything to us so that eventually it will 'become god' to us and, in turn, God will be made into 'a problem'. So the best long-term remedy for this doubt lies in practising the profound truths of the cross – the Christian principles of forgiveness, reconciliation and healing working out deeply in every area of life where problems confront us.

What is promised in the cross is not some 'cheap miracle' or 'instant cure'. To speak of healing is to speak of a deep and radical surgery in the human heart. With some people the healing is almost complete; with others the improvement is substantial. But whatever the case the essential point is satisfied. What leads to doubt is not so much the pain of a wound in itself as the memory of a wound that is clung to. It is not the unhealed wound but the wound that is never allowed to heal. The wound that is completely healed no longer provides a potential opening for doubt, and the wound that is substantially healed need not – if the strength gained from healing is coupled with a realistic understanding of how, when and where the doubt may strike again.

There is no easy short-term solution, but two things are useful to remember when helping anyone who is experiencing this doubt. The first, as always, is the importance of identifying the doubt. It is the nameless doubt that is most damaging to the mind. Unidentified, perhaps unidentifiable, it lurks below the conscious mind like a waiting shark and there is no limit to its shadowy potential for destruction. As the Chinese proverb runs, 'The doubting mind sees many ghosts.' So be sure to identify the doubt, name it, bring it sharply into focus and exorcize its ghosts. Be specific about what it is and about what it isn't. This in itself does not deal with the doubt, but it helps the doubter to see it for what it is and prevents it from being more damaging than it need be.

This is especially important for, since this particular type of doubt has no objective cause or root, it poses no final objection to faith, only an immediate objection to believing. Once this is understood the whole complexion of the problem is altered for the doubter. The problem lies not in what a person believes, nor even in how he believes, but in who he is as a believer. It is one thing for a man to see that a problem is 'entirely his own', for a man could well see this, shrug his shoulders and walk away from it. But it is quite another to realize that it is in his own highest interests to solve it as quickly as possible. The danger is not that the person should doubt that there is any truth, but that he should persuade himself that he doesn't need it. To identify this doubt, therefore, puts the onus squarely on the doubter.

Second, it is helpful to remember that the circularity of the doubt is best met by short-circuiting it. The doubt is entirely logical but the circle of its logic rests on premises which are too restricted. Since a wound and not words are at the heart of the problem, what is needed is not fresh arguments so much as fresh air. The doubter's facts are not complete, and he has not examined them for a long time. What he needs is a fresh context which makes all believing entirely natural, sheds light on the wider situation and throws the known facts into a different perspective.

The answer to bad humour is not to say 'cheer up' but to tell a good joke. We can be so depressed that the set of our minds and hearts is against laughing and false humour only entices a grimace. But given the right joke, the creative power of humour is such that the lightning speed of involuntary laughter will escape the most determined heart and mind, and people will laugh before they think of it. It is the same with this doubt. The answer it needs is to be shown something which it is utterly natural to believe.

Jesus did this with the disciples. They refused to believe the evidence of their own eyes, but he didn't rebuke them or dazzle them with supernatural signs. He simply took some fish and ate it in front of them. They were surprised into belief, coaxed back gently, rebuked by the utterly natural and simple. After all, this was what they had seen him do a thousand times. 'Ghosts don't eat breakfast!' was what convinced them Jesus was alive.

Meet doubt head-on with a solution in the order of 'Believe, don't doubt' and all you do is face one simplistic, shortsighted argument with another, and one that is cold and comfortless at that. Instead, point out gently what the doubter is doing when he doubts and introduce him to the infinite sufficiency of God who is himself the answer. Put your answer in words and 'give it flesh' in terms of compassion and patience. Then you will find that the understanding of God's truth will bring its own creative self-realization, a flooding awareness which releases repentance and faith and short-circuits the small-mindedness of doubt.

Like a theatre audience suddenly aware that it is being watched by another audience, everything suddenly changes for the person who doubts. Moments earlier he was king of the tiny realm of his problem, asking only whether he could believe in God. Suddenly the question is wider and he finds himself on his knees being asked whether God can believe in him. As God is seen for who he is, the terms of the problem change the sources of the problem dissolve. The mysterious change of heart and mind is the Holy Spirit's gift of repentance and faith.

Only one thing more needs to be added. When this doubt goes and faith comes into its own, the wonder that faith knows is in direct proportion to the absurdity of the doubt beforehand. Far from being too good to be true, there is nothing so good and nothing else so true. God proves not only better to us than our worst fears but better to us than our wildest dreams. 'Disbelieving for joy' is quickly followed by being 'surprised by joy'.

Part Three

Resolving Doubt

Chapter Twelve

A Time to Listen

Understanding doubt is like understanding the flu. It's all very fine as a study but it leads nowhere if it isn't used to prevent people catching it or to help those who have caught it. Up to this point our major concern has been to understand doubt, so the question of remedy has received only brief mention at the end of each chapter. But once we have come to grips with the nature of doubt we must put this to use. It is all-important that doubt should be resolved, for it leaves only two alternatives: if faith does not resolve doubt, doubt will dissolve faith. So it is in the highest interests of faith not only to understand but to remedy doubt. Yet the last person to be able to resolve doubt is the doubter himself. When we are in doubt we need above all to be able to share the problem, to talk it over with a fellow Christian who is able to see the thing whole and stand back to give wise and helpful advice. The chapters that follow deal principally with times when we seek to help others in doubt. But we are all in this together. Today we may be helping someone else; tomorrow we may need help ourselves.

Methods and method

As we look at the question of remedy my concern is to discuss principles which will be true for resolving all categories of doubt. This, I think, is more helpful than examining specific detailed instances, and avoids the mistake of textbook-style answers.

As soon as we say this, we are plunged into a heated discussion, not so much about methods of remedying doubt but about method itself. Today method is everything, and in the popular form of this mentality the long arm of modern philosophy is reaching over into the church and is busily reducing Christian truth to a series of techniques, 'how-to' manuals and training courses.

My quarrel with the mentality behind this approach is not that 'it isn't our style' or that it is 'crass' or 'popular', for these are only judgements of taste. Nor am I reacting to method itself and suggesting the extreme of rejecting it altogether. That would be impossible. Do anything at all (such as blowing your nose, cooking an omelette or riding a bicycle) and as soon as you think back over the way you have done it you realize you have a method. Whether it is a good method or a bad method is beside the point. Method is simply the way we do a thing.

That does not mean, of course, that all methods are acceptable. There are two basic questions we could ask of any method we use: Is it right? Does it come naturally? We will pick up the significance of the second question in chapter fourteen in dealing with another mistaken approach to remedying doubt. But our concern here is with the first question. Any method of dealing with doubt must have integrity and be in line not only with the nature of the problem *but also with the nature of the answer*. Otherwise the remedy will be inappropriate and wrong.

Where is the danger in the modern stress on method? Simply that it gains its inspiration from a deeply entrenched rationalism which suggests that all knowledge can be specified. If this were so, then it would be possible to take a truth and spell out all that it means so that it can be written down, reproduced and taught in 'how-to' techniques. This reductionism is the heart of the problem. And although it is well camouflaged in certain methods, it must be uncovered and rooted out.

Large areas of human knowledge can be dealt with usefully in this way, but since there is more to knowing than human knowing will ever know, part of personal knowledge will always be irreducible, unspecifiable, defying description in terms of methods and techniques. A style of instruction which may be excellent for teaching someone to operate a washing machine is next to useless in teaching someone to dance. Ballet is learned better from a ballet master than from a handbook.

Equally, what is appropriate in training someone to repair a car is quite inappropriate in training someone to 'repair faith'. In the deep areas of life, as one human being helps and comforts another, there is much that will never be specifiable in words, much less reduced to simple formulas and easily learned, universally applied techniques .

Yet there seems to be no end to such training today, and it is almost always hailed enthusiastically ('It changed my whole life' ... 'I grew as a person'). But the actual long-term results are often disappointing and appear to leave the church little changed. To say this is not to minimize the value of training but to warn of the damage done by the wrong sort. Nor is it that the techniques are intentionally only cosmetic solutions. They rarely rise above the superficial because they ignore the profound biblical view of the nature of knowledge.

No attempt to deal with the spiritual, the moral or the psychological must ever be outside the context of genuine discipleship. Christians seeking to help others need to remember that in certain areas only the Holy Spirit can specify the problem. Discernment comes as much through the fear of God and the wisdom of experience as from the best methods of training. Theoretical knowledge in these areas is moonshine if it is divorced from obedience of faith and conscious dependence on the Holy Spirit.

The quickest way to fall into this trap is to speak as if finding the remedy for doubt is a matter of giving textbook answers to textbook doubts. One way we do this is to talk of a doubt in impersonal clinical terms. We think exclusively in medical models of diagnosis and cure, and become detached and 'professional' about the whole thing.

Another way we can do it, though unintentionally, is to talk as if every doubt had only one logically necessary and complete answer. Riddles may have only one answer, and the sort of problems posed in crossword puzzles, detective stories and true or false examinations certainly do. For this sort of problem there is always a 'correct answer' and somebody who knows it. But human problems are rarely like that and the only way to make them so is to lop off from the terms of the problem anything that the ready-made solution is unable to handle. But this is the same reductionist fallacy in a different guise. It is both dehumanizing in practice and mistaken in theory.

In contrast to the detailed answers of a textbook approach I have outlined four major aspects of resolving doubt and some related pitfalls into which we can stumble. But again we should be careful not to understand or apply these mechanically, for they will be completely barren unless they are rooted in the life-context of a growing relationship with God and a deeply caring relationship with the person in doubt.

A lost art

The first part of helping someone in doubt is to listen. Nothing sounds simpler but nothing is harder, for the art of listening is largely lost today. One reason for this lies in the nature of modern life. We are too busy to take time to listen, and our society is too noisy to make listening generally worthwhile. With incessant noise all around we are compelled to hear too much, so we choose to listen too little. In a noisy world, speaking is much easier than listening. If we raise our voices, the noise is drowned; if we open our ears, everything else is.

A second reason lies in ourselves. We talk loudly of freedom of speech but little of the responsibility of listening. Yet the former without the latter leads to the farmyard, not to democracy. In the self-importance of our individualism we treat the world as an audience, there to listen and there to applaud. While in the lostness of our individualism we refuse to listen to others because they are not listening to us. We talk, not to say something, but because we need to be listened to.

It is always easier to observe than to obey. I recognize myself in saying this – too much in fact. I have to confess that many of these recommendations about listening are the reversal of what I have done wrong rather than a review of what I have done right.

Much is made of the 'problem of communication' today. A great mystique surrounds it, but I suspect that a large part of the problem would be slashed through in one stroke if each of us were to listen more carefully to what is being said to us. Take people seriously and take truth seriously, and we cannot avoid the question of taking listening seriously.

Listening is loving

A recovery of the skill of listening will bring rich rewards in many areas, but there are three particular benefits which listening contributes to the remedy of doubt. First, it is an expression of love in a form which is uniquely appropriate to the doubter. Doubt is devastating because it questions a believer's faith and threatens to pull out the foundations from under his whole life. Even his perception of himself may be affected, and in the pain and isolation of doubt it may be hard not to conclude that 'no one understands'.

Nothing 'speaks louder' to a hungry man than a meal, and nothing speaks more clearly to a doubter than the not-speaking of genuine listening. To listen conveys more than any words. It says to the person in doubt: 'I am taking you seriously as a person. It matters to me that you are hurting. I am giving you myself if I can be any help.'

God's care for the individual lies at the heart of Christianity. Basic to the incarnation is the fact that in Jesus, God is listening to man. He is putting his ear close to the ground of human life. He speaks to crowds, but his solutions are never mass solutions; each person is spoken to as an individual. His best-loved parables all concern individuals – the owner who delighted in finding her lost coin, the shepherd who went after the lost sheep, the waiting father who longed for his prodigal son, the good samaritan. Jesus knew a style of life thoroughly at home among crowds, yet most of his time was given to individuals, and he was always open to them – during a lunch break, when he had planned to be resting, in the night and even when he was dying.

The Gospels record that three people were raised from the dead by Jesus. In each of the three cases the person in question was not only an individual but an 'only son', an 'only daughter', an 'only brother'. Were two people ever dealt with in the same way by Jesus? Was any individual treated as a carbon copy? There is no trace of the modern tyranny of the stereotype in his dealings. Each person was unique, an individual made in the image of his Father.

This is not an easy example to follow. Too often we Christians are individualistic to a fault, without ever being personal. We are great talkers but generally poor listeners. Most of us find it easier to speak of the importance of an individual than to show it in practice by listening to one. But we are committed by our Christian faith to taking people and truth seriously, and listening is usually the first and sometimes the only chance we may have of practising the love and compassion of which we speak.

This is part of what makes caring for an individual different from handling a Bible study, preaching a sermon, or speaking on radio or television. These other approaches are no less valuable, but they are more public, and each gain in increased audience is just that – a one-sided gain in people who listen but do not speak. The effect is that eventually the speaker speaks and does not listen.

There is nothing wrong if some of our communication is on this level, but something is wrong if all of it is. Speak on without listening and communication becomes anything but. It turns into a monologue, an impersonal sales technique. Indifference is the most common way that man denies his fellow man today. But listening reverses this. It marks a man out, accepts him, affirms him and puts ourselves at his disposal.

We need to take time, even to *make* time to listen. In a hurrying age many people reveal no more than glimpses into their hurts, dropping tiny hints, sending out signals which they know can be heard or ignored. What they are saying is that they need more time later. But isn't it easy to 'pass by on the other side' by reminding ourselves how short the time is or how full the week is? Time *is* precious, but that is exactly why *never* to have time for someone may be to say he is not worth our time. Make time to listen, though, and listening will be appreciated for the precious gift it is.

A second benefit of listening is that it helps us avoid being 'reactionary'. If we do not listen to other people but only react to what they are saying, we will be guilty both of not taking them seriously and of missing the point. Instead of a judgement of considered understanding, we will merely jump to our own conclusions. Instead of hearing what the other person is saying, we will hear only our own reaction to what the other person is saying, perhaps unaware of how much our own framework, our own point of view, has silenced the other person's meaning.

There is a deeply concealed impatience, if not open arrogance, in the attitude characterized by instant replies and irrelevant judgements. Sometimes such answers are rude, sometimes they are completely wrong, but simply because we are looked to for an answer, we feel ourselves in a position of power where we need not stop to listen. Actually we may not have listened to another person at all, only to our own echo. The letter of James says this: 'But each of you must be quick to listen, slow to speak.' The context of this advice is wider than merely helping someone in doubt, but the principle still holds. The writer of Proverbs had already emphasized it: 'When you see someone over-eager to speak, there will be more hope for a fool than for him.'

A mark of this is the way that certain words or phrases or suggestions can set us off just as surely as Pavlov's dogs salivated at the sound of a bell. When we hear them ('Did I hear him say he was reading such and such a book?' or 'that he had not been to church/read his Bible/prayed for several weeks?'), our reaction is automatic and immediate. It is not so much a response – an answer that is *an answer* – but a reaction, trained, selected, trotted out on cue.

Proverbs warns against this too: 'To answer a question before you have heard it out is both stupid and insulting.' Or as the writer says earlier, 'A man may be pleased with his own retort; how much better is a word in season!' These warnings are particularly apt when we are premature in thinking we have seen the problem and know the answer.

Often as people are sharing their problems they are testing us. Do we really accept them? Is there a time limit to our tolerance? Are we as interested in them as we say we are? Are we as sensitive as we pretend? Do we know what we are talking about when we suggest answers, or is the advantage of the Christian answer only a verbal superiority?

Why should a doubter (or for that matter, an alcoholic, a drug addict, a suburban housewife or a business executive) abandon his chosen form of security for the promises of a faith we are merely speaking of? He has tough questions which deserve answers, yet, paradoxically, part of that answer initially is to have *no answer*, for the genuine answer counts only if we have genuinely listened *first*. So if we are being tested and we react rather than respond, or give answers before we have heard the real problem, we may be cut off from giving any effective answer. People lose interest if not hope when they know they are not being listened to.

The third benefit of listening is that it is the key to understanding. The good listener is like an expert wine-taster who sips the wine, savours it carefully and knows the soil, the year and the quality of the vintage. Or as Job's young friend, Elihu, expresses it, 'The ear tests what is spoken as the palate savours food.' But unlike wine-tasting the Christian calling to listen is not for the connoisseur alone but for everyone. No one can understand when he has not heard, and no one can hear unless he accepts the obligation of listening.

It is profoundly suggestive that the Hebrew word for 'obey' is simply 'to hear'. This reflects Judaism's and Christianity's emphasis on communicating in words. Words express and carry the authority of those who speak them. The Word of God is nothing less than God speaking. So when God speaks, the obedience of faith grasps the meaning and translates its implications into reality.

If we have not obeyed, then we have not heard in the Hebrew sense. Once we have the answers to What is God saying? and What of it? we must give them immediate, living embodiment. To hear is to obey. But just as obedience presupposes hearing, hearing presupposes listening. Active, eager, dedicated faith depends on equally active, eager, dedicated listening.

Listening of this calibre – a listening which is prepared to wrestle with and act on the truth and implications of all that it hears – is the absolute pre-requisite of discernment and of the utmost value in life generally. For whether it is listening to God, listening to men or listening to the lessons of human history and experience, such listening wrestles until it understands and knows what to do. As the writer of the Proverbs says, 'Listen, my son, listen, and become wise.' Or as Solomon prays, 'Give thy servant, therefore, a heart with skill to listen.'

This is especially important when listening to those who do not understand their own problem or realize how deep it lies and perhaps cannot even say exactly what is wrong. Active concentration and full attention are essential for getting to the root of the problem. Proverbs, speaking of the other side of the coin, says, 'Counsel in another's heart is like deep water, but a discerning man will draw it up.' The same can be true of the reverse situation: a man's heart is a deep well of sorrow and anxiety, but the listening man can draw it up.

Saying little, conveying much

How can listening like this be passive? Yet that is one common misunderstanding about listening. Many people give the impression that their understanding of listening is purely negative – a matter of shutting up as opposed to talking, of sitting back rather than leaning forward, of doodling or day-dreaming rather than concentrating. (Have you managed to fall asleep when talking as often as you have when listening?) But to put it like this confuses listening with being silent, and the two are very different. The tongue may be in neutral when we listen but the mind is certainly not. Concentrated listening is just as strenuous as speaking. Listening is active. To listen carefully to someone is to give ourselves to them. To say nothing is not the same as to do nothing; only a chronically garrulous age could ever think that.

A second common misunderstanding is that listening is something we do only when we are not speaking. But listening is not just a period or a stage in conversation or in helping others. It is a complete attitude, a way of relating to a person that goes far beyond the particular moments when one is merely not talking. In this sense it is just as much a part of answering doubt as it is of understanding doubt.

Some people seem to listen as if listening had no value other than providing them a momentary pause for catching their breath or guaranteeing their social right to speak again. At its worst 'I'm listening' can be a grudging admission of being forced into silence. We are listening only because it is *their turn to talk* and then it will be our turn to talk and their turn to listen.

One of the wonders of the incarnation is that in Jesus Christ, God is listening to us *even as* he speaks to us. God's Word, as it were, is also a listening ear, and the Christian who speaks to others must also be listening, asking himself, 'Is it evident to him that I am listening? Did I hear the question right? Have I genuinely understood the problem? Is my answer being understood and accepted? If not, why not?'

Listening like this is not a pause between sentences; it is merely a prelude to understanding and answering. It is part and parcel of the answer itself. As Job cries out to his friends, 'Listen to me, do but listen, and let that be the comfort you offer me.'

Listening is the first great part of remedying doubt. The one who is speaking, the one who is sharing himself is not wood or stone but a human being like ourselves, a fellow-bearer of the image of God. Listen then with everything you have – with love, with acceptance, with concentration and with stillness, without impatience or inquisitiveness. This is the listening that in saying little conveys much.

Chapter Thirteen

A Time to Discern

What is the first thing you do when you've lost something, say your car keys or your wallet? You *think*. You don't panic and rush all over the place, though you may be tempted to. You don't start an inch-by-inch investigation of your house and grounds, though you may need to do this eventually. What you do first is think.

You rack your brains, you ask yourself questions: 'Now where could I have left them? Where did I see them last? What was I doing when I last had them? By thinking carefully and asking yourself questions you narrow down the possibilities, you save yourself the futility of panicking or searching the house unnecessarily, and often you jog your memory or force your mind to a flash of insight which gives you your answer.

The same is true of remedying doubt. When we share a genuine doubt with someone we are saying in effect, 'Help! I've lost my faith. Come over and help me find it.' What we need is not only love that will stop and listen but clear thinking that will calm down panic, rule out futile answers and get down to searching in the right places.

Clear thinking, consciously depending on God for his help, leads to discernment and then to remedy. This discernment is the second major part of remedying doubt and the one we will examine in this chapter. When we first come across a problem it may appear as hopeless as attempting to crack a safe, but discernment goes to work on it, asking question after question until, suddenly, the lock flies open.

By 'question after question' I am not suggesting that we interrogate the poor person like an over-zealous policeman arriving on the scene of an accident. More important than the spoken questions are the 'silent questions' – those that we ask, not aloud of the doubter but silently of ourselves as we listen to his doubts. Even as we listen to him we 'interview ourselves listening', as it were. In forming questions and raising issues, we pursue a line of investigation which leads on to the heart of the problem and so to its answer.

Some might wonder if we are listening to a person or to a problem. But the very reason why I stressed that listening is loving was to avoid divorcing the two. Here we are building on that. The person in doubt is crying out for love *and answers*, not just love. And there are many problems which demand an ice-cold analysis, however stirred we are by the person in trouble. I love my wife deeply, but if she were in trouble she wouldn't expect me to stop thinking clearly. In fact, I would try to think particularly clearly because I love her.

It is the same with understanding doubt. We don't stop loving to start thinking clearly. We go on loving by thinking clearly too.

Is it genuine?

There are two important questions to be asked if we want to crack open the problem of doubt: What is the root of the doubt? Who is responsible for the doubt?

The first of these 'silent questions' is a major one, but we can answer it with the help of three minor questions: First, is the doubt genuine? Often there is a large difference between what is being *said* (that is, the content and claims of the doubt) and what is being *shown* in what is being said (the cause and consequences of the doubt). In other words, there is a difference between the essential root of the problem and what are only symptoms of the problem. What we must discover is whether the doubt is the result of a need for an answer or the result of a need to doubt.

Take, for example, two people who express their doubts but clearly show they feel bad about doubting. For one of the two this recurring note of guilt results from his being taught to suppress his doubts and deny them. Therefore he regards all doubt as shameful. But for the other person the guilt comes from a deliberately concealed grievance, as in the case of the man mentioned earlier who could not believe in God's love because he would not forgive his own father's lack of love. If we listen in an actively questioning manner it will help us to discriminate between the two.

For the first man the root of the problem is a doubt which

is genuine and needs a genuine answer. The guilt is only a symptom of the problem, and an unnecessary symptom at that. Such guilt is not true moral guilt but socially-conditioned guilt feelings. For the second man, however, the root of the problem is moral guilt, and his doubt is only a symptom of the deeper problem.

This is the point at which to separate those who are doubting because they need answers from those who are doubting because they need doubts. As we have seen, it is not only belief but also doubt which can be a process of rationalizing. Ironically, doubt can be as much a crutch or a means of wish-fulfillment to the unbeliever as faith can be to the believer. For doubters like this there are no reasons for their doubt, only rationalizations for their doubting. They may give intellectual reasons, but they are doubting because of an emotional need.

The proud man needs to doubt because his sense of his own importance demands it; it is not his nature to bow to anyone. The weak man needs to doubt to suggest that he is too unworthy to believe; it is his nature to bow to everyone. The unforgiving man needs to doubt God and does so by doubting that he needs God, for he knows that only the man who can afford not to be forgiven is the man who can afford not to forgive.

In the first case the doubter is saying that he does not need faith, in the second that he does not deserve faith and in the third that he cannot afford faith. But in all three cases the actual doubt is immaterial, for what each of the doubters is finally saying is that he will not have faith.

What's at the root?

Once we have discriminated between genuine and spurious doubts (between those that 'need answers' and those that 'answer needs'), we can ask a second minor question of those doubts that are genuine: What is the specific root of the doubt? For instance, someone may have a genuine doubt which on further examination is seen to have come from a faulty picture of God (part of the second category of doubts). The question then is, Where exactly did this come from? If the doubt is genuine and the person is not using this picture of God as a 'stick' to beat God with (which the first minor question should have shown), is it merely the result of his ignorance of who God is, or is it the result of the way he has been treated in life by some other Christians or by his family or whomever? Or is it the result of both?

If we can answer this second minor question, it should lead to a specific understanding of the root of the problem, and also to seeing whether the roots of the doubt are simple or compound. It is important to be specific, for the more specific the understanding the more specific and helpful the answer.

Let us say that two Christians have severe doubts about the authority of the Bible as God's Word and that these doubts have led to others. It would not be enough simply to know that they doubted God's Word; the more basic question is why? For one person the doubt might be due to a lack of understanding of what the Bible teaches about itself, and this – a problem only of lack of facts and understanding – can easily be cleared up. For the other the root of doubt might be in his presuppositions, a problem which is far more serious because it is less often detected. If the false presuppositions are left undisturbed, then no amount of biblical teaching will smoke out the doubt, for its contention is not that the Bible's view of itself is *mistaken* (a question of facts), but that the Bible's view of itself is *meaningless* (a question of framework and presuppositions).

But then again, it might just be that for one of the two the seed of this doubt was sown in some previous experience which made the doubt compound. Imagine that one of our two doubters had been a sensitive student who rightly believed in the Bible but for wrong reasons and who was therefore doubly devastated by the scorn and intellectual dismissal he found in a theological classroom. In this case the answer would need to be both intellectual and emotional, for the compound doubt has complications which an answer directed to a simple doubt overlooks.

How far has it gone?

The first minor question sifts the genuine doubt from the false, and the second minor question changes the focus from the general to the specific. Then comes the third minor question which will show what stage of development the doubt has reached. The question here (asked, remember, of the genuine doubt alone) is, How is the problem being expressed? Is it being expressed in a way which is predominantly sad or depressed or defiant or evasive or just unclear?

It is characteristic of genuine doubts in the early stages that if they are well-defined there is an acute sense of uncertainty, pain and anxiety, and a keen desire for the doubt to be resolved. If they are not well-defined, there is little sense of anything except a gnawing feeling of unreality, as we noticed with the category of doubts which stem from lack of commitment. In contrast to this, spurious doubts (and all doubt as it grows towards full-blown unbelief) are characterized by evasiveness, guilt or defiance, for though it says that it is dubious it sounds dogmatic.

Don't misunderstand me. Not all strongly expressed doubts are spurious. On the contrary, some can be the most genuine, and this is the place to emphasize an extremely important principle of listening to doubt: *expressions of doubt must be taken seriously but they need not be taken literally.* This cannot be stressed too much. The anguish of doubt can be wrung from a person in expressions which, theologically speaking, are weak, wrong or even shocking. But that is not the point. Take them literally, as the insecure, the prudish and the holier-than-thou in each of us demands and the profound problems the doubts are *showing* will be missed for the niceties or otherwise of what the doubts are *saying*. This may flatter our aspirations to orthodoxy, but it does nothing to help the problem.

Have you ever known the time when a close friend telephoned and you didn't recognize his voice? Maybe the line was bad or maybe he had a sore throat. Imagine, though, what it would be like if you recognized his voice but couldn't believe the extraordinary or surprising things he was saying, little realizing, for example, that at the other end of the line he was a hostage speaking under duress. It would certainly be him yet it would not be him. By the strange way he was speaking what he would be showing – that he was in serious trouble – would be much more important than what he would be saying.

In the same way doubt can be expressed in ways which are wild and delirious, like a hostage speaking with a pistol to his head or a sick man out of his mind with pain. Doubt like this shows that someone is hurting and in deep distress. As Georges Bernanos, the French novelist, in *The Diary of a*

Country Priest expressed it, 'Suffering speaks in its own words, words that can't be taken literally.'

So we shouldn't be shocked at the bitterness or even the blasphemy wrung out of a human heart in anguish. The essence of doubt is faith in two minds, and even at its mildest this means that to some degree doubt is faith 'out of its real mind'. Such doubt is 'faith-stress', faith that is 'not itself', faith that is crying out in pain or bewilderment or sheer fatigue. So what may be needed at that moment is not theological correction but human comfort.

'What wonder if my words are wild?' cried Job, as the poison of suffering seeped into his spirit and the shrill pain of this involuntary wildness has re-echoed down through the centuries in the cries of many believers. No one could accuse C. S. Lewis of any deficiency of faith or excess of uncontrolled emotion. Yet even he records candidly, as he muses in his journal (*A Grief Observed*) over the untamed questions in his mind after his wife's death, 'I wrote that last night. It was a yell rather than a thought.'

Who is responsible?

If we use these three minor questions, focussing them on the problem in hand with the help of the general categories considered already, it should provide an answer to the first major question concerning the root of the doubt. The second major question picks up this lead and goes on to ask, Where does the responsibility for the doubt lie? How far is the doubter himself responsible and how much is it the responsibility of others? The goal in asking this is not to blame or excuse anyone. What is at stake is a basic principle of freedom, a principle as vital in doubt as in democracy: where there is no responsibility there is no freedom.

It is never easy, either in theory or practice, to judge where a person's responsibility begins and ends. But though we may make mistakes, at least we should avoid the most obvious extremes and think carefully within the guideline of biblical principles. One extreme is to think that all doubt is the result of sin. This is a result of both poor psychology and poor theology. What it does is to confuse doubt with unbelief, exaggerating the place of doubts which are the result of sin so that one arrives at answers which are simplistic and insecure. From this point of view one can usually think of only one basic remedy: confession and repentance. This is often suggested insensitively, even cruelly. Curiously, this extreme parallels the over-reaction in secular circles which emphasizes the ideal of justice at the expense of compassion and therefore holds that everything which is considered a crime is morally culpable.

The other extreme is to say that sin has no place in the discussion of doubt. This attitude is characterized by a diminished sense of the importance of sin and a lighter estimate of the gravity of unbelief. It can lead to a remarkably tolerant attitude towards doubt that stresses its positive rather than its negative side, treating it more as a matter of psychology than theology. This mentality parallels the secular over-reaction towards the ideal of compassion at the expense of justice which has erred towards the position that all criminals are not so much morally responsible as mentally sick.

Each of these extremes is cruel in its own way, the one 'soft on doubt' no less than the one 'hard on doubt'. It is certainly cruel to hold a man responsible for what he has not done, but it is no less cruel to deny his responsibility where he has exercised it, for this is to treat him as less than a person.

A balanced Christian way lies in a third direction of seeking to ascertain where a person is responsible, knowing that only when a person is forgiven is he free and that forgiveness is known most fully only when responsibility has been faced. The key is to realize that no one is primarily responsible to God for what other people have *done to* him, whether through actions or teaching; the other people are responsible to God for this. But each person is responsible to God for what he has *done with* what others have done to him.

This distinction means that we can discriminate between doubts which are in no way the responsibility of the doubter and those that are, whether to a larger or a smaller degree. Poor teaching is the largest single cause of those doubts for which the doubter is not initially responsible. When what is taught is such a distortion of God's Word that doubt is inevitable, the basic responsibility is not the doubter's but the teacher's, and what is really God's truth will come to the doubter as a double relief. Not only will it answer the doubt, it will also ease the feelings of guilt which came from unnecessarily assuming responsibility for the doubt.

Many Christians with artistic gifts provide poignant testimony to this. For too long they were unable to escape an uneasy feeling of bad faith if not open doubt, plagued by unnecessary questions about God's approval of their artistic creativity and freedom. Somehow they could not believe that truth and beauty go together or that their art is valid unless it is being used as a tool in evangelism. But this doubt is not the artists' fault. A large part of the responsibility for this mentality must be laid at the door of an unbiblical teaching.

In most instances of doubt what comes to light is a mixture of responsibility and non-responsibility. For if the doubter was not responsible for the original cause of the doubt, he is certainly responsible for his reaction to it. Thus the continuation of the doubt, if not the initiation, may well be his responsibility. The largest single cause at this point is not poor teaching but hurtful experience. What is done to a person is painful and wrong, yet the injured person is not responsible for this but for what he does with what was done to him. However wrong the original injury was, if his reaction was also wrong and if doubt has arisen out of this, then the responsibility for the doubt (and for the grievance) is his, even though the responsibility for the original injury is not.

Spiritual discernment requires this keen sense of discrimination, an active listening which evaluates and unravels what it takes in. Jude writes in his letter, 'There are some doubting souls who need your pity; snatch them from the flames and save them. There are others for whom your pity must be mixed with fear'. The former, presumably, were those whose responsibility for their doubts was little, if any at all, but the latter were those who for some reason were culpable and whose doubt was fast ripening into unbelief. Both would need correction if their doubts were to be answered. But to the former it would come immediately as comfort, while to the latter it would come first as confrontation.

The question of responsibility must focus on both the past and the present. In terms of the past ask yourself exactly whose responsibilities (and how) have led up to their present situation. In terms of the present ask, How much should the responsibility be faced alone and how much should other people help? Notice the question is not how much *can* others help but how much *should* others help. If part of the root problem is a weakness in facing up to responsibility, too much help is as bad as too little. When we do for someone what he should do for himself we do not help but hinder. There is an element of responsibility in every doubt which no one but the doubter should face. The question is not one of endurance (how much *can* the doubter face alone?) but of responsibility (how much *should* the doubter face alone?).

This is particularly true of the fourth category of doubt, those which stem from lack of commitment. If someone's problem is rooted in a poor sense of identity or any of the other causes behind this category, then their only hope lies in awakening and exercising the responsibility of who they are. Just as a wise teacher knows when to help a child with his problem and when to make him think it through for himself, so the discerning listener will know the difference between help that is a help and too much help that is no help.

If someone's problem is partly the result of his exercising too little responsibility, any answer that takes the responsibility away from the doubter will only aggravate the problem. The nominal Christian who doubts is a case in point, for, strangely, he needs help with his believing more than with his doubting. Even if he is given answers to all his doubts, he will still doubt, because his problem is not that he doubts something but that he does not *truly* believe anything. In this situation the only remedy that will help is one which challenges him to face up to his responsibility and commit himself to the consequences of belief.

Another clear example concerns those who believe but have a poor sense of their own identity. I remember being introduced to a man who described himself apologetically as a 'hopeless case'. He was a Christian but had been plagued by doubts for years. Now he was beginning to wonder if it was a handicap he would just have to live with. His story was a moving one of repeated attempts to find answers, always ending in no answer and no relief. The doubts he expressed showed an understanding of God which was variously weak, wrong or blasphemous, but we listened without interrupting.

After a while he paused, evidently puzzled that his story of a doubt was not getting more open reaction. Then he told us that when he had recounted his story before, he had never been allowed to get beyond these initial expressions of doubt. As soon as he said this, he had given an important clue to the nature of his doubt. He had touched on deep theological problems, but none of these was worth picking up, for the real root of the problem was in his psychology, not his theology.

Those who had listened before had taken him literally and had at once confronted him or rebuked him as each expression of doubt seemed to require. But apparently no one had distinguished between the symptoms and the root of the problem. In fact with this man they were only the symptoms, and in the course of his telling the story many times they had become a camouflage for the real root which lay in his poor self-image and his unwillingness to exercise his significance.

He was the less dominant of two identical twins and had suffered a severe crisis of identity when his twin brother left home. Since then everything he had done had lacked a sense of identity and responsibility. If his faith was full of uncertainty, so was the rest of his life. But his Christian friends had listened only to his doubts and had heard them only as theological problems. Repeatedly they had answered his doubts, but since he was never satisfied they concluded that he was hopelessly diffident and prone to melancholy.

The net result was a doubly tragic situation; his doubts were not answered and his continuing dilemma of doubt was allowed to become the problem by which he defined himself. He felt he was nothing in himself. Yet the fact that he had an 'unanswerable doubt' gave him some sense of identity and a point of social acceptance which he had come to expect and enjoy.

So, as he told his story with all its uncertainty, sadness, longing and pain, the major theme of doubt was so dominant that it was easy to miss the minor theme of irresponsibility which was also carried throughout. The story was genuine, but so heart-rending that it was guaranteed to win people's sympathy and had become an unwitting pretext, an unconscious alibi which almost completely covered the trail of non-responsibility.

The initial disadvantages of doubt were being progressively outweighed by the advantages, but something he had not reckoned on was proving a still greater problem. Since there was an unmistakeable element of his own responsibility in his doubt, he was reaping the logic of his definite choice to ignore it. Using the doubt to defuse responsibility had become a style of life which increasingly refused to accept the responsibility for the consequence of anything. This in turn had grown into a habit which was being built into his character. In the end everything that presupposed responsibility – such as the element of commitment in falling in love – was being called into question, and the problems this created were spreading like a lengthening shadow over the whole of his life, reducing him to a state of uncertainty and irresolution. In this case the urgent need was not to find a new remedy but to face an old responsibility.

Jesus always addressed people in need with a clear eye to their responsibility. In doing so he sorted out those who wanted an answer from those who wanted attention. People must have been taken aback when he said to a cripple at the Sheep-Pool in Jerusalem, 'Do you want to recover?' Wasn't this ridiculous, a little redundant? Hadn't he been a cripple for thirty-eight years? But Jesus was probing at this point, and when he went on to say to the man, 'Rise to your feet, take up your bed and walk,' he was facing him with the responsibility for faith that was his.

The sheer impossibility of the command was a test of the intensity of the man's concern to be healed and the responsibility of his commitment. To exercise the responsibility of rising was faith for the cripple. To exercise the responsibility of stretching out his arm was faith for the paralyzed man. In each case their cry for help and their faith in Jesus was clinched by the responsibility of their obedience to his command, even though it seemed impossible.

Deliberate choice?

Understanding the importance of responsibility in doubt is vital for putting into perspective the effect of sin and the influence of the Evil One in doubting. Unquestionably there is a proper place for both in the discussion of doubt. Some may have wondered why we have not said more about sin much earlier. We have delayed partly because our earlier aim was to show that most common doubts are not inevitable (since they grow from a deficiency at points where God has given a wholeness in salvation) and partly because the importance of sin in doubt is either so exaggerated or so minimized that it is better to introduce it in the context of responsibility.

Two things should be clear to the Christian. On one hand, the Bible teaches that doubt can be the result of sin and that it can be sin itself. Doubt is not just a matter of faulty epistemology or poor psychology; it can be the result of a deliberate choice to disobey God and reject his truth. Whatever other alienation this causes, it does cause separation from God and therefore gives a sense of his absence which is the source of much doubt.

The prophet Isaiah answered a popular complaint against God, exposing it as a rationalization by which the people were trying to justify their evasion of God's demands: 'The Lord's arm is not so short that it cannot save nor his ear too dull to hear it; it is your iniquities that raise a barrier between you and your God.'

Whether sin is the root or the result of doubt, whether its point of entry is through an action or a reaction, does not matter at this point. All that is important is to see that sin and doubt can be integrally related, so that no understanding of doubt is really complete unless the possibility of sin is taken into account.

On the other hand, it is equally important to make sure that the place of sin is not exaggerated. A large part of the burden of our inquiry has been to prevent just this problem. This is a special danger to people who seek to help others in doubt but who are themselves insecure as believers. When we are insecure, the anxiety which is caused by our own uncertainty can be blamed not on the internal deficiency of our faith but on any factor which is seen to threaten it externally. So our answers to doubt, while apparently solicitous and forthright, may mask a hidden fear of doubt which has the effect of forcing us to see everything in black and white and make simplistic judgements.

A particularly bad form of this (and one to which even the most compassionate and discerning of listeners is prone when tired) is the unconscious habit of putting someone into a category to dismiss him rather than describe him. What sounds like an explanation can then be used as an excuse. During the Vietnam war there was an army saying which illustrates this, 'If it's dead and isn't white, it's Vietcong.' This is as subtle as it is evil, and God alone knows the unknown number of civilian deaths which were covered by those words. Within the wider definitions of war which were used to justify killing, this little 'category dismissal' tidied up all the loose ends so that there was a justification and a legitimacy for even the ugliest and most unnecessary acts of murder.

But this is only a blatant example of what we are all apt to do when we categorize someone. All we may be doing grammatically is to explain the state that a man is in, but what we may be doing logically (if only by our tone of voice) is excusing ourselves from doing anything about it. Exaggerating the place of sin in order to explain doubt is typical of this. Other examples can be seen in the misuse of descriptive terms like *carnal* and *backsliding*. What we are saying is that another Christian's problem can be explained by his 'sin' or by the fact that he is 'a carnal Christian' or a 'backslider', but what we mean is that the problem is the other person's responsibility and not ours. Terms like these are helpful if they are accurately used, but they should never be used to cover an excuse. Otherwise, we are using a descriptive category as a handy waste-paper basket into which we drop our discarded responsibilities. The more carefully labelled a person is, the more easily he can be dismissed.

Perhaps the question which the disciples asked Jesus when they saw the blind man by the roadside was like this: 'Who sinned, this man or his parents?' Probably the disciples were only too aware of what could not be done. In order, therefore, to escape the unconscious moral pressure of doing something themselves, they asked Jesus who was responsible.

Jesus, however, was conscious of two things at the same time. He knew what could be done and should be done, so he answered in terms of the immediate resolution rather than the ultimate responsibility: ' "It is not that this man or his parents sinned," Jesus answered; "he was born blind so that God's power might be displayed in curing him." ' Then in the decisive act of doing something about it, he showed that his explanation, unlike theirs, was not an excuse.

The 'father of lies'

If some people may have wondered why there was no earlier mention of sin, others may be puzzled that the influence of the Evil One has not been more fully stated. Again, the reason is that this is not the main purpose of our inquiry. Besides, there is so much unhealthy exaggeration about Satan. It is wiser, I believe, to introduce the subject also in this context of responsibility.

The Christian who seeks to understand the relationship of the Devil to doubt must keep two things in balance. On one hand, the Bible is emphatically clear that the role of the Evil One in stirring doubt is completely in keeping with his character. He is described by Jesus as 'the father of lies'. His first recorded words (in Genesis), 'Did God say ... ?' are calculated to cast doubts on Eve's faith in God. The most commonly used names given him are *Satan* which means the 'adversary' and the *Devil* which means the 'slanderer'. If doubt begins with the temptation in the Garden of Eden, it ends only with the overthrow of the Evil One at the end times.

The recorder in Revelation describes how 'the great dragon was thrown down, that serpent of old that led the whole world astray, whose name is Satan, or the Devil'. As this announcement was made, a loud voice rang out in heaven, 'This is the hour of victory for our God ... For the accuser of our brothers is overthrown, who day and night accused them before our God.' So we should have no hesitation in seeing that behind, beneath and beyond all finite and human causes of doubt lies the influence of the Evil One. All doubt is to his advantage, for to have someone in two minds, to have him stretched to the breaking point between faith and unbelief, is to have him half-way towards his desired goal which is unbelief. As C. S. Lewis's elderly devil, Screwtape, in *The Screwtape Letters*, writes to his nephew Wormwood, 'For the first time in your career you have tasted that wine which is the reward of all our labours – the anguish and bewilderment of a human soul.'

On the other hand, we must be wary of exaggerating the power and influence of the Evil One. For one thing, the undue place which is given to the Devil today, even by Christians, has served to diminish the sense of Christ's power and victory. Too much of the talk of the Devil gives him too much room in people's imagination if not in their theology. It is quite true that the Devil seeks to undo God's work, but it is also true, as John's first letter says, that 'the Son of God appeared for the very purpose of undoing the devil's work'.

Nothing is more characteristic of Christian faith than its emphatic affirmation of the complete victory of Jesus Christ over the powers of darkness. Biblical doctrine and Christian experience are one. Christ is Victor and there is no power in heaven or earth, in the present or the future, that can stand against him. As Paul writes to the Colossians, 'On that cross he discarded the cosmic powers and authorities like a garment; he made a public spectacle of them and led them as captives in his triumphal procession.' The Devil may appear to have a lot of rope, but the end of that rope is in the hands of God.

For another thing, to blame too much on the Devil is another form of excusing human responsibility. Perhaps this partly explains the extraordinary modern phenomena of 'sympathy for the Devil', or the wave of popular feeling which likes to identify itself with Judas and makes him the patron saint of the unjustly condemned and the popularly misunderstood. Attitudes like these are the result of bastard emotions begotten by a generation which has never squarely faced the responsibility of its own knowledge and actions.

A Christian equivalent of this can be seen in the frequent assertions that this or that happened to people because they were 'under attack from the Devil'. I would certainly not deny that this can be so and that very often today it is. The point I am making is that by referring wrongly to the attacks of the Devil, some people are guilty of smuggling in an excuse under the cover of an explanation. Some have developed this mentality to such a degree that a handy rule-of-the-thumb translation for 'under attack' is 'I am tired' or 'Things are not going well.' In cases like this it is not biblical realism that demands that they blame the Devil but the self-indulgence of their own private surrealism which would create any reality to avoid the responsibility of the true one.

The grip of the Devil on a life can be strong and real, like a plaster cast on a broken arm. But some Christians who have had this grip broken are like a man who has had a cast for so long that he has forgotten how to use his arm, so that even when the cast is taken off he nurses his arm and protects it. There are Christians who have known genuine liberation from genuine oppression but whose faith is as weak as if they were still in bondage. They excuse themselves by blaming the Devil's attacks. At this stage, however, it is not the Devil they should blame but themselves. The cast is off but the muscles of their faith will remain weak until they are exercised and built up again. The same principle holds true: where no responsibility is faced, no freedom is found.

These, then, are the 'silent questions' we should ask, the line of thought our investigation should pursue. Think these questions over carefully. Don't learn them by rote or ask them mechanically even if they are the right ones. Make them your own. Put them in your own words. Let them be so natural to you that you think hard but not self-consciously when using them. Then they will lead towards discernment. Skill in answering doubt depends largely on skill in questioning doubt.

Chapter Fourteen

A Time to Speak

Which is more infuriating, someone who never listens to a problem or someone who claims to understand it perfectly but gives no answer? If we listen carefully to someone in doubt and claim to understand the problem but never give him a satisfactory answer, the longing hopes of the doubter will be driven into despair. When we fail to listen we leave a person in his doubt, but when we only listen we add despair to his doubt. Now he knows that we have no answer and, worse still, he suspects that there is no answer at all. Nothing is more infuriating than a Buddha-like smile that seems to know but never says.

Between these two extremes – of not listening or never answering – lies the time when listening and discerning grow naturally into answering, when understanding a problem shifts over easily into tackling it. This is the third major part of remedying doubt, and the one we will examine in this chapter – the time to speak, when we help the doubter by saying what is wrong and what can be done about it.

A helpful answer

If you have wrestled through with the issues this far, the question of what to do and say should be comparatively clear. In fact, if what we have discussed is basically correct, it should lead to a working knowledge of how doubt grows and can be understood. This in turn will encourage a practical wisdom in dealing with doubt. Such wisdom should make the elaboration of detailed answers to specific doubts unnecessary.

Better to have a grasp of basic principles and grow in wisdom and practical experience as we put them to use than to carry around a detailed set of instructions and find that they do not fit life. The fact that we are not specific in advance is the very reason why we can be specific at the time.

Those who are more specific than they need be ahead of time end up being more vague than they should be at the time. The problems of life are more complex than their instructions led them to believe.

Does this mean that the answer is left to the uncertainty of the moment when it is needed? Are we to rely on good will and spontaneity to see us through? Not at all. The same hard thinking that leads to discernment is also needed in giving an answer. But first let us consider what a good answer is and second the way it should be given.

A helpful answer is one that provides an appropriate and practical solution to the correctly perceived problem. To be more than a 'mere answer', such a response will need to contain certain basic components. First, before answering the doubt, it must unravel and explain it, going behind the doubt to show why and how it happened. Second, it must not only stop the doubt in its tracks but show where those tracks would lead to if not answered, so that the logic and consequence of doubt are clear. Third, it must reveal the responsibility of doubter for his doubt, so that he can face up to his responsibility and thus find freedom. If these other components are also there an answer will become a genuinely helpful and lasting solution, pointing the way out of the doubt and ensuring that the problem does not occur again.

These are the essential characteristics of a good answer. They are the natural outgrowth of listening and discerning and should be so filled out in the specific situation that they meet the need, providing an answer to it or giving guidelines that point towards one.

But the manner in which this answer is given is all-important. It is not simply a matter of the right words.

Compassion is a life-line

The first characteristic of the way an answer should be given is compassion. Accept the person in doubt, penetrate into his pain, show him encouragement, sympathy and love and that will always speak louder than words. If as we answer we are the slightest bit insecure or self-righteous or have our own problems with belief, we may be threatened, if only subconsciously, by the doubts that are expressed. Sooner or later this will show in the way that we respond to the doubts. If we lack the love that 'covers a multitude of sins', our answers will have a hollow ring that betrays our best intentions.

Compassion in the one who answers is a hallmark of the practice of Christian truth. To the person in doubt, however, compassion is far more than a means of identification; it is a life-line. Whatever its root may be, the effect of doubt can be devastating to the believer (assuming that his faith was real and not spurious, and that his doubt is genuine and not a rationalization). With one damaging blow at the underpinnings of life everything begins to come apart, and there are few parallels to the feelings that follow – a dizzying sense of disorientation, a strange numbness of feeling, a sensation of being paralyzed and completely at a loss.

The one who claims to have 'lost his faith' and says it is 'nothing' shows only that his faith was worth next to nothing before he lost it. But the one whose faith was genuine in the first place knows this is not so. What was nearest to his heart has left a vacuum. The one certainty which guaranteed all other certainty has itself become uncertain, and he is plunged into an unfathomable sea of uncertainty. As Proverbs says, 'A man's spirit may sustain him in sickness, but if the spirit is wounded, who can mend it?'

This is why, although a period of doubting is a time of weakness, it is the strong believer and not the weak believer who is most devastated. This is also why it is those ages which know the greatness of faith that also appreciate the depths of doubt. Our own age, by contrast, treats doubt as of little importance and shows that it has little understanding of faith.

Compassion ministers directly to this devastation which is the faith-stress of doubt. Doubt is a crisis to faith because faith is not only trust, an active grasping of God's faithfulness, but 'a trust held in trust'. When we believe, we make an understanding commitment to what we believe is the truth of the matter ('that he exists and that he rewards those who search for him' – Hebrews 11 : 6). But we also commit ourselves to the consequences of that knowledge and assume responsibility for what we now know. Paul writes to Timothy, 'I know who it is in whom I have trusted, and am confident of his power to keep safe what he has put into my charge, until the great Day.' He then concludes, 'Guard the treasure put into our charge, with the help of the Holy Spirit dwelling within us.'

When we believe, we are 'holding in trust' God's character

and the entire range of his trustworthiness. Just as a medieval knight in a tournament might have carried his lady's portrait or a husband today a photo of his wife, so the Christian faith is a trust held in trust. Faith itself is no more God than the lady's portrait is the lady, but, in being true to the one whom the portrait represents, the knight is true to his lady. It is the same for the believer. In believing, he is most true to who God is.

Faith can be viewed either as an active commitment to God or as the wedding ring of the believer's commitment. But the effect is the same. In a world that denies God the situation is never easy, and the precious trust held in trust is sometimes carried dangerously. The knight must actively fight for the honour of his lady; the husband and wife must resist a thousand temptations if they are to remain true to each other. An insult to either the portrait or the ring is a threat to the trust. Similarly, for the Christian the battle of faith is to hold in trust the honour of God's character and to live through the faith-stress which is doubt's pressure on this trust.

Imagine a small boy in Dickensian London, running an errand for his master. As he makes his way home through the long, dark streets, clutching a package he has been given to take to his master, he grows tired, becomes discouraged, sometimes wondering if he is lost, perhaps fearing the possibility of attack or injury or theft, but always hurrying on towards home with his master's instructions in mind. This is the Christian's path through life.

To believe is to bear that trust and, however difficult or dangerous the circumstances, to carry it home till the end of life. The faith-stress of doubt is the result of pressures which imperil the whole errand and call in question both the Master who initiated it and the one who is running it. When, in the crisis of doubt, the believer cries out in strange and unrecognizable sounds, it is not surprising. Instead of speaking clearly, faith is stammering with fright or choked with pain. But such doubt is still *faith* stammering, *faith* stumbling, *faith* being strangled. Whatever pressure it is under and however strange it sounds, it is not unbelief – at least, not until it gives up and turns back or goes over to the other side.

Are we being 'soft on doubt' by saying this? Surely not.

We are understanding doubt as Jesus did. Warning Peter of his approaching denial, a test he would fail miserably, Jesus adds, 'But for you I have prayed that your faith may not fail; and when you have come to yourself, you must lend strength to your brothers.' Of course Jesus is saying that Peter's denial was a betrayal of trust. But isn't he also saying that Peter's denial wasn't Peter being fully himself? To believe with a single-minded, whole-hearted attention to truth is to be 'most oneself'; it is to be in one's 'right mind' about truth. But when the believer doubts and is in two minds, he is not strictly 'himself', and it is this crisis of identity which is the deepest damage of the faith-stress of doubt.

This is the reason why doubt must always be taken seriously but need not be taken literally. Like a soldier denying his true allegiance under torture or like a sufferer 'out of his mind' with pain, the believer may do or say something in the agony of his doubt which shows that he is not quite himself. This does not necessarily excuse such expressions of doubt, but it explains them, for in speaking more of what a doubter feels than of what he believes it tells us *what* is wrong with him, or at least *that* something is wrong.

Love a person for himself and you can ignore for the moment what his doubt is saying and still take him seriously as a person. When we respond only to the contents of a person's doubt, we are treating him seriously only in so far as he is a believer or doubter. But when we respond also to the personal causes of the doubt, we are taking him seriously as a person.

No solvent to doubt will rival the power of love and compassion. Answer a man with compassion and you reach a level below that of theological error. When we answer without them we are only 'Job's comforters', people who answer without having comfort or compassion, and that is no answer. As Job himself expressed it,

> Devotion is due from his friends
> to one who despairs and loses faith in the Almighty;
> but my brothers have been treacherous
> as a mountain stream,
> like the channels of streams that run dry.

Or, as he says later with understandable bitterness,

> If you and I were to change places,
> I could talk like you;
> how I could harangue you
> and wag my head at you!
> But no, I would speak words of encouragement.

What is true for every genuine doubter is especially true of those who have comforted others and now need comfort themselves. Because they have helped others, they know all the answers and none seems right. No state of mind may seem more helpless. They can answer themselves intellectually, and yet their answers are cold and comfortless because they know them too well. 'Physician heal thyself' mocks them. Nothing seems more hollow than the fact that their answers are true, and to know that they have been helpful to others is a source of irony more than encouragement.

It is hard to be a teacher, director or leader. But who will teach the teacher, direct the director, lead the leader? When they are in doubt themselves it challenges not only their competence and experience but the deeper sense of their identity and calling. This is why doubt can represent a particularly severe threat to leaders. How easy it is for them to fall into the trap of defining themselves by their job or role or gift! So the director, for example, is a person only because (and so long as) he directs. If he himself should need directing, then he is doubly at a loss – once because he needs direction and twice because this wipes out his point of identity.

The same is true too of the minister or leader, and particularly so since part of the sensitivity which true leadership requires is often gained from the rough school of life's wounding experiences. The danger is that in times of tiredness or discouragement pressure is put on the leader's own weakness and his motivation may undergo a subtle shift. Alongside his positive desire to help will grow an unnoticed negative desire to help in order to seek help. When this happens, the helper needs help, or eventually he will be tempted to feel utterly useless. If he cannot help, he is not only helpless, he is no one. A minister who needs ministering or a leader who needs to be led may feel as useless as salt that needs salting.

Situations like these form a Gordian knot which no

amount of theological expertise will unravel. But it can be slashed through in one stroke by love and compassion. Love treats the person seriously as a person who happens to be a helper, not as a helper who is therefore a person. Or to change the picture, when someone is caught in a private dungeon of despair, heavy theological keys may be needed to bring complete release, but there is nothing like love to raise him to his feet, give him a new sense of hope and value and spur him on to find his way out.

Waffle and candour

The second characteristic of our answer should be frankness. Not all frankness is in the service of truth, but those who are sure of the truth can afford to be frank. Candour and realism do more than speak against doubt; they add their own recommendation to faith. As Proverbs says, 'A straightforward answer is as good as a kiss of friendship.'

Waffling vagueness is often a clue that the person trying to help is out of his depth. Some people never seem to come to the point, and one suspects they are not sure what it is. Their attempts to help are couched in pious generalizations, lengthy circumlocutions, beating round the bush. Other people turn on doubt and unleash a withering round of spiritual fire, explaining, answering and warning. This is extremely impressive for a short while, until we realize they are blazing away into the darkness.

Still others are aware they have no answers, but rather than admit it, they trail off lamely into expressions such as, 'I'll be praying for you.' In such instances this is not to be taken literally; it is only an expression of sympathy and should be translated, 'I wish I could do more, but I'm afraid I'm stuck.'

In most cases there is nothing wrong in being unable to help. What is wrong is the dishonesty of not admitting it. We should aim for a candour that corroborates the truth of what we are saying. Four extremely simple points may be a help with this.

First, if we are unable to help we should say so. Otherwise the hesitancy or confusion we express, however we try to disguise it, will rub off on our Christian faith. Without meaning to we will be suggesting that Christianity is no stronger than our muddled explanations or poor defence of it.

Where we can't help we can at least recommend someone who can – a friend, a minister, a helpful book or taped lecture which deals with the problem. If we are straightforward and open in admitting that we are unable to help, we will not have to mask those guilt feelings which come from a sense of failure we have not admitted. True, we haven't been able to help, but by admitting it we have localized the problem. It is not that Christianity has no answers but that we as individual Christians do not know what the answer is. Any recommendations then come as a natural step and not as a desperate move or a poorly concealed attempt to palm off the doubter on someone else.

Of course, if we do recommend something, we should beware of falling into a stereotyped formula or suggestions based entirely on people and books that have been helpful to us. Even if several people share the same problem, they will not all respond to the same remedy, in the same way.

Recommending books is a case in point. The one thing more damaging than never suggesting any books is indiscriminately to outline lengthy reading-lists to each person in doubt. For every doubt which might be answered with the help of a reading-list, many more would be made worse. Doubts are best met first by love and time and care, and not by a list of books. Our recommendations should not be indiscriminate or routine even for those who value and know how to use books.

Second, if there is no one who can help as far as we know, it is good to face this and clarify what it means. All it means is that no one can help *at the moment*, and that is quite different from saying that no one can help *at all*. There is an important difference between putting doubt in cold storage and repressing it. There are many situations in life where we cannot find an answer when we want it, not for any sublime reason such as the mystery of God's dealings in this world but simply because we have been temporarily cut off from advice or help.

Take, for example, a student on a university campus, cut off from the biblical teaching of his home church. Or, conversely, consider a student who has become a Christian at the university going home for the vacation and finding no one who can appreciate or answer his intellectual questions. The best way to handle the doubts that arise in such cases is to advise people to put them in deep-freeze until they can get to a friend or a book or someone with the wisdom and experience to answer the problem.

This is not to repress the doubt but to suspend judgement on it for the time being – but only until we have access to the people or the materials which will allow us to come to a responsible conclusion. There is a definite place for verification in Christian faith, but if Christianity is true it is not because it is instantly, totally verified at every moment or even at any moment. No human knowledge is of this order of certainty.

This has practical implications for the problem of doubt. For one thing it means that like all rational people the Christian has the freedom to be wrong at times, and the fact that he can be wrong does not necessarily mean that all is up with his faith. For another thing, it means that the Christian is free to wait when he wants to know for sure. Like all thinking people the Christian has the right to weigh new facts and new theories and wait before making his judgements. There is no need to panic every time a new or hostile hypothesis is published. This leads to reactions which are hasty, unduly emotional and a waste of energy. There is no need to panic at all. A hundred hostile questions do not make one doubt. It is unhealthy to repress doubts, but we can keep them in cold storage without losing integrity.

No easy cure

Third, we should never imply that the answer to doubt will be easy. Doubts are sometimes easier to detect than solve and easier to diagnose than cure. Only the simplest of doubts is simply solved, and the resolution of some doubts may be painful. Some people have been living with doubts for so long that they have grown used to them and would miss them. So for them the problem must get worse before it gets better. But unless they are warned, the first discouragement may make them give up, for they may prefer the expected pain of a known problem to the unexpected pain of the as yet unknown answer. Frankness here is not only constructive but in the long run healing.

The essence of a problem lies in a situation or a state of affairs that cannot readily be cleared up. So to tackle a problem is to come to grips with the state of affairs which produced it. Put simply, if doubt is a problem so also is its resolution and to face that frankly has all the realism of a bucket of cold water thrown in one's face. But such realism is necessary in life. Only one thing is worse for a climber than being lost and that is to know it but not dare to admit it. For a climber to find his way again involves at least the admission that he has gone wrong and the willingness to retrace his steps.

Resolving doubt is like this. It involves a 'second time around' which increases the necessary effort and looks much harder than the first time. The first time he believed, faith seemed simple, but now that it seems to have failed and he sees that nothing is ever quite that simple, he is sure it must be hopelessly complicated. Where everything seemed easy before, everything seems difficult now. What faith saw as possible, doubt says is impossible. Where faith was carefree and spontaneous it is now burdened and self-conscious. The danger is that the doubter may succumb to a paralysis of introspection which we might call the 'centipede complex'. This is well pictured in the little nineteenth-century poem:

> The Centipede was happy quite,
> Until the toad-in-fun
> Said 'Pray, which leg goes after which?'
> Which worked her mind to such a pitch,
> She lay distracted in a ditch,
> Considering how to run.

The toad's taunt is a common feature of the debate which rages within us when we doubt, and it has an added twist when behind the questions we ask of ourselves lies the concealed mockery of the Evil One. 'Give up,' he suggests. 'There's no way you can do it! You'll never make it! Think of the time. Think of the pain!' It is this whirlpool of inward-looking defeatism that can be avoided by a realism which marks out the perils of the river before the journey begins so that they come as no surprise. Frankness and candour also save our answers from being pat, for no doubts are removed by a wave of the wand, and we should refuse to offer easy answers, appealing short-cuts or solutions with a 'money back' guarantee.

Of course, there is the opposite danger of being so brutally realistic that we unnerve the poor person in doubt. This would be worse. To him everything seems up in the air, nothing seems solid. But in fact, only the doubter is up in the air, and this little exaggeration of the Devil's is a lie whose spell needs to be broken. Much can be solidly counted on. For example, it is the common experience of doubters that in searching they do find. Even the doubter's previous doubts have been resolved. Introduce reminders like these – not as a substitute but as a support for the proper answer – and they will comfort and encourage, offsetting the more discouraging aspects of the situation.

Fourth, be careful to steer a course between over-simplifying and over-complicating your answer. Both dangers have little to do with how simple or complex a problem is. The question they raise is how open or closed we are in our attitudes.

The simplistic answer is not the mark of simplicity but of insecurity. And the over-complicated answer is often not the mark of a complex mind being brought to bear on a problem too small for it, but of a small mind being brought to bear on a problem too complex for it. In either case a dose of candour is effective. Each may have its origins in purely psychological factors.

When we are dealing with the problems of another human being we always need to remember that nothing is ever quite that simple. Over-simplification is a special danger for anyone who is unsure of what to say or how to say it. Also, though this is less obvious, it is a temptation for the person who has heard a particular problem many times before and who is therefore too quick to label and classify it, or for a person who is too tired to do anything but slip into an easily categorized solution. The mistake in each case is to think only of the general categories and not of the individual details and differences.

There are two obvious but important differences between the man with the answer and the man with the problem. The first is that to the man with the answer, the answer is 'obvious'. But to the other man, though he may hear the answer with his ears and understand the syntax and logic of what is said, the answer is anything but obvious. Of course, when the answer is obvious to him too, the problem is no longer a problem.

The second difference is that to the man with the answer the problem is objective. It is not *his* problem. We can share our problems and help each other in them, but no one can completely get under the skin of another man's problem. As Shakespeare said, 'Everyone can master a grief but he that has it.' The simplistic answer that forgets this can insult a person's identity as well as his intelligence. In the end neither the person nor the problem is taken seriously.

Thus in the interests of openness and humility, we should acknowledge that however right we think we are, the answer may not be as simple as we have suggested, and it certainly will not strike the doubter as simple until he has made it his own. Some doubts can give pain even after they have been answered. There are times when the pain of doubt is like the discomfort of a badly fitting shoe. If the shoe has rubbed in several places at once, the pain will still be there when the shoe is taken off, and the tenderness may even continue when a better fitting shoe is put on. The sore spot will be there for a while.

We have concentrated on the general style of answering and not on specific answers. But again, unless we do answer the doubt and answer it decisively with discernment and love, there is little point to all we have discussed. We must come to the point and then as simply and clearly as we can lay out the answer. Without this answer – appropriate, practical and specific – all else, in a certain sense, is air.

It is a deep privilege to be there when doubt is resolved, and a believer is sure of God again. But if God uses our efforts to answer another person's doubts, it is by his grace. The danger we face when we have been a help to someone is that we confuse our faith in God with our ability to answer doubts about God. Once we do that, we are not trusting God but our faith in God. Christianity then becomes no more true to us than our best defence of it, no more helpful to us than our ability to explain it. But we are not to rejoice in the fact that doubts submit to us but that, as Jesus said to the disciples in a parallel situation, our 'names are enrolled in heaven'.

Chapter Fifteen

A Time to Warn

One last possibility remains and that is that the doubter will prefer to doubt rather than to believe.

All our discussion has been based on the double assumption that if Christianity is true there is a sufficient answer in Christ to every conceivable doubt, and that if his doubt is genuine the doubter will be open to the possibility of resolving his doubt in the interests of faith. The reason we assume the latter is not that faith expects any special favours, such as the courtesy of a second chance, but that the essence of doubt is its open-endedness. Genuine openness must be prepared to turn either way, back to faith or on to unbelief. Both faith and unbelief have closed on what they believe to be the truth of the matter; doubt is open about the question at hand.

At a certain point, however, it may become plain that a person simply will not believe no matter how clear or conclusive an answer has been given. Then comes the time to warn. This is the last of the four parts of remedying doubt and the one we will examine in this chapter.

It may well be that these occasions are rarer than some people think, and it would certainly be an injustice to mask a failure to help someone with the excuse that they refuse to be helped. Still, this can be the case, and it is as dangerous to ignore that fact as to exaggerate it. Sadly, the possibility remains that with all the time and love and understanding and careful answering in the world, and with every genuine rational reason for doubt cleared up, the person may still choose to doubt it. It is unmistakably his choice to doubt. The problem is no longer that he cannot believe but that he will not believe, and when this is clear the real problem has been smoked out. To be without an answer to doubt is one kind of problem, but to have an answer yet refuse to accept it is another. The real explanation is now separated from excuses, and the genuine responsibility for the doubt is cordoned off by itself.

The choice to doubt may be seen at different stages in different types of doubt. It is usually apparent earliest and most obviously in doubts that are rationalizations, but it is a sleeping danger in all doubt, and it is here that doubt's destructive potential lies. Doubt, as we have continually indicated, is the uncertain state of being in two minds, of being ambivalent, indecisive, irresolute, equivocal, of hedging one's bets between certainty and uncertainty, knowing and not knowing, faith and unbelief. This certainly has its own problems, but great as they are they are not the deepest problem. The deepest problem is that doubt will not stay that way for ever. At some point a person cannot help coming down on one side or the other, either on the side of faith or on the side of unbelief. When he does, he is no longer open but closed.

Both the comfort and the warning of doubt lie in the fact that doubt is not final but temporary, not static but dynamic. The logic of doubt has the force of a question-mark. It is always asking, Will faith resolve doubt or will doubt dissolve faith? The dynamics of doubt are the dynamics of rolling dice, a spinning roulette wheel, a coin tossed in the air. For a moment they hover between one thing and another, between 3 and 6, heads or tails; the next moment there is no question. Doubt too is up in the air, but it will not stay there for ever. Sooner or later it will come down either as faith or as unbelief. There are no other possibilities.

Of course, doubt is different from dice or a coin because the crucial factor is not chance but choice. Here we are back to the same sobering point. If someone chooses to doubt in the face of every possible answer to his doubt, then the logic and consequence of his settled choice lie in one direction only – unbelief. So the real danger of doubt is not in what it does but in where it goes. If doubt is bad when it is uncertain and unsettling, it is far worse when it is settled and certain unbelief.

Terminal doubt

Doubt is double-minded, but since it will not stay that way for ever, no one may doubt everything all the time. We must believe something in order to doubt anything. So we can 'doubt for ever' only something which is not essential. But over the essential things of life we are forced to come to some conclusion for the sake of our own world view, without which we could not live or function.

This is where the central issue of doubt comes up again. Is doubt to dissolve faith or is faith to resolve doubt? For however long the mind is in two minds, it will eventually be 'made up' one way or the other. However much it feels 'up in the air', it will eventually 'come down' somewhere. Even if the debate is lengthened by the most protracted filibustering, the motion is bound to come to vote sometime. And the more crucial a place the question has in the doubter's life, the more it is impossible to abstain. So the answer to faith's motion can only be aye or nay.

When doubting is in its terminal stage, be prepared for the solemn responsibility of warning a person. However genuine or deep the doubts originally were, and however cogent and compassionate have been the answers put forward, a stage may be reached when every justifiable reason for doubting has been removed (and possibly several unjustifiable ones too). Yet the doubter still deliberately chooses to doubt rather than to believe. This is the moment when doubt is in mortal danger of becoming unbelief. It may call itself doubt for a long while afterwards, but the undecided openness which is characteristic of doubt has gone. There may still be undecided openness towards possible new beliefs (though strictly speaking this is not doubt so much as agnosticism), but in relation to the old belief the decision is made and the mind is closed.

When that happens (and only God knows *exactly* when it happens; all we sometimes see are the results), the stage of doubting is followed by the state of unbelief. 'While there's life there's hope!' could be rendered here as 'While there's doubt there's faith!' While the door is open even a crack, the possibility of faith is not excluded. But when the door clicks shut on faith, however quietly, unbelief has won. What was once a sudden cry of doubt has choice by choice matured into a settled creed of unbelief.

If faith and unbelief mean nothing at all, this moment will be of little consequence. But if the difference between faith and unbelief is the difference between light and darkness, and is decisive for our whole lives, then this moment makes all the difference. This is appreciated by the biblical writers and helps to explain the seriousness with which they view what is virtually the last stop on the line before unbelief, the stage of discontented grumbling or murmuring.

The New Testament word for this (*gonguzo*) is a Greek word with onomatopoeic roots which captures well the complaining groundswell of grumbling. In its secular usage the word describes a legal claim arising from discontent of someone who feels he is not receiving his due. But as it was generally used by the Greeks, it said nothing at all about the objective grounds of the claim. It is used more often of a thankless grumbler or a grasping opportunist than of someone who has genuine grounds for complaint.

In the Septuagint the same Greek word is used as the opposite of the word *obey*. It speaks of a disobedience and deliberate unbelief which has no way of denying God intellectually but which sullenly drags its feet at every opportunity and keeps up a grumbling murmur of dissatisfaction which is the nearest it can come to rejecting God. The word is especially important since it is used to translate the Hebrew word *lûn*, which is crucial in the classic description of Israel's murmuring against God in Exodus 15–17 and Numbers 14–16.

Almost as an entire nation the people of God were in two minds. They felt caught between their past in Egypt and their future in the Promised Land. Instead of maintaining a disciplined tension of faith strung between promise and fulfilment, between word and action, they collapsed and sagged limply into thankless grumbling and complaining. This is given voice in a series of petulant claims that justice is not being done and that God must fulfil his promise completely and at once.

The net result of their complaining is the creation of a contemptuous picture of God. He is reduced to the level of man – stripped, relegated and demoted, without sovereignty, without mystery, without judgement. It is this that God deals with, both as a challenge and as an affront. Faith honours God as God and lets God be God, but the murmuring which is the last stop before unbelief denies everything about God short of denying his existence. Man's estimate of things is made out to be more real or more just than God himself. The order of creation is reversed and man plays god to God. Man calls the shots and directs the shooting. This attitude of disobedience, although it stops short of denying God, is at the heart of the murmuring which characterized the perennial obstinacy of God's people.

But no Christian has reason to throw stones. We are not exempt from the same possibility. Writing to those under the New Covenant, the apostle Paul in 1 Corinthians gives a sobering list of warnings from Old Testament history, and he uses the same Greek word to drive home his lesson: 'Do not grumble against God, as some of them did.'

We face the same danger as they did, for our own expectations can be so moulded by our desires that we grow restive and are quick to demand rather than to ask, and grumble if we do not receive. If God's way, God's actions, God's timing do not fit in with the way we see things or want things, then so much the worse for God. We have a case against him, a grievance which can be taken to court, and grumbling is a way of letting everybody know the legitimacy of our case.

Crossing the frontier

Grumbling is not the only way that doubt can beat a respectable retreat into unbelief. In fact, it is more common in cultures or periods when Christian faith is so identified with the intellectual consensus that there are almost no intellectual alternatives to faith. Disbelief is then forced into a sullen attitude of reluctance or grudging complaint that lacks the finesse of a rationally arguable alternative to faith. Our own age, of course, is not like that; today there is no shortage of arguable alternatives. This is probably why the more obvious style of 'grumbling into unbelief' is found more rarely today and usually in the areas or pockets where the Christian faith is still held strongly.

Some Christian families are a prime example. Think of an older teenager dragged off reluctantly to church or forced to sit quietly through family prayers. The expressions of restlessness or recalcitrance backed up by low, almost inaudibly muttered comments show that no other options may be open, yet there is always the protest of grumbling.

But where a thousand alternatives to faith do exist and are openly bidding to take over at the first sign of doubt, the retreat from doubt to unbelief is a much more refined and sophisticated process. The essential movement and ultimate direction are the same as with grumbling, but the psychological and intellectual camouflage is vastly improved. Bring on the heavy artillery of 'Modern scholarship now holds . . . ,' 'Ever since Freud it has been impossible to believe that . . . ,' and even the strongest claims to faith feel the ground tremble. How easy it is then to disbelieve!

Someone may reject Christ because he prefers the playboy philosophy. But then let him say so. He has no right to say that he is rejecting Christ because he no longer believes in the resurrection. The latter is dishonest and his bluff must be called. The better the camouflage the harder it is to detect doubt's swift run to cross the border into unbelief.

Still, there are other signs, less obvious, perhaps, than open grumbling but just as plain to the discerning listener. One sign is the telltale way in which questions are asked, for though he wants no answers he does not stop raising questions. In fact, he raises question after question, but his aim is not so much to find the truth as to call in question. The questions are placed like a series of carefully laid smoke bombs, designed to cover a well-planned line of retreat. Their aim is not so much to find something as to fence off something, not so much to get to grips with the problem but to get out of the grip of the answer.

By throwing blame on God, by charging God with a lie, by sueing God for breach of promise or lecturing God on his failings, he raises clouds of smoke and successfully manoeuvres his retreat. Martin Luther touched on this: '[There is] no poorer, lowlier, and more despised pupil on earth than God. He must be everybody's disciple. Everybody wants to be his schoolmaster and teacher.'

Another sign is the uneasy apprehension when the reality of God's presence is felt, for there is still some fear of God in unbelief. Both faith and unbelief are able to ignore or drown out the fear of God most of the time (the former to its loss and the latter to its gain). But they cannot do it all the time. So when God's presence is unmistakably real, each has its own reaction.

The two types of fear are as different as night from day. The fear of God in the believer draws him nearer, whereas the fear of God in the unbeliever drives him back. The fear of God makes the believer search himself, whereas the fear of God in the unbeliever quickly accuses God before he can be accused. The fear of God in the believer makes him trust, whereas the fear of God in the unbeliever makes him frightened and suspicious. As Pascal puts it, 'The right fear comes from faith, false fear from doubt... Some fear to lose Him, others to find Him.'

The demarcation between doubt and unbelief is like a frontier between two countries. Sometimes it is difficult to know when one has reached it. Have you ever driven in Europe? Some of the signs marking the border are imposing and unmistakeable but others on the smaller roads are nondescript and easy to miss. Some loom up suddenly, without any warning, while others never seem to come at all, and over the last twenty kilometres a dozen or more petrol stations are able to advertise themselves as the 'last petrol this side of the border!'

In a similar way it is easy to miss the frontier between someone's doubt and unbelief or to realize suddenly that without any prior warning you are there. But if that point should come, it is our solemn responsibility to warn the person about what he is doing and what the consequences of his decision are. There are few times in life so solemn as the moment when a person faces up to what he knows of God's truth consciously intending to turn away.

Checklist

What should be our response to a person in this situation? On the one hand, we should be held back by reluctance, a sense of God's restraint that acts to curb the impulsive or wrong reasons for which we might attempt the right thing. Here are some questions to act as a simple checklist. Are we as certain as we can be that we are right, that this stage has been reached? A warning like this is far too serious to use as a shot in the dark or as an expression of sour grapes that comes from our failure to help. The right truth at the wrong moment is not only pointless when it is given, it is often blunted for later moments.

Another question: Are our motives clear? No motive in this life will be absolutely pure, but certainly the fully- or half-conscious wrong motives cripple our attempts to help people and make a mockery of the truths and principles we set out to defend. If there is pride, resentment or jealousy in our hearts when a warning is needed, we will either be afraid to say anything at all ('I am *just* as bad as he is, so what right do I have to say anything?'), or we will say something but in a wrong and unhelpful spirit. These are the particular expressions at *this* stage of the old error of being too soft or too hard on doubt.

(Most subtle of all is the self-righteousness which grows when a humble, helpful spirit seeks to say what is right, is sure it has said what is right and then takes pride in being sure it has said what is right!)

A third question is this: Are we as clear as we need to be about what we are saying? The mistake to avoid here is to say what we have no right to say, what it is none of our business to say, or what is quite beyond the scope of our knowledge to say. We are definitely *not* to say precisely where the person is standing before God at that moment. Nor can we say how God will judge that person ultimately. These are beyond our knowledge, and they are God's business anyway, not ours.

We are not sitting in judgement on him; we are saying something about judgement to him. By saying too much we are not only in danger of being wrong but of taking on ourselves a responsibility which should be his. On the other hand, in saying the right thing and in refusing to go beyond our brief we are helping him to understand the situation and we are challenging him to face his responsibility.

This is not easy. The doubter-turning-unbeliever is doing wrong, but unless he faces up to it, he is likely to mask his guilt by flinging back at us the accusation that we are judgemental, authoritarian or just plain meddlesome. This can hurt our pride or undermine our confidence, making us retreat from the exposure which confrontation involves. That is why these questions are important. In clearing away the clutter of wrong motivations and approaches, they free us to speak in love with quiet, direct authority.

The questions should make us cautious. But to balance the deep reluctance they bring remember that we have an equally heavy responsibility to speak out. Every person is ultimately responsible for his own position before God, but to know that a person is in this position and *do nothing* is to share that responsibility before God. We will have been watchmen who gave no warning. We are not guilty of anyone else's sins, but we are answerable to God for our uncaring silence. This responsibility for what we know, which is a burning drive in all evangelism, is just as important in confronting doubt. If ever someone stands poised between life and death, it is at this moment when his doubt is changing into unbelief.

The strength of what we say comes from the various strands we weave together in our warning. The first strand is concerned with making sure that all rationalizations in the doubt are shown up for what they are. The doubter must see that his camouflage is discovered. No one is taken in by the false reasons he is giving for his doubt. If he is allowed to get away with it and his dishonesty remains unchallenged, his position will have a lie at its heart and his heart will be impervious to the truth. If the lie is accepted and the doubt is rationalized, it will have a justifiable explanation. But when the rationalization is exposed, the well-insulated explanation becomes an obviously bad excuse.

The second strand of our warning comes in pointing out to the person the real reason for his doubt. In doing this the false reasons are stripped away and the attention is focussed on the real reason. Why is the person doubting? Is it a mask to conceal guilt? Is Christianity being rejected only because it stands between him and something he wants? The doubter must be allowed no illusions. He must be given no hiding-place. As God says to Israel through Ezekiel, 'You say that the Lord acts without principle? Listen, you Israelites, it is you who act without principle, not I.'

The third strand woven into the warning comes in pointing out the consequences of unbelief. We suggested earlier that not only should doubt be stopped in its tracks but that we should indicate where those doubts lead. If we have done this, then to repeat and amplify the warning here is natural and not unexpected. It is not that we are suddenly 'getting nasty' (as it is easy to do when others find unconvincing what we are convinced by), but that we are developing the fuller significance of a truth already mentioned.

The burden of this is sobering, for what we are saying to the doubter is that he is free to choose but that God will leave him to the consequences of his own settled choice. This, in fact, is what God's judgement is. So the judgement of a person's own belief is not arbitrary but self-chosen. This needs to be expressed and applied to the immediate situation until its lesson comes home.

The last strand woven into the warning is an emphasis on the promise of God's forgiveness and restoration *at any stage* if there is true repentance and faith (backed also by an offer to help and to pray at any stage). Without this final strand our warning will have no specifically Christian content. We will be no better than Jonah who was willing to pronounce God's judgement but unwilling to share his mercy. Forgiveness and restoration are, after all, the whole point of the warning. What we say about judgement is true, so there is no manipulation in saying it. But our interest is not in the factual starkness of the truth but in the truth rightly responded to. The emphasis on what the situation *is* is only in the interests of what the situation *might be*. This above all makes the risk of such grave speaking worthwhile. There are few joys like the joy of seeing someone turn back to faith at this late stage.

This brings us full circle in the problem of doubt – from faith through doubt to faith again, or from faith through doubt to unbelief. There is no other place to end. Between the single-mindedness of faith and the single-mindedness of unbelief, doubt is the loss of vision, the blurring of focus which makes two minds out of one. And this leaves only one question: Is this faith one that will mean the resolution of doubt or is this doubt one that will mean the dissolution of faith? All the compassion, clarity and cogency of our persuasion and our prayers is to weigh down the scales in favour of the former.

Part Four

Two Difficult
Doubts

Chapter Sixteen

Keyhole Theology
Doubt from insistent inquisitiveness

Have you ever determined not to do something and then gone back on your original intention? Sometimes you prove two things at once – that your original intention was wise yet that without breaking it you would have missed something. So far we have steadily refused to be sidetracked into a full discussion of any particular doubt. Perhaps now with the main burden of the discussion completed, we can relax and look at two common specific doubts.

For some people these two examples may prove helpful in themselves. For others they will only illustrate my earlier point: doubting in general can be discussed adequately in print, but specific doubts are answered better by talking to people.

The two doubts I have chosen are common, and serious enough to be a problem even for the strongest believers. The first is the doubt of insistent inquisitiveness, or as it might be called 'keyhole theology'.

Think of detective stories and the importance of keyholes in the days before electronic eavesdropping. Far more than a mere security device a keyhole was a unique source of information. Without it what lay behind the heavy door was a mystery. With it a glimpse into the room was possible and so was a chance to hear the conversation inside. How many criminal trials, at least in novels, have turned upon the evidence of a keyhole?

But keyholes can be as misleading as they are useful. The few words overheard may be vital – but what if the context which explained them is lost? What if there is a mysterious other person in the conversation, sitting just out of sight? Who is he? What is he saying? Use the keyhole to jump to a wrong conclusion and you may be further off track than if there is no keyhole at all.

Franz Kafka captures this in *The Castle*. Minor servants

grew desperate after the lifelong attempts to get beyond the impersonal outer circle of castle bureaucracy. To compensate for their loss of dignity and hope they fell back on a fantasy world of absurdly-involved and pathetic explanations, a world where guesswork stood in for knowledge, where elaborate arguments were built on silences and firm conclusions were drawn from a glance or a raised eyebrow.

As the hero K says to Pepi, 'You chambermaids are used to spying through keyholes and from that you get this way of thinking, of drawing conclusions, as grand as they are false about the whole situation from some little thing you really see.'

That is the trouble with keyholes. You don't always see enough to come to a conclusion, but once you've seen a little it's difficult to resist trying. This mistake is the essence of keyhole theology. There are times when we see glimpses of God's ways but not enough to allow us to make conclusions about what he is doing and why. Yet we cannot resist jumping to conclusions. Being insistent as well as inquisitive, we refuse to suspend judgement and our wrong conclusions so misrepresent God that we end by doubting him.

Suspended judgement

What exactly does it mean for faith to suspend judgement? Could this be a well disguised form of irrationality smuggled in at a late hour? Perhaps doubt is a problem of too much thinking after all? Emphatically not. The hoary rumour that doubt is a problem of too much thinking has surely been laid to rest. Most doubts, as we have seen, have far more to do with wrong thinking or no thinking at all than with too much thinking. In each case a genuinely critical, mature way of thinking has an essential role to play in pointing towards the remedy. To think and not understand is one problem; not to think and have no chance of understanding is a greater one. A keen mind will rarely remain idle and satisfied. If the faith by which it lives does not allow it room to move, the mind is apt to exact its own revenge. A good mind denied by bad faith will self-destruct with insecurity, guilt, fanaticism or doubt.

The Christian wholeheartedly supports genuine rationality. But we must add a qualification to give this balance. Christianity is second to none in the place it gives to reason, but it is also second to none in keeping reason in its place. We never know the value of a thing until we know its limits. Put unlimited value on something and in the end you will exhaust it of all value. This is as true of reason as it is of natural resources such as oil.

This is why Christianity is thoroughly rational but not the least bit rationalistic. It also explains the curious fact that it is rationalism, and not Christian faith which leads to irrationality. If we forget the limits of a thing, we fly in the face of reality and condemn ourselves to learn the simple, ironic lesson: more without limits is less; less with limits is more.

We have emphasized all along that the Christian faith is warranted belief and is therefore profoundly rational. This means that we have sure and sufficient reasons at the point of coming to know God (the point of original assent), but this is not the case for every question in life. Man is finite and the world is fallen, so there will be many areas of mystery that are opaque to a searcher, however curious or persistent he is. At such times we see through a glass darkly or, as it were, through a keyhole partially. It is not that it is rational to come to believe and irrational to continue to believe, as if the break between rationality and irrationality were a matter of time and stages. Rather the truth is this: we can always have sure and sufficient reasons for knowing why we can trust God, but we cannot always know what God is doing and why.

To put it another way, the rationality of faith is implacably opposed to absurdity but has no quarrel with mystery; it can tell the difference between the two. Christianity's contention with rationalism is not that it has too much reason in it, but that it has very little else. When a Christian comes to faith his understanding and his trust go hand in hand, but as he continues in faith his trust may sometimes be called to go on by itself without his understanding.

This is where the principle of suspended judgement applies. At such times if the Christian's faith is to be itself and let God be God, it must suspend judgement and say, 'Father I do not understand you, but I trust you.'

Notice what this means. A Christian does not say, 'I do not understand you at all, but I trust you anyway.' Rather he says, 'I do not understand you *in this situation*, but *I un-*

derstand why I trust you anyway. Therefore I can trust that you understand even though I don't.' The former is a mystery unrelieved by rationality and indistinguishable from absurdity; the latter is a statement of the rationality of faith walking hand-in-hand with the mystery of faith. So the principle of suspended judgement is not irrational. It is not a leap of faith but a walk of faith. As believers we cannot always know why, but we can always know why we trust God who knows why, and this makes all the difference.

The only snag with this is the obvious one: what is eminently reasonable in theory is rather more difficult in practice. In practice the pressure of mystery acts on faith like the insistent chafing of a painful rub. It isn't just that we would like to know what we do not know but that we feel we must know what we cannot know. The one produces frustration because curiosity is denied; the other leads to genuine anguish. More specifically, the poorer our understanding is in coming to faith the more necessary it will be to understand everything after coming to faith. If we do not know why we trust God, then we will always need to know exactly what God is doing in order to trust him. Failing to grasp that, we may not be able to trust him, for anything we do not understand may count decisively against what we are able to trust.

If, on the other hand, we do know why we trust God, we will be able to trust him in situations where we do not understand what he is doing. For what God is doing may be ambiguous, but it will not be inherently contradictory. It may be mystery to us, but mystery is only inscrutable; what would be insufferable is absurdity.

Let's change the picture from a detective story to a wartime situation. In a fallen world a believer is in the same position as a patriot in a country occupied by a foreign power. If he resists, he faces not only the enemy but the torturing questions raised by the moral ambiguities in the only style of opposition open to him. The anomalies and dilemmas of this are captured in Basil Mitchell's celebrated parable of the resistance fighter:

> In time of war in an occupied country, a member of the resistance meets one night a Stranger who deeply impresses him. They spend that night together in conversa-

tion. The Stranger tells the partisan that he himself is on the side of the resistance – indeed that he is in command of it, and urges the partisan to have faith in him no matter what happens. The partisan is utterly convinced at that meeting of the Stranger's sincerity and constancy and undertakes to trust him.

They never meet in conditions of intimacy again. But sometimes the Stranger is seen helping members of the resistance, and the partisan is grateful and says to his friends 'He is on our side.' Sometimes he is seen in the uniform of the police handing over patriots to the occupying power. On these occasions his friends murmur against him: but the partisan still says, 'He is on our side.' He still believes that, in spite of appearances, the Stranger did not deceive him. Sometimes he asks the Stranger for help and receives it. He is then thankful. Sometimes he asks and does not receive it. Then he says, 'The Stranger knows best.'

A situation like this is not easy for war-time faith, and talk of the theoretical difference between ambiguity and contradiction is apt to sound academic and comfortless. Other questions matter much more. Is God really on our side? How can we tell when he is in disguise? Isn't it dangerously confusing if he seems to dress up as the enemy? Why does he sometimes appear to be flying the wrong flag? Surely we cannot *only* trust? Can't we also know? What if we have been duped, deceived, led into a trap, betrayed? Can we trust a God who seems to behave like a divine Pimpernel, popping up in the strangest of disguises, using the most paradoxical of means? Unless he shows some stability or continuity that we can see, how can we rely on him, how can he be counted on? How can we know he is different from the eastern notion of god which turns life's reality into a fancy dress ball and human personalities into the multi-million disguises and fantasies of the divine? In short, how do we know God can be trusted?

At root there are only two basic questions for faith – Is God there? and Is God good? But it is precisely the answers to these questions which are most savagely mauled by the mystery of evil. If faith is not strong enough to suspend judgement, it will press reason and logic too far and create such a distortion of God in its own mind that either this god would be the devil (Baudelaire) or else the only excuse for such a god would be that he doesn't exist (Stendahl). The dilemma of the believer in a fallen world is like this. Expressing the crisis of meaning which exile in Babylon meant for the faithful Jews, Jeremiah used this very picture: 'The Lord played an enemy's part and overwhelmed Israel.'

This is where the principle of suspended judgement operates. Face to face with mystery, and especially the mystery of evil, the faith that understands why it has come to trust must trust where it has not come to understand. Faith does not know why in terms of the *immediate*, but it knows why it trusts God who knows why in terms of the *ultimate*.

The resistance leader knows best; he can be trusted through thick and thin since he is not a stranger but a friend. Jesus said to his disciples before his crucifixion, 'You do not understand now what I am doing, but one day you will.'

So the suspended judgement is not irrational. It stems from sufficient understanding, and it will result in complete understanding. For the moment it need not insist. It can trust. At such times everything around us will pressure us or call on us to make judgements. The situation may be riddled with apparent contradictions, but since we know that not all the facts are available, it is not only wrong but foolish to make judgements and press reason too far. As Martin Luther advised in such situations, 'Faith should close its eyes and should not judge or decide according to what it feels or sees.'

Two aspects of suspending judgement must be emphasized. The first is that it should never be confused with an embargo on asking questions. There is nothing wrong with raising questions, pursuing possible answers and searching for evidence. All these are processes of thought which stop short of making judgements. The problem is not that the judgements of faith are themselves improper, let alone blasphemous, for judgements are part and parcel of the thinking process which God has given us. The problem in this situation is not that we make judgements on God but that we make judgements at all when we have insufficient grounds on which to do so. Once again it is not the result of too much thinking but of the wrong sort of thinking.

Notice also how it is that the fallacy of making an unfounded judgement grows into the blasphemy of making a judgement on God. The real temptation to doubt does not come in *not believing* God but in believing what is *not God*. The danger is that we press judgement too far and our speculation creates such a distorted picture of God that we cannot continue to believe in good faith. To believe the wrong thing is always halfway to believing nothing. Our misrepresentations of God are so pathetically inadequate or monstrously hideous that to believe in him any longer is unnecessary or repugnant. Even in the middle of his grief C. S. Lewis was able to recognize this.

> Not that I am (I think) in much danger of ceasing to believe in God. The real danger is in coming to believe such dreadful things about Him. The conclusion I dread is not 'so there is no God after all' but 'so this is what God is really like. Deceive yourself no longer.'

In the dark

There are two situations that make it especially difficult to suspend judgement. The first is when it seems that God is not guiding us. If we were able to be more logical under pressure, the question would not be 'Can God guide me?' or 'Has God guided me?' but 'Is God guiding me *now*?' However, the thrust of the predicament is so immediate and so insistent that the logical distinction is blurred. If it seems that God is not guiding me now – and if this is sufficiently painful, it is easy to forget that he has guided before and hard not to wonder if he is able to guide at all.

The pressure is painful because of a feeling that God is not guiding us at the very moment when so much is at stake. If his honour is not in question, then at least our lives and reputations are. Everything in us becomes very emphatic. We need to know in order to decide. We cannot juggle factors indefinitely or delay a decision for ever. It's embarrassing to be unable to answer the inquiries of our friends. It's demoralizing to lose a sense of direction and feel we are drifting. Have we missed the way by mistake? Have we done something wrong?

There is no end to such haunting questions, and the longer they are unanswered the louder they mock. Faith tosses and turns like a man delirious in a fever. Everything has become unreal, nothing is impossible. Doesn't God care?

Is God there after all or have we been mistaken all along?
Everything screams at us to choose, to decide, to act, just to
do something. If only there were a word, a sign, a token,
anything at all from God to help. But there is only silence
and impenetrable darkness.

Bunyan's Pilgrim experienced this when Atheist mocked
him about his journey to the Celestial City. Hearing that he
was heading for Mount Zion, Atheist roared with laughter
and Christian was shaken by his explanation:

Christian   What is the meaning of your laughter?

Atheist   I laugh to see what ignorant persons you are,
to take upon you so tedious a journey and yet
are like to have nothing but travel for your
pains.

Christian   Why man? Do you think we shall not be received?

Atheist   Received! There is no such place as you
dream of in all the world.

Scorn is a deadly argument and Atheist's taunt makes
Christian wonder. But Bunyan's point is not only that scepticism can stir doubts in a believer but that every believer
has his own private sceptic sitting in on the inner delibera-
tions of his heart. For long periods he may be silent, voted
down in argument or quieted by reason, but give him just a
few moments of uncertainty over guidance and he will be up
on his feet again, questioning vociferously. Are we really being guided as we thought? How do we know we're on the
right track? Is there any such destination as the place we
think we're going to?

Here faith may have to suspend judgement on what God
is doing. Faith may not know why, but it knows why it trusts
God who knows why. We do not trust God because he guides
us; we trust God and then are guided, which means that we
can trust God even when we do not seem to be guided by
him. Faith may be in the dark about guidance, but it is never
in the dark about God. What God is doing may be mystery,
but who God is is not. So faith can remain itself and retain
its integrity by suspending judgement. Jesus underwrites
such faith when he promises, 'I am the light of the world.
No follower of mine shall wander in the dark.'

Jesus does not say that we will never *walk* in the dark,

but that we need not *wander* in the dark, or have a way of life at home in darkness – a distinction which sounds trivial if you don't know what it is to feel the anguish of such a situation. The darkness is no less dark and the dilemma no less agonizing, but neither is ultimate, for the outcome lies with God. This has been the experience of countless believers who have suspended judgement although they did not know the whys and wherefores of God's guidance. Part of Job's dilemma was at this point:

> If I go forward, he is not there;
> if backward, I cannot find him;
> when I turn left I do not descry him;
> I face right, but I see him not.
> But he knows me in action or at rest;
> When he tests me, I prove to be gold.
> My feet have kept to the path he has set me.

David writes, 'Even though I walk through a valley dark as death I fear no evil, for thou art with me.' But perhaps the most illuminating biblical example is Isaiah's challenge:

> Which of you fears the Lord and obeys his servant's commands?
> The man who walks in dark places with no light,
> yet trusts in the name of the Lord and leans on his God.
> But you who kindle a fire and set fire-brands alight,
> go, walk into your own fire.

The believer who trusts God and suspends judgement is contrasted with the man who cannot trust God and therefore must create his own light with his own self-made sparks rather than trust God and wait in the dark. Jeremiah in Lamentations speaks of the same predicament: 'It was I whom he [God] led away and left to walk in darkness, where no light is.'

A situation like this is easy from every perspective except the inside – and that, unfortunately, is the one that counts. Anticipated in theory or remembered in the past, the menace is negligible – no worse than a fog rolling back in the sun or a nightmare that recedes when we wake. Everything is always so obvious afterwards. God's ways are not our ways. God's thoughts really are higher than our thoughts. That is when we can say with Augustine, 'You were guiding me as a

helmsman steers a ship, but the course you steered was beyond my understanding.' But the hard question is whether
we can say, 'Father I do not understand you, but I trust you'
while we are *still in the darkness*. That is the challenge faith
faces in suspending judgement, and that is the time doubt
raises its voice.

Through fire and rain

The second situation, even more devastating, is the experience of suffering, whether physical or mental. Pain and suffering can be considered from many angles, all of which
should be adequately explained to give a comprehensive
answer to the questions they raise. But our interest here is
not with ultimate metaphysical questions, nor with wider
practical approaches in facing it, but with the narrower
question of the doubt that we experience when we trust God
and suspend judgement.

Suffering is the most acute trial that faith can face, and
the questions it raises are the sharpest, the most insistent
and the most damaging that faith will meet. Here as nowhere else the supreme challenge is issued to suspend judgement. The basic principle is the same (we do not know why
but we know why we trust God who knows why) and our
basic prayer is the same ('Father, I do not understand you,
but I trust you'), but the price we are asked to pay is unique.

Can faith bear the pain and trust God, suspending judgement and resting in the knowledge that God is there, God
is good and God knows best? Or will the pain be so great
that only meaning will make it endurable so that reason
must be pressed further and further and judgements must be
made? To suspend judgement not only seems hard but ridiculous. At first it makes the problem worse. To suffer is one
thing, to suffer without meaning is another, but to suffer and
choose not to press for any meaning is different again. Yet
that is the suicidal submission that faith's suspension of
judgement seems to involve.

As suffering continues, the fire heats, the temperature
mounts, the pressure increases, and the unbearable anguish
threatens to choke faith and turn its cry into a scream of
doubt. To suspend judgement and simply trust is the hardest thing. Faith must reach deep into its reserves of courage

and endurance if the rising panic of incomprehensible pain is not to be overwhelming.

In Job we have the world's classic sufferer, the one in whom every sufferer knows he has at least one brother. But much of Job's agony was that he was racked by this very dilemma. Was he to trust God and suspend judgement, or was he to doubt in pressing for an explanation? At first he passed the test with honours. Disaster hit him, his children were killed and his fortunes ruined, but his faith in God remained undeterred. 'Throughout all this Job did not sin; he did not charge God with unreason.' Job did not know why, but he knew why he trusted God who knew why, and in suspending judgement he trusted. The resistance leader knew what he was doing.

But this, of course, was only the first round of the testing and, as events unfolded, agony was piled on agony and there was no relief. His wife encouraged him to curse God and die; his friends accused him heartlessly; his brothers held aloof; his relatives faded away; his servants forgot him; his slaves refused to answer him; children despised him; and he came to stink in the nostrils of his own family.

Each degree of mounting pressure served to heighten the dilemma. If he trusted God and suspended judgement, he had to be silent. But every moment he continued in silence was taken as a tacit admission of his guilt. Yet to defend himself he had to explain the suffering, and to do this he had to press reason to conclusions he had no desire to entertain and no right to make. This tension was the torturous rack on which Job's faith was stretched to the breaking-point. It is little wonder that his self-defence is a demonstration of faith mixed with doubt.

On the one hand, Job's faith reached heights of unrivalled courage, as when he cried, 'But in my heart I know that my vindicator lives and that he will rise last to speak in court.' On the other hand, his chosen style of defence led him into the bitter blackness of self-pity and doubt, as wrong as it is understandable. In his reply God rebuked Job for defending himself in a way that accused God: 'Dare you deny that I am just or put me in the wrong that you may be right?' In doing this Job had dissolved the moral universe in one stroke and had brought down upon himself even more spiritual agony because he had made himself out to be more just than God.

What was the root of Job's mistake in not suspending judgement? Was it his blasphemy? Not really. That was only the result. At the root of his problem lay a fallacy in his thinking (the notion that he had enough information to make proper judgements in such a situation). Once this fallacy was accepted, the blasphemy was an inevitable result. If this is so, it is curious to see that both Job and his friends made a very similar mistake.

Job's friends believed that God in his justice pays every man his desserts *in this life*, and therefore they presupposed a one-to-one ratio between sin and suffering: Job was suffering; Job must have sinned. Job roundly denies this. But in the absence of any knowledge of a final judgement *after death* he has no way to deny it. So in defending himself he demands from God a one-to-one ratio between suffering and explanation, between pain and meaning. Thus both Job and his friends press reason too far and make judgements where they have no right to. The two errors lead in opposite directions, but they are both minted from the same coin.

Jeremiah shows us a different way altogether in Lamentations. Experiencing a personal crisis at the thrust of his ministry brought him deeper into misunderstanding, he cries, 'He has broken my teeth on gravel; fed on ashes, I am wracked with pain; peace has gone out of my life.' But Jeremiah does not go on to judge God and demand an explanation. Instead he rests his case with God and suspends judgement for the moment. He adds, 'The Lord, I say, is all that I have; therefore I will wait for him patiently.'

John Bunyan makes a similar point in *Pilgrim's Progress* when Interpreter takes Christian and shows him a fire burning in a grate, with a man standing in front of the fire flinging water on it. For some reason the fire does not go out but blazes higher and higher. Interpreter then takes Christian behind the wall and shows him the secret. A second man is secretly applying oil to the fire to counter the work of the man with the water. Seen from one side nothing but water is put on the fire, but it still blazes higher because the oil is more effective than the water, even though it is secret.

Interpreter explains that the fire is a picture of the work of God in our lives. The man on the outside with the water (who is all that can be seen) represents the Devil, while the man with the oil can behind the wall represents the work of Christ in maintaining faith. Interpreter concludes, 'And in that thou sawest that the man has stood behind the wall to maintain the fire, this is to teach thee that it is hard for the tempted to see how this work of grace is maintained in the soul.'

Knowing why?

There is one thing we must not skate over too quickly, or in our haste we may not notice until too late that the ice is thin. If suspended judgement turns on the principle 'we do not know why but we know why we trust God who knows why', it is all-important that we *do know why we trust God*. 'Of course,' we say, 'I know why I trust him!' but this can be the sort of self-assurance which wears threadbare after the first few moments of suffering.

Sometimes we have no way of knowing how much strain our faith can take until we actually suffer. Only then do we know whether our faith is grounded where it should be. Very few of us pass the test of suffering well. When the chips are down and we do not know why we can trust God, we may find very soon that we do not see why we should.

I must emphasize that a full discussion of how we are able to trust God is beyond our concern here. What matters here is to show how significant trust in God can be in a time of suffering.

First, I must repeat that if all religious issues were boiled down to their essence, there would be two inescapable questions: Is God there? and What is he like? Our view of the existence of God and the character of God are the truths which determine all our other answers.

For the Christian there is no completely satisfying answer to the question 'How may I be sure that God is there and that God is good?' which is not finally anchored in Jesus Christ. 'And 'proof' of God's existence or argument in favour of his goodness which ends elsewhere is bound to be inconclusive or wrong. However cogent and compelling they may seem as arguments, in the long run they will prove both intellectually weak and emotionally unsatisfying, and there is nothing like suffering to show up this flaw.

The test of suffering reveals whether our 'knowing why'

is an irreducible bedrock conviction grounded in the revelation of God in Jesus Christ, or whether our faith is resting to any degree on what is not foundation, but superstructure or just plain sand. In this connection we can make two equal, though opposite, mistakes, both of which end in making God so remote that we do not know why we can trust him in a time of suffering.

The first mistake is to see Jesus as so much one with God the Father that we forget that God became man in Jesus and is one with us in our humanity. So there is no one who stands between God and man. The danger then is that God will become remote, in our feelings if not in our theology, and that in his remoteness his silence will be mistaken for his absence.

God's silence hurts. Human beings suffer, they look up, they cry out, they pray, they tear their hearts out, but there is no answer. The heavens are brass, the gates are locked, the phone is busy, and in the ringing nothingness of silence they wonder if God was ever there. 'Be not deaf to my cry,' says the Psalmist, 'Lest, if thou answer me with silence, I become like those who go down to the abyss.' Or as Gerard Manley Hopkins put it in his Last Sonnets:

> And my lament
> Is cries countless, cries like dead letters sent
> To dearest him that lives alas! away.

What is difficult enough for the believer who knows why he trusts God is almost unbearable for a believer who is uncertain or for a nominal believer. No generation bears more eloquent testimony to this than our own. In his play *The Devil and the Good Lord* Jean-Paul Sartre portrays Goetz, a butchering soldier-turned-saint who grows disillusioned by his spiritual ineffectiveness and God's silence. Eventually he wonders if his creed is true or whether it is only his own voice shouting out loud to cover God's silence. Finally he bursts out,

I prayed, I demanded a sign. I sent messages to Heaven, no reply. Heaven ignored my very name. Each minute I wonder what I could BE in the eyes of God. Now I know the answer: nothing. God does not see me, God does not hear me, God does not know me. You see this emptiness

over our heads? That is God. You see this gap in the door?
It is God. You see that hole in the ground? That is God
again. Silence is God. Absence is God. God is the loneliness of man.

This terrible cry of an uncertainty that trails off into unbelief is echoed many times in modern drama and literature.
But even this fades in comparison with the eyewitness
descriptions of those who have faced the silence of God in
real experience. One example is Elie Wiesel's account of
Auschwitz in *Night*. A Hungarian-born Jew, Elie Wiesel
was a survivor of both Auschwitz and Buchenwald, and his
book is a searing account of a small boy encountering un-
masked evil.

Never shall I forget that night, the first night in camp,
which has turned my life into one long night, seven times
cursed and seven times sealed.... Never shall I forget
those flames which consumed my faith forever. Never shall
I forget that nocturnal silence which deprived me, for all
eternity, of the desire to live. Never shall I forget those
moments which murdered my God and my soul and
turned my dream to dust. Never shall I forget these things,
even if I am condemned to live as long as God Himself.
Never.

And what of the Christian? Is he different because his
courage is greater or his theological explanations more
nimble? Far from it. A Christian too recoils from such a
snake-pit of evil. He feels the same pain, the same agony, the
same questions, the same silence. A Christian does not know
why either, but (and here alone is the difference) he knows
why he trusts God who knows why.

And how is this? Because of another Jew, a Jew not in his
youth, but in his prime, who freely took on himself the full
desolation of God's silence so that after suffering in our place
he might restore us to his Father, that then we might be
sure that God is there, and God is good.

For the Christian the cry of Jesus, 'My God, my God, why
hast thou forsaken me?' will always have depths of meaning
which the human mind can never fathom. But one thing at
least it means. No man can sink so low that God has not
gone lower still. As C. S. Lewis puts it, 'Sometimes it is hard

not to say "God forgive God." Sometimes it is hard to say so much. But if our faith is true, He didn't. He crucified him.' This is how it is that doubts about the Father are silenced in the Son. God may become remote to us in times of suffering if he is not 'the God and Father of our Lord Jesus Christ'.

Do you catch the intimacy in that little give-away description of God? Jesus was known and loved by the disciples. To them he was *our* Lord Jesus Christ. They had followed him, lived with him, learned from him. They loved him and they would lay down their lives for him. But who was God whom they had never seen? Quite simply he was 'Jesus Christ's Father', and so they called him 'the God, and Father of *our* Lord Jesus Christ'. Didn't Jesus himself say, 'Go to my brothers, and tell them that I am now ascending to my Father and your Father, my God and your God'? Hadn't he taught them to pray 'Our Father in Heaven'?

So the truth of the incarnation is not just good theology; it is practical comfort and assurance. Jesus identifies with us in our humanity, and now we know that God is for us in Christ. The Resistance leader can be trusted. He went through torture too.

This, however, can lead easily to the opposite mistake which is to see Jesus as so much one with our humanity that we forget that in his deity he is still one with God the Father. We may identify him so completely with ourselves that he is not the Father's volunteer but God's victim whose death is a meaningless sacrifice.

As this extreme sees it, Christ has become one with us, so in his greater suffering there is comfort to all lesser suffering; but the comfort is meagre and short-lived. Its value is relative and not absolute, for it has achieved nothing finally. God the Father is still angry and implacable, or distant and remote. So, although Christ's death is a magnificent statement, a heroic gesture and an inspiring symbol, it is essentially tragic, wasted and futile. After all, if he is not God, why should the death of one Jew be different from the death of six million other Jews?

Arthur Koestler's dramatic soliloquy *The Misunderstanding* is a typical modern expression of this mistake. It pictures Christ on the road to Calvary, carrying his cross painfully and issuing a challenge to God to look down from heaven and care or to look away for ever:

> Are you the one who is playing these games with Adam's seed? Or are you only absent-minded and asleep? Soon I shall know when this stake and I change places, when instead of me carrying it, it will carry me. That will be the test, your trial. Then I shall know.
>
> If that is the case and you are only distracted or asleep, I shall put your sleeve in my pain until you wake up and my purpose is achieved. But if you are that deaf and dumb spirit, then pulling your sleeve will be a gesture of a fool, and dying will be hard.

Is the cross just a vicious trap into which Jesus was led by God? Is it only a bad joke played on him by an indifferent deity? Is it merely a travesty of justice so extreme that protest and revolution will never want for a hero? Is Jesus God only because he is the poorest and most suffering of men? These are the questions which clamour for our attention if we make this second mistake. And it is obvious that, though dramatically opposed, the result is still the same. God is still remote, and his silence, which this time, is silence to Christ as well as ourselves, is taken as proof of his absence.

This extreme, like the other, depends on a caricature of Christ. It emphasizes only a half-truth. In contrast the Bible, which spares nothing in stressing Christ's identification with man, does not stop there. Jesus freely became man for a purpose – a purpose which cost God the Father as much as it did God the Son, a purpose which was successfully carried out and vindicated by the resurrection. Not surprisingly it is those whose faith in God is anchored in the incarnation – God become flesh, crucified, risen – whose faith can pass through the fires of suffering. For there is no question however deep or painful which cannot be trusted with the God who is the Father of Jesus Christ.

This is true not only of questions raised by suffering but also of unanswerable intellectual questions which tax the power of speculation by pushing it beyond its limits and raising anxiety for faith. (For example, Why did God create man if he knew that ... ?) There are questions which in this life are unanswerable. There are facts which we cannot explain but must never explain away. Faith can suspend judgement on these. There is no question which we cannot leave with God if he is the Father of Jesus Christ.

Injustice

It would be tempting to leave the question here – but impractical too, for the essence of suffering is experience, not thought. If the suspended judgement cannot be applied, it is useless. There are two situations where suspended judgement has practical applications. The first is when we suffer because of the injuries or hurts which come from other people.

The Christian view of life is not romantic but realistic. Life in the fallen world involves injuries. No one passes through unscathed. We will all be injured. We will all meet with injustices. Across the fabric of our lives thousands of these 'little murders' leave their marks of wear and tear. The challenge each time will be the same: Where we do not know why, will we trust God and suspend judgement or will we demand to know why and go on to say why anyway?

'But surely,' you say, 'when we suffer under other people, isn't it quite clear what is wrong? Why should we suspend judgement then? Wouldn't we do better to stand up for our rights and speak out against wrong?' This is a natural response perhaps, and not altogether wrong. In fact, it would be quite right were it not that in many situations we simply do not know exactly who was wrong and why.

For example, it is very easy to see that what the Nazis did was wrong, and it is not too difficult, though definitely harder, to see why they did it. But that still leaves other important questions unanswered: Why was it that those particular people suffered? Or, as the victims of the Nazis must have put it themselves: Why is this happening to us?

Just as long as there is one question like this still unanswered, there is at least one question on which human judgement must be suspended and moral judgement qualified. But our tendency is to make judgements on all questions regardless of whether we are able to or not. What then happens is that the judgements we are entitled to make are used to mask the judgements we are not entitled to make. So we make what would otherwise be perfectly good judgements but vitiate them with the concealed anger, resentment or rage which spills over from the bad judgements we have no right to make.

Thus under a pretence of morality we mystify our own wrong and perpetrate the evil and hypocrisy we are out to combat. For into the morality of the immediate judgement, which we have every right to make, we unconsciously inject the immorality of ultimate judgement, which we have no right to make.

One example of this, which is clear because it is so exaggerated, is the type of revolutionary fervour which tirades against the slightest injustice in a completely disproportionate manner. This is passionate but not moral. It is hardly a response to the immediate injustice and certainly not a very helpful one. The immediate injustice is little more than a peg on which is hung the full-blown rage at what is considered to be the ultimate absurdity and injustice of life or a particular social system. This is not only immature and hypocritical; it is also counter-productive. It destroys the possibility of justice it seeks to promote and has little value except to let off steam.

When suffering becomes entangled in the complex mesh of human relationships, it is not easy to make good judgements. Most people go ahead anyway, letting the chips fall where they may. Others search themselves so conscientiously that they end up in self-paralysis, afraid to make judgements at all. But if you are conscious of this dilemma, suspending judgement provides a short cut through this maze.

We are not primarily responsible to God for what another person does to us; he is responsible to God for that. We are responsible to God for our reaction to what others do for us. This is the key to the principle of responsibility in retaliation. If we forget this, not only will we be resentful rather than forgiving, reactionary rather than self-controlled, full of self-pity rather than trust; we will also make judgements when we have no right to make them.

In the Sermon on the Mount, Jesus said, 'You have learned that they were told, "Eye for eye, tooth for tooth." But what I tell you is this: Do not set yourself against the man who wrongs you.' This speaks directly to our hearts. If we set ourselves against someone, we will soon set ourselves *up* against him. What happens next will run according to the classic we/they rules. *We* suppress our own wrong and forget it or project it onto *them*, so that when *we* judge *them* (even if only in the hollow but psychologically vital internal judgements), we make judgements we have no right to make. We will in fact be 'playing god' to them, for behind any moral judgement is an evaluation of the moral situation which is essentially an intellectual judgement.

This need not issue in crude and open revenge. It can as easily produce subtle hypocrisy or secret resentment. But whatever the result the root is the same, a refusal to suspend judgement in situations where the mystery of evil means we cannot judge adequately. Eventually we will either have to accuse God or usurp his place in judging others. So faith has its part to play in forgiveness, and it does this by suspending judgement. Where it does not know, it lets God decide.

This is a constant biblical theme. Joseph forgives his brothers the genuine injustice they did to him: 'Am I in the place of God?' he says. 'You meant to do me harm; but God meant to bring good out of it.' Joseph was not a cloistered saint. He was far closer to the modern business-man. In fact these are business-like words. Joseph is liter-ally minding his own business and leaving God's business to God.

Paul makes the same point in his letter to the Romans: 'Never pay back evil for evil.... Do not seek revenge, but leave a place for divine retribution; for there is a text which reads, "Justice is mine, says the Lord, I will repay." ' Or, as he writes later, 'Each of us will have to answer for himself. Let us therefore cease judging one another.'

A different way of expressing this is to say that suspended judgement is the silent partner of both faith and meekness. The challenge to faith posed by suffering is related to the challenge to meekness posed by injury. This is not coinci-dence. Faith in God despite suffering is helped by the meek-ness of faith, just as meekness in the face of injury is made possible by faith in God. The reverse is equally true. The man who is not meek does not really trust God, and the man who cannot trust God will not be truly meek.

If we resolutely refuse to make judgements we have no right to make, then we will hold no one, neither God nor man, responsible unfairly. Instead of the normal retaliation in kind by which human wrong answers wrong, we have the chance to lift the situation to a higher level where the retaliation against wrong is love and not hatred, forgiveness and not resentment, trust and not doubt. Faith's determination to suspend judgement is therefore a most important lesson in what Hebrews calls the 'school of suffering' or in what Paul refers to as the change of heart brought by bearing 'your hurt in God's way'.

When I said that we are not primarily responsible to God for what another man does, but rather that he is, I emphasized the word *primarily*. Of course, we have secondary responsibilities. Our primary responsibility in every situation, without exception, is to forgive others as God has forgiven us. But Christian forgiveness is not soft or indulgent, and in many situations we have a secondary responsibility too, according to our callings in life. Always forgiving is not the same as never punishing. A forgiving father should not mean a spoiled son. Forgiving magistrates should not mean a permissive society. What they should mean is that discipline is controlled by justice and compassion; for a forgiving heart is free of anger and prejudice and needs no mask to cover its hypocrisies.

What about a second type of situation, in which it would be fruitless or impossible to place the responsibility on anyone? Some injuries are not only unjust but inexplicable. If there is no one to blame, even the small satisfaction gained from blaming someone else is denied to us, and the situation is fundamentally demoralizing. Nothing is harder to bear than suffering which is apparently meaningless.

The seeming injustice of such suffering is that someone should answer for it but no one is answerable. So we are left, it seems, with one of two choices. Either we must find the answer within ourselves by resigning ourselves to it or condemning ourselves for it, or else we must answer back by accusing, or at least questioning, someone else. It is difficult to hold an impersonal universe personally responsible, and nothing less than personal responsibility will finally do. The only remaining option is that God be called to the bar and charged with the injustice of all suffering which is otherwise inexplicable.

How odd it is that those who emphatically deny that God is there are often the first to assert that he is not good! 'Why does God allow ... ?' can be an atheist's theoretical question designed to challenge the credibility of faith, but just as easily it can be his passionate personal challenge to the irrationality of suffering. If God is allowed to be personal nowhere else, he must be personal here. In this sense blame is an extremely useful index of belief, for everyone believes in God at least as much as he shows by his blaming God for suffering he cannot explain.

This can be said of us as believers too. If suffering without explanation creates doubt, doubt is a makeshift explanation for suffering. If we are hurting and can get no answer from God, the best way to get back at God is to doubt his goodness. We then have a picture of God we can throw the blame at. Doubt becomes a counterfeit answer to suffering, for if God is like that, he is to blame. Now at least one of the questions raised by suffering is crossed off our list.

It is always easier to hurt most those we know best. In the same way there is nothing like doubt to gather up and throw back the bitterness faith feels when it is left in the lurch by the isolating experience of unexplained suffering. Reflecting on his own dark thoughts after his bereavement, C. S. Lewis admitted, 'All that stuff about the cosmic sadist was not so much the expression of thought as of hatred. I was getting from it the only pleasure a man in anguish can get; the pleasure of hitting back.'

If there is just one person we can blame, and if we can do this in any way at all, even in the most unconscious and hidden of grudges, then there is at least some shelter from the heat of the questions raised by apparently meaningless suffering. But if we suffer, and there is absolutely no one to blame, we are stranded like a naked man left to face the sun on the fiery anvil of the desert sands. Little wonder that faith is sorely tempted to curse God and die!

Faith is not repression

To suspend judgement at this point is like walking in the dark along a narrow path with a steep cliff on either side. If there are dangers on the side of answering back, there are also dangers on the side of not answering back, and these must be marked off just as clearly. The danger in suspending judgement is that we go on to deny the emotional reality of our experience and inadvertently turn faith into repression.

To suspend judgement on *why* something is happening

is completely different from denying *that* something is happening. The former is faith, the latter is repression. It is not the business of faith to deny reality but to order it. Denying reality is a mark of make-believe not of living faith. The sort of faith that needs the protective gloves of evasion and euphemism condemns itself to a timid, sickly existence. Such faith is a pale and delicate imitation of true faith, a counterfeit which encourages hypocrisy and heartlessness in the name of surface appearances and the niceness of orthodoxy.

Biblical faith, in contrast, is full-blooded and down to earth. Look at Jesus and you see God's face wet with human tears and God's heart roused with outrage. To trust God did not mean for Jesus the denial of the evil and brokenness of the world but the absolute refusal to make this determinative. The temptation to deny reality is the Devil's clever attempt to turn suspended judgement inside out. It goes through the same motions and makes the same gestures, but it achieves the opposite result. To deny reality does not answer the problems raised by reality; it only affirms that they are insuperable to faith and insists that they remain so.

There are elements of unhealthy repression in many areas of contemporary faith. What we saw earlier in relation to doubt is equally true of Christian attitudes towards other emotions, such as feelings of failure, depression or grief. Over much of the stiff, tight-corseted unnaturalness that poses as Christian faith we might engrave the sound advice of Shakespeare in *Macbeth*:

> What man, ne'er pull your hat upon your brows.
> Give sorrow words; the grief that does not speak
> Whispers the o'er-fraught heart, and bids it break.

Augustine demonstrated the honesty and freedom of a better way. Writing after his mother's death, he admitted, 'The tears which I had been holding back streamed down, and I let them flow as freely as they would, making of them a pillow for my heart. On them it rested, for my weeping sounded in your ears alone.' He owed to his mother not only his physical birth but his spiritual birth too, and at her death he was not ashamed to express his profound grief.

This mistake has been brought sharply into focus today by the exaggerated teaching on thanksgiving. In its extremes it strains for a praise which is unnatural. The new emphasis on praise and thanksgiving is so welcome that it seems churlish to question it. But when the biblical injunction to 'give thanks whatever happens' is taught with an insistence on literalism, it not only contradicts much of the Bible, it can also be psychologically damaging. Yet Christians are being instructed today to praise God even for evil.

This is a dangerous travesty of biblical teaching. Jesus did not give thanks for everything. Face to face with evil he was outraged; face to face with suffering and sin he wept. And if it were not for that anger and those tears and the resolute road to the cross which they marked, we would not realize how outraged by evil God is and how seriously he takes sin.

The dilemma is not the result of tension between the Biblical view of things and our experience of things, as if faith were opposed to reality. The dilemma comes from the tension between the biblical view of evil (a reality which God hates and is not to be thanked for) and the biblical call for faith to thank God whatever happens. One way out of the perplexity which this tension creates is to think of each experience in life as a unit, and to consider it in terms of its unity and diversity.

When an experience is considered in terms of its over-all unity, the only appropriate response to God is unreserved trust and thanksgiving. There is no situation so evil that it is irredeemable by God. From this perspective it is always right to trust God and give thanks. Jeremiah expresses this sense of trust in God's sovereignty even over evil when he says in Lamentations,

> Who can command and it is done,
>   if the Lord has forbidden it?
> Do not both bad and good proceed
>   from the mouth of the Most High? ...
> let us lift up our hearts, not our hands,
>   to God in heaven.

But if the same experience is seen in terms of its diversity, it may well be that the different elements which make it up include that which is evil, painful and disappointing or, as the case may be, good, beneficial and delightful. Each of these individual elements calls out its own appropriate response, and in many instances this response should not be thanks. Outrage is appropriate in response to genuine wrong, tears in response to grief, shock in response to an unexpected disaster. Don't force yourself to thank God *for these things* or you will be harder on yourself and softer on evil than God is. It is not that *even* the Christian need not give thanks for these but that the Christian *especially* should not give thanks for them.

So when we say we must give God thanks 'whatever happens', we must not make ourselves wiser than God who tells us to do it. Perfectionism is twice as dangerous as permissiveness. The disaster it precipitates is deadly, faster and more discouraging.

There is no need for the extremes of wooden literalism. The balance of faith and realism is as true to Scripture as it is comforting to us. Augustine, as if anticipating the current teaching, wrote, 'Who would wish for hardship and difficulty? You command us to endure these troubles, not to love them. No one loves what he endures even though he may be glad to endure it.' Martin Luther puts it equally strongly: 'God has not created man to be a stock or stone but has given him five senses and a heart of flesh, so that he loves his friends, is angry with his enemies, and commiserates with his dear friends in adversity.'

If God has made us this way, do we really think he will ask us to live in a way that is unnatural to the way in which he has created us? If he has made us capable of the full range of human emotions, are they to be denied in practice? Part of God's mercy is his integrity. We can be sure that he will never forget our humanness, and we should do no less with ourselves.

The wonder of Christian faith in time of suffering is its humanness. Where the Muslim resigns himself, the Buddhist and the Hindu withdraw, the stoic endures and the existentialist fights in vain, the Christian can exult. But the fierce joy of Christian exultation is not triumphalism. Nor is it superficial. We exult because in knowing God we know of the outcome, but this is no protection from the pain of suffering in between. 'We are tossed on a tide that puts us to the proof,' wrote Augustine, 'and if we could not sob our troubles in your ear, what hope should we have left to us?'

Chapter Seventeen

Kept Waiting
Doubt from impatience or giving up

Do you find it easy to wait? Most of us don't because waiting *does something* to us. Two years ago my wife and I were waiting in the casualty department of a busy city hospital. We were struck by the change in the way people waited. Those who were alert and eager, almost impatient, were those who had arrived most recently. They sat up every time a name was called out, expecting it to be theirs. But gradually they became like the rest, who had been there longer. Resigned, staring blankly, those who had been there longest sometimes even missed their names when they were called.

Waiting also tells us something. It shows what our relationship is to the person or the event we are waiting for. Would a man wait for his fiancée in the way he waits for his income tax bill? If he did, it might not tell us much about his fiancée. But it would tell us volumes about his opinion of her. Some people can keep us waiting for hours and we don't mind. But if others are only a minute or two late we get impatient. Why should *he* keep *me* waiting? Waiting shows us what we think of the person who keeps us waiting.

The last doubt we will examine is like this, though the question is, What do we think of *God* when he keeps us waiting? This doubt comes when a particular vision God has given us seems utterly impossible or hopelessly delayed. The hardest thing to do then is to wait and work on. Waiting does something to us, and it tells us something about our relationship to God. In a nutshell, the lesson of this last doubt is that suspending judgement does not mean suspending operations.

This doubt and the previous one are closely related. The ability to suspend judgement and the ability to wait and work on are basic skills of faith. Each is an art which presupposes and complements the other, and both are automatically challenged whenever faith is challenged, though in different ways. In suspending judgement faith stays true to God by not doing what it is tempted to do; whereas in waiting and working on faith stays true to God by doing what it is tempted not to. The two doubts are different sides of the same coin and they are both extremely difficult. In refusing to suspend judgement faith may lose hold of God's character; in refusing to wait it loses sight of its own calling.

A world view on fire

Every Christian should be a visionary. When we come to know God, the illumination of his truth breaks into every part of life. Our world view is changed and our sense of calling is wholly transformed. A Christian world view begins to operate. But vision is more than this. Its key idea is not operation (the essence of a world view) but inspiration, or operation raised to the level of inspiration.

Commitment to God's truth is commitment to God's vision of things. So Christian vision is a Christian world view that has caught fire and is ablaze with the knowledge of God. God's character and God's calling transcend the immediacy of seen reality, reinterpret the entire picture and call us to realities that are beyond and above. This is the vision of faith, insight that leads to through-sight, so that in all circumstances, despite all appearances, what is seen with the finite and the visible is the eternal and the invisible.

This vision of faith takes the flow of time and history and charges them with a dynamic of hope, freeing the Christian to wait for God with meaning. If time were only cyclical, a process of infinite change, it would quite literally be going nowhere. Life's highest goal would be detachment, not involvement. The pursuit of purpose within time would be eternally thwarted. On the other hand, if time were only linear, a mere sequence of moments, either man would have to conquer time and impose his meaning on it or time would conquer man. Like a jailer it would hurry him down the corridor of the years to the death sentence that awaits him at the end.

But the Christian view of time is different from either, not because our experience of time is different but because our evaluation of time is transformed by the vision of God's truth. Faith which sees this is therefore able to bring together both the vision and the vehicle by which it is achieved, so that the means of faith and the end of faith form an unbroken link. Faith not only sees, it substantiates what it sees. It is concerned with the reality beyond and with making it real here and now. As the celebrated eleventh chapter of Hebrews begins, 'Faith gives substance to our hopes, and makes us certain of realities we do not see.'

This means there is a creative tension within Christian faith. The Hebrew word for faith has the same stem as the word for hope and the root meaning of both is tautness or tension. Faith which lacks this is less than it should be. The Christian view of things is pitted ultimately against the vision of other faiths and world views. It stands over against every perception of reality which is finite from end to end. Faith sees the infinite as well as the finite – or it sees nothing. The tension of faith results from its being stretched between God's promise and God's fulfilment, and if one or other of these is thought to fail, the line of faith will sag or snap.

Faith's calling is to live in between times. Faith is in transit. It lives in an interim period. Behind faith is the great 'no longer'. Ahead of it lies the great 'not yet'. God has spoken and God will act. Christ has come once and Christ will come again. We have heard the promises and we will witness the event. However long the waiting takes, it is only the gap between the thunder and the lightning.

Faith's task is to join hands with the past and the future to hold down God's will in the present. The present moment is the disputed territory for faith, a no man's land between past and future, ground either to be seized by obedience or lost to disobedience. Visionary faith stakes out its possession of the land and does so with energy and enthusiasm that come from its knowledge of what the reclaimed land will one day be.

Picture in your mind a couple walking through a bare unfurnished house. What makes them so excited and keen to buy it? It isn't what they see but what they see in what they see. Being creative and full of ideas, they see what it might be where others see only what it is. The vision of faith is like this. It has ideas about the future which are God's ideas. God himself is the one who 'summons things that are not yet in existence as if they already were'. Vision is not a matter of seeing what is and asking why. It is far more a matter of seeing what had never yet been and asking why not.

Are you a visionary? Is your Christian faith merely functional and routine, or does it inspire you, throwing light and meaning on all you do, moving ahead of you like a pillar of cloud and fire? We are called to be down-to-earth as Christians but not to be earthbound.

The defence never rests

Hebrews 11 is the great Honours List of such faith, a stirring catalogue of men and women whose vision of God called them to live and work over against the customs, values and priorities of their generation. They marched to a different drummer. Their sights were on a different goal. Their home was in a different country. They looked forward to a different city. By their faith they called the entire world in question, and Hebrews says of them, 'Those who use such language show plainly that they are looking for a country of their own.'

The secret of visionary faith lies in that sentence. How is it that they managed to transcend their times, surmounting the immediate, living over against the generally accepted, looking beyond the impossible? They were not an elite. The secret is simply that their whole lives were speaking and acting with the language and logic that is proper to faith.

The language and the logic of visionary faith is a demanding style of argument. It is not difficult to understand but difficult to substantiate, for once it is stated it can be substantiated only in life. So anyone who is not prepared to back his words with his life will find that his use of the argument will be too costly or quite ineffective.

This style of argument is illustrated in *Strong Poison*, an early novel of Dorothy Sayers. The story opens with Harriet Vane in the dock, on trial for the murder of a writer with whom she had been living. There is a strong, apparently watertight, case against her. The prosecution, who do not know her personally, are pressing for a verdict of guilty. Undeniably she had the motivation and the opportunity. All the known facts of the case are against her. She should hang.

But into the grave situation steps the hero, Lord Peter Wimsey. He believes in her innocence and therefore he is sure that, although the known facts are against her, the known facts are not all the facts. So what he does is to set out to discover and demonstrate the missing facts which would change the picture completely. Arguing with his colleagues he says, 'There must be evidence somewhere, you know. I know you have all worked like beavers, but I am going to work like a king beaver. And I've got one big advantage over the rest of you ... I do believe in Miss Vane's innocence.'

This is the daring style of argument used by visionary faith. The believer knows why he trusts that God is there and that God is good. In accepting the consequences of this knowledge, he rises to a life-calling which sets him against the grain of the contemporary social reality and tests to the limits the obedience of his faith. Time and again he believes God and is prepared to obey even though is does not visibly pay or work. Other options repeatedly seem easier. Worse still, they sometimes seem more natural, more logical, even more right than God's way.

At such times is the believer to trust God and so maintain the tension of faith in the face of pressure? Or is he to bow to the current odds and, in trying to ease the strain on faith, destroy the tension altogether, replacing faith with doubt? This is the challenge to the visionary and his reply is audacious. Knowing why he trusts God, he trusts and waits. The *known* facts are against God, but the known facts are not *all* the facts.

Lord Peter Wimsey's defence highlights two things which are important to this style of argument. The first is that it does not matter how overwhelming the case appears to be so long as we know why the accused is innocent. If we are unsure of this, our argument will collapse. We could never be sure that the known facts of the case were *not* all the facts, and any arguments to counter the apparently watertight case against the accused might sound no stronger than wishful thinking.

But this is only what we have underlined about faith in God all along. If there is 'no reason why' when faith is present, there will certainly be 'no reason why not' when doubt arrives. If we say that we trust God, there is no virtue in siding with him *in the end*, belatedly hurrying forward, as it were, to congratulate God when the verdict is given in his favour. Knowing why we can trust God, we should be like loyal friends who believe in his integrity *all along*. The final vindication adds nothing to faith except the chance to turn round and say to doubt, 'Didn't I tell you?'

The second point is equally simple. Lord Peter's line of defence needed substantiating. Merely to state it might have meant an interesting headline ('PEER SPEAKS UP FOR MURDERESS'), but it would not have cleared Harriet Vane of the charge. It is the same with faith. Without obedience faith is no more than an interesting theoretical statement. To become credible it must be 'real'-ized in practice. This is the point of saying that even when the vision is delayed faith must wait and *work on*. There is a form of waiting which is an act of faith, and another which is an act of laziness, carelessness or despair. Only the former is related to the obedience of faith.

This style of argument is common in the Bible, and there are striking illustrations of it that are just as telling as those in Hebrews 11. One is the Old Testament belief in the physical resurrection of believers, despite the fact that this had neither a solid precedent in history nor a full theological explanation until the resurrection of Jesus centuries later. This belief was not wishful thinking, a romantic sidestepping. The Hebrews were blunt and frank about death.

All known facts pointed to one conclusion: death is the end. The Psalmist said: 'But remember this: wise men must die; stupid men, brutish men, all perish.... For men are like oxen whose life cannot last.' However if there is an undying value to the person who is made in God's image and who trusts God, then the known facts were obviously not all the facts, and Isaiah could say:

But thy dead live, their bodies will rise again.
They that sleep in the earth will awake and shout for joy;
for thy dew is a dew of sparkling light,
and the earth will bring those long dead to birth again.

Another remarkable example of this style of argument can be found in Jeremiah's prayer to God during a crisis. It was the tenth year of the reign of King Zedekiah over Judah. Jerusalem was in the merciless grip of the Babylonian siege. Jeremiah himself was in prison and God had just informed him of the imminent fall of the city. On every hand the outlook and prospects were bleak. No time must have seemed less suitable for long-range planning, let alone confident business enterprises. But this was the exact moment when God told Jeremiah that his cousin would come and offer to sell him the family land, and that he was to buy it.

If Jeremiah had not known why he trusted God, an order like this would have sounded ludicrous, unreal, completely out of touch with the facts of the situation. If ever there was a time not to buy and sell property, it was then. But when his cousin came, Jeremiah obeyed God and bought the land. The known facts of the situation were all against it, but if God had told him to do it, then clearly the known facts were not all the facts and do it he must. By his act of obeying God he argued with appearances and defied the obvious and his perplexity is evident in his prayer:

> Look at the siege-ramps, the men who are advancing to take the city, and the city given over to its assailants from Chaldaea, the victim of sword, famine, and pestilence. The word thou has spoken is fulfilled and thou dost see it. And yet thou hast bidden me buy the field, O Lord God, and have the deed witnessed, even though the city is given to the Chaldaeans.

This is faith's characteristic style. God's word is normative and all else is judged by it. The waters may be dark and swirling, but faith steps from one stepping stone of God's Word to another. Visibility may be poor, but faith pursues the vision from one glimpse to another, undeterred by whatever stands across its path. If God says so, God must know why. Then the argument is not with God but with the contradictions of the situation that deny his lordship.

So Noah listened to God and built an ark. So Abraham left home and country and lived in a tent, waiting for a more permanent city. So Sarah conceived a child, though she was well past the age. So Moses crossed the Red Sea as if it was dry land. And the letter to the Hebrews comments, 'They were not yet in possession of the things promised, but had seen them far ahead and hailed them. . . . That is why God is not ashamed to be called their God.'

The stiffest test

But, and this after all is the point, this style of argument is extremely demanding. Not only does it provide no insurance against doubt, it increases the risk. There is always the possibility that the tension may be stretched to the breaking point. So Noah who built the ark by faith also fell into a drunken stupor. So Abraham who trusted God with the life of his son would not trust him with the safety of his wife. Most of the heroes of faith knew defeats like this.

What would you say is the hardest test for visionary faith – crisis, disappointment, disaster or delay? Unquestionably it is delay. Nothing is harder for faith than waiting. That may sound surprising. Surely there is nothing easier to do than wait? Can't any old lazy bones do that? True, there are forms of waiting which involve no effort at all. They are simply a matter of hanging around. But that is not the kind of waiting required in visionary faith. Because it is visionary, it can see more than is yet substantiated; because it is faith, it can wait for it. But being visionary faith, it is out to substantiate all that it has seen, so it can hardly wait for it.

Crisis and failure are much less painful to the vision of faith than waiting. In fact they are important only because they involve waiting. If I remove the word *crisis* and substitute the word *setback* instead, you will see at once why a crisis is a problem for vision. It sets back the vision, and every postponement means even more waiting. Do you know someone who says he has no problem with waiting for his vision? He might ask himself if he has a vision worth waiting for. Equanimity can be a sign of indifference as much as faith. A sure mark of Christian vision is its godly impatience and holy restlessness.

Just as a plane presses at the sound barrier and shudders with the impact as it breaks through, the visionary throughsight of faith takes on itself the crushing weight of the contradictions of reality. Often there is a moment just prior to breakthrough when the pressure is most intense and faith seems to shudder with the strain, threatening even to disintegrate. This strain is what causes doubt. The immense weight of contradictory reality crashes against faith like a shock-wave so that momentarily the clarity and singlemindedness of the vision is lost and faith is thrown off course into a dazed state of double vision.

If this was true of those heroes of faith whom Hebrews describes by name, could it have been any different for those unnamed ones who were 'tortured to death, disdaining release, to win a better resurrection'? Or of those who had to 'face jeers and flogging, even fetters and prison bars. They were stoned, they were sawn in two, they were put to the sword, they went about dressed in skins of sheep or goats, in poverty, distress, and misery.' Do we imagine that they were never in two minds? Do we believe they had no second thoughts?

Jesus is the pioneer of visionary faith. 'For the sake of the joy that lay ahead of him, [he] endured the cross, making light of its disgrace.' Yet even he experienced anguish of spirit as his obedience to God's will put him at odds with the will of the world. Looking into the horror of the cross, he cried out, 'Now my soul is in turmoil, and what am I to say? Father, save me from this hour. No, it was for this that I came to this hour.'

And when his cry of abandonment rang out from the cross itself, we may remind ourselves that he was quoting and fulfilling the Old Testament; we may reassure ourselves that it was not a cry of despair but instead a prayer to God; we may rejoice that its sequel was the cry of triumph, 'It is finished.' But we must never be so blinded by sentiment that we minimize the horror, the alienation and the bitterness of that hour. There, if ever, Jesus must have been tempted to doubt.

This is no easy lesson. It is one thing to be fired by a vision and get up out of an arm chair. It is another to be fired by a vision and walk through fire and rain. It is one thing to be stirred by the reminder that every crisis is an opportunity to demonstrate faith. It is another to translate the vision into reality and to pay the price of doing so. Yet for visionary faith only the latter counts.

The book of Revelation looks forward to a time when 'there shall be no more delay ... the hidden purpose of God will have been fulfilled'. But that day is still in the great 'not yet' for us, and until it dawns every exultant 'Hallelujah!' will sooner or later be followed on the Christian's lips by an impassioned 'How long, O Lord?' The latter expresses the unique pain and distress as the vision of God is thwarted or denied by the reality of a world in rebellion.

'Our trust in God will be perfect,' wrote Martin Luther, 'when life and death, glory and shame, adversity and prosperity, will be the same to us.' But isn't this another way of saying that our trust in God will never be perfect in this life? The only alternative in this life to the inevitable ups and downs of human experience is not perfection but the zombie-like trance of total detachment. Perfection is impossible, detachment is wrong. So long as we live, we will know the ups and downs, and their challenge to faith will be the same double option we have seen all along: Will faith be stimulated or stymied by each crisis?

Speaking of a robust faith, Pascal says, 'There is some pleasure in being on board a ship battered by storms when one is certain of not perishing. The persecutions buffeting the Church are like this.' But what is true of the church in persecution is not always true of the individual Christian in time of doubt. Doubt is lonelier than persecution.

A better test for faith is to catch it off guard in a time of failure, upset or delay, and watch its reactions then. The off-duty reaction is the one that shows the calibre of faith. 'Though he slay me, yet will I trust in him' is both credible and proper when Job says it, because he had almost been slain and he was still trusting. But it is quite another matter for someone to say it if he never expects God to slay him and has made very sure that the possibility is unlikely to arise.

The corrosion of waiting eats first into the sense of total involvement with our work. We are forced to stand back and think about it rather than do it. Waiting eats next into the timetables we have set for ourselves, delaying them, setting them back, making us wonder if they are feasible or if they are worth it. Soon it is eating into the worthwhileness of what we are doing. If it cannot be done as we originally intended, or if it looks as if it will never be finished, is it worth doing at all?

Before long the corrosion eats into our souls and we ourselves are called in question. Will we ever finish the work God has given us? Has God shown us what he wants us to do next and we've missed it? Will he ever show us? Perhaps we are unready? Perhaps we will never be ready? Perhaps we are useless to God?

No wonder it seems easiest to stop waiting. This puts a stop to faith and necessitates doubt, but at least it stops the torture of waiting. Whether we act in panic or impatience, at least we have the satisfaction of taking things into our own hands. It may even release us from the temptation to blame God. One moment longer and we might be saying, 'Who does God think he is to keep us waiting?'

The agonizing wait stretches a believer on a rack. If he maintains faith, he feels tortured even more and no one seems to come to his rescue. All that is wanted, his torturer says, is that he recant and deny that anyone will come to his aid. The believer's faith is then caught: Heads-I-win, tails-you-lose. If he maintains faith there seems to be no guarantee that his rescuer will come to his aid, and his situation is torture only because he does maintain faith. On the other hand, if he recants, he will be free and he will be his own rescuer. So the choice is flattering. This is the way doubt reasons with faith under the trial of waiting, and if faith gives in, its recanting is doubt.

Prevention and cure

What is the best preventative for this doubt? First, it is vital to check the vision. Only the genuine vision can be expected to come true. History is strewn with the ruins of follies that were the result of private lines to God. Is the vision from God himself? Is it in accord with the rest of God's revelation of himself? How much of selfish and impure motivations are also mixed in, which need to be purified first? When the testing comes it may be too late to answer these questions. Better to ask them before and be sure of the answers.

Of course, a vision will fail if it is false. It may also fail because it is not practised as it should be. One pale version of visionary faith is the talk of hope which preoccupies itself with an object of hope (such as the second coming of Jesus) but never expresses that hope in action. Without something to hope for, we are literally hope-less. Without a reason to hope for it, we are only hoping against hope. But even with the best object and the best reason in the world hope is still not fully Christian unless it issues in a dynamic of living which demonstrates the hope in action.

One counterfeit of visionary faith is the comfortable idea that waiting is only a matter of waiting in situations where, humanly speaking, we have to wait anyway. Thus some people wait only when it is impossible to do anything else. But this removes the dimension of faith from waiting and reduces it to resignation. Activism and resignation are equally a denial of faith in God, though in different ways. It is not so hard to wait when we have to, when everyone else is waiting too. But can we trust God and wait when everyone else is moving on, going somewhere, doing something? Or must we take things into our own hands, decide for ourselves, and make the best move we can? That is the test.

Second, it is important to feed and exercise faith. Seeing the vision is like being born, a once-for-all experience. But maintaining the vision is like growing; it needs daily nourishment. The stiffer the test the better faith's diet must be and the more strenuous its exercise. The more tension faith faces in some areas, the more relaxation and refreshment it needs in others. The more it is opposed by the powers of this world, the more it must experience the powers of the age to come. Waiting for God is absolutely dependent on waiting on God.

A comparison of two biblical incidents shows the possibilities clearly. The first occurred during the ministry of the prophet Elisha when Samaria, the capital of the northern kingdom of Israel, was under siege by Benhadad, king of Syria. When the situation became desperate the king of Israel cried out, 'Look at our plight! This is the Lord's doing. Why should I wait any longer for him to help us?' Once his ordinary human endurance had run out, he could wait no longer since he had no faith. But if it was God's doing, as he said it was, then to refuse to wait for God was illogical. Yet the reaction was human. Waiting was so intolerable that something had to be done to break the hopelessness of waiting. In taking things into his own hands, he demonstrated that waiting was showing up his lack of faith.

The second incident took place in an equally grave situation as the southern kingdom of Judah was attacked during the ministry of Isaiah in the ninth century BC. King and people were shaken like trees in the wind, but Isaiah took his stand against the mounting panic and the repeated attempts to find help apart from God. 'Have firm faith, or you will not stand firm,' he says. Or as he expanded on this later, 'Come back, keep peace, and you will be safe; in stillness and in staying quiet, there lies your strength.'

Isaiah is the prophet of faith. When he condemns Judah,

it is not for its wickedness alone, but for its shortsighted reliance on untrustworthy gods. Each crisis sends the people reeling in fresh panic and shows that their trust was not in God in the first place. In contrast Isaiah was the living example of his own teaching. If faith is a radical reliance on God, it is undaunted by circumstances, unaltered by the odds. Even when it faces what is humanly impossible, faith can still stand at full stretch. Such faith is the antithesis of self-reliant humanism. When the strongest self-reliance has broken down, such faith will still be standing.

Isaiah's supreme expression of this is in chapter 40. Appropriately it follows from the awesome vision of God's character and power. Other faiths may fall short, other people in their prime may grow weary, 'but those who look to the Lord will win new strength, they will grow wings like eagles; they will run and not be weary, they will march on and never grow faint.'

Faith that waits is not resigned. Nor is it hoping against hope. Faith's logic is not couched in tentative expressions, such as *probably, perhaps, if, depending on* but in courageous affirmations with all the force of *nevertheless* or *yes, but*. These are the affirmations which pit faith against despair and snatch victory from the jaws of defeat. This is the faith which becomes a source of vital new energy given by God, an energy at once supernatural and miraculous, that makes the impossible entirely possible. For a faith like this, waiting is not the falsification of hope but merely the duration between the promise and the fulfillment, between the 'no longer' and the 'not yet'.

Thus the known facts may all be against God. But knowing God, we know that the known facts are not all the facts. So where we are going gives strength to what we are doing; and what we are doing is a sign of where we are going. Seeing God we can wait, and trusting God we can work on while we wait. This is the vision to which we are called.

Picture a small boy frustrated with a jigsaw puzzle because he is certain that the pieces do not fit the picture on the box. We are like this when we doubt. Each doubt makes us feel that this time we have found a real problem with God. But shake the pieces up a little, rearrange the one or two that we have put in the wrong place and everything changes. It is not the fault of the puzzle or the picture but the boy.

It is the same with our doubts. What we begin by calling God's problem ends up being seen as our problem which God solves. As our discussion draws to a close let this conclusion linger in our hearts and minds: The problem of doubt is not ultimately a matter of God's faithfulness but of our faith, just as the answer does not ultimately depend on our faith but on God's faithfulness.

This should make us prepared to take all our doubts to God straight away, though with the help of Christian friends. Doubts which are not resolved will inevitably blame God in the end. But is it right to allow each doubt to blame God in the beginning? Any current doubt will tend to thrust us away from God, but our experience of his resolving our previous doubts should encourage us to come nearer. The first reaction of our hearts should echo William Cowper's prayer, 'Decide this doubt for me.'

If we are resolved to discard all inadequate grounds of trust, to abandon everything that will not hold us up, to reject all spurious foundations until our feet are on solid rock, then our faith will be single-minded and whole-hearted, a radical reliance on God which grips, and is gripped by, the faithfulness of God when all else fails.

We cannot guarantee that our faith will not fail, even when faith is single-minded. And when we are in two minds, we cannot enjoy God and we do not feel we can count on him. But God is more certain, more faithful and more gracious than our doubting views of him. So the better we know ourselves the more inappropriate we know it is to trust in our own promises or vows. When all is said and done, we are still ignorant, weak and sinful. How much better it is to pray. When we pray even the most devastating doubt remains faith and does not become unbelief. Each of us, however confident we are, may be a doubter, so Martin Luther's 'doubter's prayer' should strike a chord in all our hearts:

Dear Lord,
Although I am sure of my position,
I am unable to sustain it without Thee.
Help me, or I am lost.

WHOSE PROMISED LAND?

Colin Chapman

It is not easy to be dispassionate about this issue.
Whose is the promised land, the land the Israelis call
Israel, the Palestinians call Palestine? What
arguments, claims and counter-claims lie behind the
pioneer spirit of the settlers, the conflict, the
violence, the refugee problem, the uprooting of
families?

This book outlines the claims, then traces the story
behind them, going right back to the time of the
Bible, the basis for the Jews' claims to the land.
What do the Bible's prophecies mean? How were the
promises and prophecies made to ancient Israel
understood by Jesus and the first Christian
community? How should they be understood today?
Is there a way forward?

Colin Chapman has been working with university
students in different countries in the Middle East
since 1968. He has had to face the issues first-hand.
His aim in this book is to be fair in facing the issues
and constructive in putting forward a way of peace.

ISBN 0 85648 956 5
£3.95/$7.95

THE JOURNAL OF
John Wesley

Abridged by Christopher Idle

In his Journal, John Wesley gives his readers a vivid picture of his life in eighteenth-century Britain and America. Wesley's account, originally written in code and later published in instalments, records the journeys of the man who regarded the world as his parish. Covering fifty-six years of his life, the Journal chronicles his controversial open-air preaching, his inner doubts and conflicts, his journeys on horseback and by ship, and his encounters with many people — the famous, the infamous and the ordinary.

This new abridgement of Wesley's Journal has been made by Christopher Idle, Rector of the London Dockland parish of Limehouse. His fascination with John Wesley and George Whitefield, who both preached many times in his present neighbourhood, goes back many years.

'Part travelogue, part spiritual diary, Wesley's comments during his 250,000 miles of travel make highly entertaining reading.'
Daily Telegraph

'For the first time, an accessible, abridged version of the eighteenth-century spiritual classic.'
Methodist Recorder

'Christopher Idle has performed a labour of love and given us a selection of the Journal . . . The whole enterprise is very well done.'
Kenneth Slack, BBC Radio 4

ISBN 0 85648 850 X
£4.95/$7.95

George Whitefield
AND THE GREAT AWAKENING

John Pollock

George Whitefield was a controversial but
outstanding preacher during the Great Awakening of
the eighteenth century. He was barred from church
pulpits by the scandalized clergy, but he took to the
open air where thousands gladly flocked to hear him.
By the time he was twenty-three, his preaching had
taken London and Bristol by storm, and he had made
the first of seven visits to the New World.

Whitefield's fame as an evangelist has often been
overshadowed by his contemporary, John Wesley.
This book takes a fresh look at the man who in many
ways started the work that Wesley continued.

John Pollock is well known for his biographies,
including a life of the slave-trade abolitionist,
Wilberforce, The Apostle, a life of St Paul, and
Shaftesbury: The Poor Man's Earl. His books have
been translated into thirteen languages. He lives in a
small village in Devon, England.

'John Pollock is able almost to make us feel that we
could be standing on the far edge of one of the great
crowds listening to his burning words.'
Western Mail

'A compact, readable, swift-moving biography of the
grand itinerant.'
Christian Century

'John Pollock's vivid biography brings Whitefield
clearly before us as man, preacher, and evangelical
trail-blazer.'
Sunday Telegraph

ISBN 0 7459 1018 1
£4.95/$7.95